Second-Hand Cultures

MATERIALIZING CULTURE

. . . .

Series Editors: Paul Gilroy, Michael Herzfeld and Danny Miller

Barbara Bender, *Stonehenge: Making Space*

Gen Doy, *Materializing Art History*

Laura Rival (ed.), *The Social Life of Trees: Anthropological Perspectives on Tree Symbolism*

Victor Buchli, *An Archaeology of Socialism*

Marius Kwint, Christopher Breward and Jeremy Aynsley (eds), *Material Memories: Design and Evocation*

Penny Van Esterik, *Materializing Thailand*

Michael Bull, *Sounding Out the City: Personal Stereos and the Management of Everyday Life*

Anne Massey, *Hollywood Beyond the Screen: Design and Material Culture*

Wendy Joy Darby, *Landscape and Identity: Geographies of Nation and Class in England*

Joy Hendry, *The Orient Strikes Back: A Global View of Cultural Display*

Judy Attfield, *Wild Things: The Material Culture of Everyday Life*

Daniel Miller (ed.), *Car Cultures*

Elizabeth Edwards, *Raw Histories: Photographs, Anthropology and Museums*

David E. Sutton, *Remembrance of Repasts: An Anthropology of Food and Memory*

Eleana Yalouri, *The Acropolis: Global Fame, Local Claim*

Elizabeth Hallam and Jenny Hockey, *Death, Memory and Material Culture*

Sharon Macdonald, *Behind the Scenes at the Science Museum*

Elaine Lally, *At Home With Computers*

Susanne Küchler, *Malanggan: Art, Memory and Sacrifice*

Second-Hand Cultures

NICKY GREGSON AND LOUISE CREWE

Oxford • New York

First published in 2003 by
Berg
Editorial offices:
150 Cowley Road, Oxford, OX4 1JJ, UK
838 Broadway, Third Floor, New York, NY 10003-4812, USA

Berg is the imprint of Oxford International Publishers Ltd.

Library of Congress Cataloging-in-Publication Data

Gregson, Nicky, 1958-
    Second-hand cultures / Nicky Gregson and Louise Crewe.
        p. cm. — (Materializing culture)
Includes bibliographical references and index.
        ISBN 1-85973-672-6 (cloth) — ISBN 1-85973-677-7 (paper)
    1. Secondhand trade—Social aspects. 2. Material culture. I. Crewe,
Louise. II. Title. III. Series.

HF5482 .G74 2003
306.3'4—dc21

                                                            2002014678

British Library Cataloguing-in-Publication Data

A catalogue record for this book is available from the British Library.

ISBN 1 85973 672 6 (Cloth)
        1 85973 677 7 (Paper)

Typeset by JS Typesetting Ltd, Wellingborough, Northants.
Printed in the United Kingdom by MPG Books Ltd, Bodmin,
Cornwall.

For Isabella, Sacha, Willow and Mave

Contents

Illustrations   ix

Acknowledgements   xi

1 Introduction   1

Part I: Spatialities of Exchange   17

2 Geographies of 'Location'   19

3 Constituting Difference   51

4 Spaces of Shopping Practice   85

Part II: Practice of Second-hand Consumption   111

5 Redefining Rubbish: Commodity Disposal and Sourcing   115

6 Transformations: Commodity Recovery, Redefinition,
       Divestment and Re-enchantment   143

7 Gifting and Collecting   173

8 Reflections/Further Directions   195

Appendix   205

Notes   219

Bibliography   231

Index   251

Illustrations

Figures

2.1   The oppositional imaginings of retro retailers   34

Plates

2.1   Car boot sale, South-east England, September 2001   25
2.2   Car boot advertisement: Nottinghamshire, September
          2001   26
2.3   Sunday morning juxtapostions: middle-class suburbia
          and the boot sale   32
2.4   Nottingham, Lace Market   35
2.5   Charity shops on the high street   40
2.6   Charity shops on the high street   41
2.7   Charity shops meet 'the alternative': Manchester,
          Oldham Street   46
3.1   Car boot sales: selling paraphernalia   55
3.2   Phil and 'the stall'   57
3.3   Atomic 1   63
3.4   Atomic – interior 1   64
3.5   Atomic – interior 2   64
3.6   Atomic – interior 3   65
3.7   Luna – the window   66
3.8   Fun, play and laughter 1   68
3.9   Fun, play and laughter 2   69
3.10 Regulation 70s   70
3.11 Charity shop logos   75
3.12 Charity shop logos   76

5.1   Dumped outside Imperial Cancer – the donations in
          rubbish sacks   122
6.1   Rupert   169

Acknowledgements

This book has been a long while in the making. Its origins lie in two ESRC funded projects (R000221288 and R 000222182) conducted in 1994/5 and 1998/9 respectively, and in the publications that stemmed immediately from them. Our thanks go to all those who have commented on this work along the way, and especially to friends and colleagues in the Department of Geography, University of Sheffield and the School of Geography, University of Nottingham. We also wish to thank our two RAs – Beth Longstaff and Kate Brooks respectively – for their different but equally invaluable contributions to the two projects. Most of all though we want to thank each other, for making this collaboration so rewarding – and Patsy and Edina for the wackier moments of inspiration.

Introduction

'The Mission'

A few years ago now, responding to an end-of-grant report, one of our referees commented that we seemed to be on a mission. Although we hadn't thought about it in such terms, at least until then, there is a sense in which the observation is accurate – both personally and academically. Certainly, we have both invested excessive amounts of time in various second-hand worlds over the past six years – and longer – participating in them, buying, selling and observing. And we have spent even longer talking with others about them, analysing this 'talk' and writing about it. So, if time is an indication of investment and commitment then this is indeed a mission. But there is an academic mission here too that it is important to acknowledge: that from the outset of the research we have been concerned to show that second-hand worlds matter.

In part, as others have argued, that they matter is an empirical issue. Located by Miller et al. (1998) as part of the 'second generation' of consumption studies, and represented as a necessary counter to the key pioneering texts (Douglas and Isherwood, 1979; McKendrick et al. 1982; Miller, 1987; McCracken, 1988; Campbell, 1987), second-hand sites have been identified as critical in building up stocks of grounded knowledge about practices of consumption and their variation across particular sites. So, we have studies of nearly new sales and classified advertisements (Clarke, 1998, 2000), work on garage sales (Freedman, 1976; Gordon, 1985; Herrmann and Soiffer, 1984; Parrish, 1986; Soiffer and Herrmann, 1987), swap meets and flea markets (Belk et al. 1988; McCree, 1984; Maisel, 1976; M. Miller, 1988; Razzouk and Gourley, 1982), as well as our own research on car boot sales, charity shops and retro shops, existing alongside studies of shopping centres (Miller et al. 1998) and festivals such as Christmas (Miller, 1993). More than this though, our work has been concerned to demonstrate that second-hand worlds matter

1

theoretically. Initially, back in the mid-1990s, we cast these arguments around what we saw as critical omissions to accounts of consumption cycles and spaces of exchange. Correspondingly, we argued then – as we still would – that goods have both a use and an exchange value that extends well beyond the first cycle (Gregson and Crewe, 1994), that open up extensive biographies in things that are not just historical but geographical (Appadurai, 1986; Koptyoff, 1986), and invariably symbolic. Moreover, and simultaneously, we were concerned to move beyond accounts that sought to identify particular sites – spaces, usually of consumption – as emblematic, symbolic of their time, as metaphor – notably the department store and the mall (Baudrillard, 1988; Bauman, 1993).[1] So, we were concerned to argue that consumption occurs in sites and spaces that are ordinary and mundane in their location and in their situation within everyday life, and that consumption is frequently practised here in relation to some very ordinary sorts of goods – for instance, everyday clothing, household goods, books, toys and so on (and see too Miller et al. 1998; Miller, 1998).

Beyond this though, and as our work has developed, we would want to make additions to these arguments. Specifically, we would claim that theoretically second-hand worlds matter for two further reasons. First, because they allow us to develop new insights around exchange. As Miller (2000) has suggested recently, one of the key points about the clutch of recent work on second-hand sites has been its destabilization of dualistic accounts of exchange grounded in the opposition drawn between 'the market' and 'the gift' (Callon, 1998; Carrier, 1995; Carrier, 1997; Dilley, 1992; Gregory, 1982; Mauss, 1954; Schrift, 1997; Strathern, 1988). Dealing with worlds where the fundamental principles of exchange cannot be assumed to be the same as in market exchange – that is, where money works to decontextualize goods and where goods are divorced from who is doing the buying and selling (Sayer, 1997) – exchange here must be reworked, through goods that have been 'cast off', 'cast out', 'given away', 'donated' or, indeed, that have either outgrown or that have outlived their original consumers. Exchange here then is about alienable goods and ways of reappropriating them – to sell and to consume. And it is also, as Miller again argues, about the 'birth of value': ways in which people create the conditions for value to emerge, in the context of transactions.

Thus far we would agree with Miller. Where we differ, in an additive sense, is in terms of how this connects to a second issue, space. As our work has progressed, a question that has preoccupied us increasingly is the connection between second-hand exchange and the production of space. An integral part of our argument, then, is that included among the principles and premises of second-hand exchange is the attempt on the behalf of both buyers and sellers to produce spatialized practices of exchange. At one level this is about no more than the relatively banal point that the sites and spaces of second-hand exchange are variable in terms of their constitutive practices. Beyond this though, such variation signals that what we are looking at here is attempts to inscribe meaning in second-hand exchange; to constitute routinely – through practices that are situation-specific – particular sets of premises and principles[2] of exchange. Space, then, and the practices that bring this into production, are integral to this. And indeed, one of the key aims of this book is to show just how critical this is, for the practices and premises at work here vary from those where the differences between 'first' and 'second-hand' are increasingly being written out of certain spaces of second-hand exchange to spaces where it is precisely this distinction that is being valued, in multifarious ways. Furthermore, such are the differences between readings of second-hand exchange that, for those trying to sell second-hand goods, it has become increasingly important to attempt to regulate against their co-incidence in space – through working with the constitution of selling space/s. So, we find particular instances of second-hand retailers mobilizing existing geographies of retail location to impart meaning to the goods they sell, notably through their proximity to and distance from spaces of first hand exchange. And we show too how retail interiors are constituted in ways that also signal proximity and distance – through the adoption of regimes of representation that either accord with standard retail conventions or that use these to constitute interior spaces oppositionally. Yet, there are limits here. Notwithstanding the constitution of these distinctive geographies, those selling second-hand goods are shown to be unable to regulate out counter-readings of second-hand exchange. These spaces of exchange, then, are shown to be characterized by transactions that, in their premises, both accord with and go against those desired – for example, by purchasing for 'fun' that which is being retailed for knowing recontextualization, or by attempting to bargain in a charity shop.

Where this takes us is to argue that the premises constituting second-hand exchange are as much shaped by buyers as they are by sellers. Correspondingly, another of our concerns here is to examine what buyers are trying to achieve through purchasing second-hand. In part this is shown to be located in second-hand goods themselves, and to be intrinsically connected to subject positions. So, purchasing second-hand can be about capturing 'difference' – in which case it is invested with the now classic Bourdieu-ian markers of distinction and taste (Bourdieu, 1984). Or it can be about capturing 'value' – in the sense of 'the bargain', with its connections to the imperatives of thrift. Equally however, it can be about social respectability, a need born of financial necessity. But second-hand exchange for buyers is also shown to be about spatialized practices of shopping. These practices are grounded in particular forms of knowledge and are argued to rely on constituting distinctive geographies associated with first and second-hand shopping. Moreover, these geographies are shown to invest second-hand spaces with meanings that differentiate them radically from first hand spaces. For example, these spaces can be seen to be about a moral economy of redistribution, but they can also be seen to be about treating the self through practices of shopping. And they can also be read as being about a temporary suspension of conventional social relations of exchange, as a form of carnival.

Together, these findings establish unequivocally that 'second-hand' matters; that for both buyers and sellers (although importantly, not all sellers) the goods and spaces of second-hand exchange bring an entirely different context to transactions to first-cycle exchange and that this context is critical to the creation of 'value'. It is one of our aims here to demonstrate this. But more than this, what we show here is that there is discordance – rupture even – between the premises of buyers and sellers, that exchange is being carried out in particular sites in ways that are not necessarily co-incident. Not only then are buyers' practices frequently far messier than those assumed by second-hand retailers and invested in their constitution of discrete distinctive selling spaces, but the increasing regulation of these spaces is argued to mitigate against these practices, to go against the conditions for value creation. Indeed, in attempting to regulate out certain readings of second-hand through particular spatializing practices, second-hand retailers may well have written out the very spatialities of 'difference' that enable buyers to constitute value through second-hand transactions. Second-hand worlds, then, allow us to see that space matters, intrinsically - not only in creating the context for value creation through transactions but to constituting the limits of these second-hand worlds.

The second reason that second-hand worlds matter theoretically is that they allow us to develop existing accounts of consumption. Currently, two accounts prevail in the literature, those that locate understandings of consumption within a commodity chain approach, and those that hinge consumption to the constitution of identities and subjectivities.[3]

Taking second-hand seriously however, provides problems for both. The commodity-chain tradition relies on a narrative that understands consumption exclusively in relation to its connections back through retailers' supply chains to production. Constituted primarily in relation to accounts of globalization, these accounts are motivated primarily by a critique of first-world consumption patterns and their dependence on inequalities in third-world production, and continue to privilege production over consumption. Moreover, in so doing and in failing to take seriously the practices of consumption, they reinstate the very separation between production and consumption that they set out to break down. Acknowledging the second-hand market, though, introduces further difficulties for such approaches, notably that this is an arena at some remove from production activities. So, while all second-hand goods can be invested with biographies that link them to production, and indeed might reflect the conditions of their production in their durability (even their value), they exist in a relation to production that is mediated by the first cycle of consumption, and particularly by practices of consumption.

There is perhaps no better example of this than the second-hand car market where, notwithstanding the ways in which differences in production feed through to shape second-hand value (compare for instance Mercedes with Vauxhall), it is the practices of consumption (associated here with mileage and general 'wear and tear') that exert key effects on price. And we would argue similarly with respect to many other types of goods. Indeed, while the brand and the label certainly work to confer value in the second-hand clothing market – Nike, Chanel, Paul Smith, cK, Levi 501s, Windsmoor, and even 'M&S' being particular instances that spring to mind from our research – their value is always mediated by condition. Too worn, too 'bashed-about', too shabby and the brand or label loses its allure. Or, to take an even more extreme case: retro clothing, where much of the value is located in the imagined histories and biographies of consumption – of who wore this clothing, where, to which (authentic) events and so on. Similarly with household goods, books, bric-a-brac, vinyl. Missing and/or torn pages, scratches and 'knocks', 'chips', or even things like visible signs of overuse (frequently turned knobs, missing teapot lids and so on) all require negotiation, and are all associated with the traces of first-cycle consumption practices.

For us, then, one of the key points about second-hand is that it works to question the privilege accorded production within commodity-chain accounts, and to show that the practices of first-cycle consumption actually matter, to the very constitution of the second-hand market. What people actually do with things, how they use them, is as important to producing commodity biographies as the geographies of the commodity chain.

Although we have more sympathy with approaches that locate the importance of consumption in questions of identity formation and subjectivity, there is little doubt that second-hand poses difficulties here too. Chief among these is the representation of the act of purchase as an act located intrinsically within the first cycle of consumption, and as an act that is constitutive of social relations. While we would not want to deny the importance of the latter – indeed, we would agree that a very great deal of consumption is about acquisition (much of it first hand) that is about domestic provisioning, appropriate mothering and so on – the existence of the second-hand market shows that we ought not to be taking for granted that acquisition will always be through the first cycle. Instead, we need to problematize this, to ask in which conditions particular goods might be acquired through the second-hand market, where, how, by whom and for whom. And we need to think too about how the existence of spaces of second-hand exchange relate to practices of first-cycle consumption; to acknowledge that consumption includes the work of 'casting out' and giving away, and that it is as much about constituting alienable goods as it is the inalienable.

Correspondingly, one of our concerns in this volume is to explore the processes and practices by which and through which goods enter spaces of second-hand exchange, and what happens to them in consumption. Some of this is shown to be about the work of second-hand traders and retailers, for whom much of the 'work' is literally sourcing goods to sell. Involving complex linkages between various second-hand outlets – whereby retro retailers routinely visit boot sales and charity shops, or boot sale traders 'mine' jumble sales, as well as house clearances – these worlds are argued to be embedded primarily in local and/or regional geographies, although in the case of retro traders they may extend nationally or internationally. At the same time though, the goods offered for sale in second-hand sites are all ones that have been 'cast out' by someone. Part of our concern here then is to address just how and why goods come to be cast out, by whom, and in the process opened up to further cycles of consumption. This we show to be inextricably bound up in gendered practices of 'good housekeeping' – of monitoring consumption patterns, wear and use – and linked to acquisition, in the sense that 'casting out' is frequently allied with making room for more. But it is also shown to depend on the constitution of 'deserving others' and to be subject to practices of self-surveillance. What gets cast out, then, to where is argued to be a highly regulated, disciplined practice, one that depends on being able to 'cast out' respectably and on being able to replace and/or substitute goods. It is a practice that is argued to be associated with particular subject positions and class positions, and works to constitute critical differences between and within places in terms of the goods that appear 'for sale' in various second-hand sites.[4]

Turning to acquisition, one of the arguments that we make here is that acquisition through the second-hand market can involve practically any item – the one significant exception being food[5] – and that there is huge variation here, from goods that may change hands many times in a highly regulated manner (houses and, to a slightly lesser extent, cars being the obvious instances), to goods whose temporal durability is more limited – witness the relative scarcity of clothing from the 1960s and earlier – or goods that are only rarely exchanged (of which the 'art' market provides a good example). Another point that we make about acquisition through second-hand, however – particularly of the sorts of goods that concern us here – is that this is intrinsically connected to practices that reveal the work of consumption. Buying second-hand, then, is argued frequently to involve consumers in additional 'work'; far more so than is common with comparable goods purchased first hand, and this is shown to vary in relation to particular facets of material culture. Our main example here – and this is indicative of the spaces of exchange we researched – is second-hand clothing. Unlike clothing purchased first hand, most second-hand clothing has actually been worn. The goods therefore bear the traces – the imprints – of their previous owners; their bodies have literally left their marks, through personalized ways of wearing, smell and so on. Consequently, we show how these items require rituals of divestment – cleansing, purification and personalization – to enable them to enter new cycles of consumption. By way of comparison, other types of goods – and household consumables/tools are our prime example here – frequently require more conventional forms of 'work' – fixing, mending and repair – to enable reuse. Like divestment rituals, these activities entail working with various forms of practical knowledge, but in this case there is rarely a body to negotiate. Rather, objects are being restored, returned to working order. Again, this is totally unlike first hand acquisition, where the failure to work means the return of the good to the shop. Finally, we use the example of goods purchased for transformation. Here the work of consumption is shown to produce something else instead and to rely on the possession of sets of practical, skilled knowledge, often in conjunction with elite or specialist taste aesthetics. More akin to practices of first-cycle food acquisition and subsequent transformation into 'the meal', this is nonetheless an activity that differs again from many first-cycle practices. So, while material fabric, wool and DIY goods (paint, wallpaper and so on) are all bought first hand to be worked on to be transformed into something else (dress, jumper, made-over room), rarely are they bought – as they are second-hand – to be cannibalized, cut up. Here, then, we see the purchase of the object for its destruction.

Looking hard at what happens to second hand goods post-acquisition then starts to open up the partialities of accounts of consumption that rest exclusively on first-cycle practices. But, as we show, working on things and with things is not the only set of practices occurring within second-hand consumption that differentiates this from first hand. Another is associated with the ways in which – for some – second-hand goods are acquired precisely because of their previous use; a use that is imagined, that is located in a historic past, and that is valued above 'the new'. Often associated with the middle classes and used as a marker of distinction and discernment, these practices of consumption allow us to see not only why certain goods are acquired second-hand, but to unlock the importance of commodity biographies and to examine appropriate practices of second-hand consumption. Again, this is shown to vary in relation to particular facets of material culture, but one general tendency is clear: that practices of second-hand consumption for the middle classes are at their most appropriate when they juxtapose items purchased first and second-hand. So we show, for example, how wearing a combination of 'new' and 'retro' is constituted as 'knowing chic', while wearing primarily second-hand is to raise respectability fears; and we show too how the practice of purchasing 'trash' relies not just on being able to mobilize irony, but also on the presence of other things that display that 'trash' is indeed being bought appropriately, ironically. More generally, we use this to suggest that commodity biographies exist not just in a linear, temporal relation of first/second-hand, but in a spatial relation of articulation expressed in practices of consumption – in wearing, in display – where the certainties of the one unlock the potentials of the other, safely, in a framed, controlled juxtaposition of meaning.

At the same time as being purchased for use, items acquired second-hand are also bought for their symbolic value, as gifts and as part of collecting rituals. These two practices interest us in that they are clearly about constituting inalienable goods through the second-hand market, for self and others. And what we are interested in particularly here is the limits, as well as the possibilities for both sets of practices. In part heavily dependent on the sites we researched – in six years for example we have never realized the classic second-hand myth of 'I bought it for £1 and sold it for £30000!'[6] – the arguments we put forward here suggest that collecting needs to be seen as a ritualized form of practice. That this is both a pleasurable way of being in second-hand spaces of exchange – for 'the chase' – and a mode of acquisition, and that it can encompass some very ordinary goods (kids' toys, CDs for instance) as well as the more extraordinary (rare books, ceramics, antiques and so forth). Gifting, by comparison, and particularly gifting for key points in the gift economy – notably Christmas and individuals' birthdays – is argued to be hard work, very hard work. Entailing the unpredictability of the second-hand market as well as the need to buy something at the moment that anything appropriate is spotted, this form of acquisition requires routine 'traipsing' to satisfy, and is characterized by much frustration as trips fail to realize suitable purchases. In contrast, where gifting can work through second-hand is in offering up the impromptu, unplanned gift, of the 'I saw this and thought of you' form. This we argue to be a form of gifting that works in much the same way as through the first cycle, where what is being exchanged is shoppers' skills and knowledges in interpreting others' taste, and not just commodities per se.

Staking out that second-hand matters, and how, raises inevitably broader issues to do with our approach to and understanding of consumption, the relation of 'second-hand' to consumer culture, and 'the consumer'. Although this is not the place for an exhaustive discussion of these issues (for a useful review, see Slater, 1997), a few comments are in order.

Consumption, Consumer Culture and 'the Consumer'

Defining consumption is one of those academic endeavours that defies, indeed calls into question, its very purpose. Conjoining purchase, use, production and distribution, the global and the local, the relations between subject and object worlds, not to mention questions of need, choice and citizenship, consumption encompasses the conditions and the constitution of social life. Nonetheless, more manageable 'bites' are possible, and – along with many others – we regard consumption as about questions of acquisition and use of things (objects), but of less tangible things too including services (health, education and so forth). And we see acquisition and use to be culturally constituted; 'needs', wants, desires even, are intrinsically connected to the conditions and politics of their provision (market, state, third sector) and specific practices of use themselves impart meaning/s, not just to material objects but to services, leisure, time, space and place even. A concern with second-hand however, means that, for us, consumption remains – at least in part – about the relations between people and things. Rather than pursuing accounts that approach this relation by attempting to destabilize, even dissolve, the human/non-human distinction (notably actor-network theory and its derivatives: see Latour, 1993; Bingham, 1996; Whatmore, 1997, 1999), we (still) see this as a dialectical relation, in which people do not just appropriate things but in which people and things are positioned through objectification. Consequently, we follow Miller (1987), who – working from Hegel – defines objectification as entailing processes of externalization (in practice, the distancing of goods and services from the conditions and institutions of their production) and sublation (their reappropriation by society/ies through social subjects). Indeed, we would want to push these arguments slightly further: to argue that the biographies of things highlighted by 'second-hand' are indicative of the importance of the recursivity of objectification. The use of things, then, is not a straightforward, linear and finite act of objectification – something that is still implicit in many accounts of consumption practices – but something that may encompass multiple temporalities (and spatialities) of possession, that may involve multiple social subjects and contrasting – or at the very least changing – cultural milieux, and that may take place across different societies. Correspondingly, and as befits any dialectic, the process of objectification needs to be articulated repeatedly, recursively, in accounts of the practice/s of consumption. It is our hope that something of this comes across in what follows.

Talk of the biographies of things takes us on to the relation of 'second-hand' to consumer culture. One of our primary motivations in beginning this research was that 'second-hand' provides the potential for critique, resistance even. So, to buy and consume using the second-hand market could be argued to be a counter to many of the labels that mark out the 'consumer society' – its consumerism, materialism, the ceaseless desire for (and destruction of) 'the new' and so on (Campbell, 1992; Miles, 1998). And similarly, such activities could also be located within ethical and/or 'green' consumer movements – as part of a commitment to reuse, to sustainable forms of consumption, to using resources (and things) to their fullest potential (Bedford, 2002; Bookchin, 1990; Dobson, 1991, 1995; Elkington and Hailes, 1998; North, 1995; Trainer, 1985; cf. Imrie, 1989).[7]

Although primarily focused through consumer boycotts and campaigning on the commodity chain, the conditions of labour behind the brand, and on ethical trade,[8] 'second-hand' has the potential to be cast as another critical political moment within consumption; one where politics is located not in consumer knowledge/s that connect to the act of purchase, but in an act of purchase that is associated with maximizing the temporality of goods' durability.

When we set up the research, we expected to encounter a lot of this type of talk (and practice), especially among certain facets of the 'critical' middle classes, and we anticipated that 'second hand' goods and their consumers might be seen, and see themselves, as part of an alternative, critical consumer culture. What we actually found though was very different. So, although some did talk like this and act in such ways, they were – and are – but a very small minority among our respondents. Instead, consumption through the second-hand market turns out to be shaped by many of the very same motivations that shape consumer culture more generally. We see here then how thrift – saving money by working at consumption – is a prime imperative. About capturing relative value through 'the bargain', this works in much the same way as in first hand exchange, in that it is 'the bargain' – as much as, if not more than the good – that constitutes value. 'Distinction' too figures. Indeed, what is being sought through 'second-hand' frequently bears a marked similarity to the practices that shape designer purchasing and consumption in the first cycle: difference, taste and individuality. At first sight what this appears to suggest is that consumer culture – the meanings and practices that shape consumption – transcends the first/second-hand distinction, and that value, distinction, and indeed the brand are core consumption imperatives, permeating, constituting and even defining our relation to things in ways that seemingly obliterate the biographies of things. But, as we show here, while meanings might look identical, it is consumption practices that are of greater import. What matters for many acquiring goods through the second-hand market is the spaces through which goods are acquired. For many, then, consumption through the second-hand arena is 'clever' consumption, a set of practices which reveal and display heightened consumption knowledge/s and skills, and which encode the extent of investment in consumption. And space here, in the form of the distinctions between first and second-hand retail sites, is critical to sustaining such consumption practices. Correspondingly, rather than transcending the first/second-hand distinction, our research suggests that this distinction matters profoundly to the enactment of consumer culture.

From a very different perspective, we see too how the first/second-hand distinction works to highlight the ways in which the biographies of things intersect with consumer subject positions. As we show, 'clever' consumption through second-hand arenas and second-hand goods is not something that is necessarily pleasurable. It can be, and often is, resented; it is often hard work; and it is associated strongly with living on a limited income. For such individuals, second-hand goods (and retail spaces) can be a site of alienation. They signal that to be compelled through force of circumstance to consume second-hand goods is to be excluded from that which is desired, participation in the 'consumer society'. Resonant with Bauman's arguments about the importance of consumerism to the constitution of the 'new poor' (Bauman, 1998), this indicates that as well as signaling critical facets of contemporary consumer culture, 'second-hand' works to highlight the striations and inequalities within contemporary consumer society.

In terms of consumers: accounts of 'the consumer' within the consumption literature have moved a long way recently from the 'dupes' and 'heroes' of previous representations (Ewen, 1976) and from assumptions that consumers are individual agents, to acknowledge that consumption is about social relations, that it is also about sociality (Maffesoli, 1996) and that it encompasses the crowd (Slater, 1993), the mass, as much as the dislocated, isolated figure of the flâneur (Bauman, 1993; Wilson, 1991, 1992; Wolff, 1985). Moreover, there has been a move to recognize that consumers actually know a very great deal about what they do by way of consumption, and that they can articulate this discursively. As our work has progressed, however, we have come to develop a particular account of 'the consumer', one grounded in discourse and its links to material practices – that is, to what consumers actually do in their acquisition and use of things. It is important that we say rather more about this at this stage.

There are two points that we want to make at this juncture. First, this representation rests on a very close linguistic reading of what people actually say – in this case about 'second-hand'; how they talk about this, specifically as individuals and generally; the types of phrases that occur, significant ones as well as repetitive ones; the narratives that they use and those they don't; the silences; the discourses they cite and their dispositions toward these. We remain, then, totally committed to a model of inquiry that continues to take talk seriously, even if it does not make the mistake either of seeing this as the end point of analysis or of automatically equating talk and action. Second, this representation relies too on linking talk with practice – the latter being examined through both talk about what is done and, as critically, through observation. This too is regarded as citational of discourse. What this means is that we prefer readings of 'the consumer' to begin from a more general reading of the subject. So, rather than assuming a particular social relation between the consumer and things, or seeing the consumer as a means of transferring 'the social' onto 'the material', we err toward a more provisional, partial and fragile reading of the consumer that demonstrates in which conditions, where and when, particular consumer identities and subjectivities emerge. As we show, the spaces of second-hand exchange are particularly significant in this respect.

Having said something about the theoretical motivations for the research, we turn to our sites and our reasons for their selection.

The Sites

One of the benefits of conducting this research over a relatively long time-frame has been the way it has enabled site selection to take place alongside developments in our own understanding of second-hand worlds. When we began the research, car-boot sales were an obvious choice, and not just because they were then mass-participation, popular events reckoned to attract over one million people each weekend. Located for the most part in fields on the urban fringe; temporary, in that the regulatory context permitted only fourteen events on any one site per annum; and transient, in that they literally appear and then disappear, these sites seemed to us, at the time we began the research, to be the antithesis to the high street and the mall, and particularly to the 'cathedrals of consumption' that then prevailed in the literature. Often muddy, at the whims of the weather, pervaded by the smell of 'hot dogs' and 'burger vans', and characterized by piles of ordinary household goods and clothing, they were (and are) a long, long way from the likes of MetroCentre or West Edmonton Mall – or, for that matter, Wood Green or Brent Cross. Moreover, they turned out to be critical in other ways, particularly in their subversion of conventional, first hand social relations of exchange and in how they began to open up our understandings of consumption practices. Car-boot sales then took us to worlds where the rules and principles of exchange were remade; where people could both buy and sell, literally in the same space – mostly for cash, but sometimes without any exchange of money; where understandings of conventional 'guarantees' were suspended; and where prices were indicative rather than fixed, the basis for bargaining and haggling. Consequently, participation in this world – while it could be no more than idle looking – was shown to be grounded in specific sets of knowledge, and not just practical, accumulated knowledge about how (and where) to buy/sell but consumption knowledges too. So, car-boot sales led us to explore possession and personalization rituals; to practical (gendered) knowledges about how to mend or even transform particular goods; and to the beginnings of an engagement with the complexities of second-hand clothing, and with material culture.

It is these themes that have been critical to the subsequent choice of charity shops and retro shops as further case studies. So, one of the things we wanted to do here was to look at second-hand sites that are less transient in their location within the retail landscape; that are relatively 'fixed' in their spatial form, in shop units – even if they might occupy short-term leases – and that are positioned correspondingly in the interstices or on the edges of existing retail geographies, rather than on their margins.[9] Moreover, we wanted to examine sites where exchange relations appeared more in accordance with 'the market' – where buyers and sellers remained distinct, and where money was the only form of exchange, yet where imperatives other than 'the bargain' could be anticipated to be at work. Charity shops, then, were an obvious choice. With their transparent connections to both specific, named charitable causes and to acting charitably through donation, they provided an instance where second-hand exchange looked as if it might be interwoven with discourses of 'charity'. By contrast, retro shops – with their connection to second-hand 'style' – provided a clear opportunity to explore further the material culture of the self-stylized 'alternative'. More than this though, the significance of these two sites lies in their relation to second-hand exchange, in their contrasting, radically divergent, interpretations of 'second-hand'. So, whereas charity shops have come to be recast increasingly through 'charity-retail' – a practice that questions the distinction between 'first' and 'second' hand – retro shops, like car-boot sales, are by contrast founded on the distinction between first and second-hand, positively using this to create value – in this case around recontextualization.

Nor does the interrelatedness of our choice of sites stop at exchange. In terms of consumption, we wanted particularly to be looking at sites where less emphasis was placed on practical knowledge (the ability to mend/transform goods) and where rather more was placed on practices of appropriation and knowingness.[10] In short, we wanted to be looking at spaces with large quantities of second-hand clothing that enabled us to explore more fully than was possible with car-boot sales, issues

of divestment and personalization, recontextualization and the importance of imagined histories (and geographies), and of fashion in second-
hand clothing. Again, given their stock balance, charity and retro shops
were the obvious choices – although we would note that contemporary
trends around 'vintage clothing' make this a rather more significant
site now than it appeared in late 1997 when we wrote the research
proposal.

Structure of the Book

'The mission' discussed above provides the core structure to the book.
However, we supplement this with an appendix containing a fuller
discussion of our methods. Still rarely acknowledged within research
monographs such as this, explicit discussion of methods is nonetheless
important – to the development of arguments, to exposing what can
as well as what cannot be said, and to representing research as practice
(see too Hermes, 1995). Chapters 2 to 4 inclusive tackle spatialities of
exchange. Chapter 2 focuses on the geographies of 'location' and examines how and why second-hand spaces are located on the margins and
in the interstices of conventional retail space. Chapter 3 is concerned
with elaborating the distinctions between our three sites of exchange
and their encoding, not just in the principles of exchange but in the
regimes of representation used to constitute shop interiors. Together
these two chapters work to establish the various premises and principles
of second-hand exchange and their inscription as spatialized practices,
and to establish the discordance between the practices of retailers and
of certain second-hand shoppers which threatens both the context for
value creation and the future trajectory of second-hand worlds. In
Chapter 4 we consider this further, exploring in depth the various
practices of second-hand shoppers, practices that we show to weave
together a number of second-hand sites in ways that both blur their
distinctions and maximize their distance from the spaces of first-cycle
exchange. Chapters 5 to 7 turn to questions of consumption. In Chapters 5 and 6 we focus on developing our account of the biographies of
things. Chapter 5 examines how goods come to be in second-hand
spaces of exchange, specifically how they are both cast out from households and sourced by traders, devalued and reclaimed for potential
revaluation. Chapter 6 moves on to consider the rituals and practices
through which goods purchased in second-hand arenas come to be
reappropriated in consumption practices. Chapter 7 is concerned with
the distinctive consumption practices of gifting and collecting, and their

articulation through 'second-hand'. Finally, in Chapter 8 we turn to reflect on likely futures for second-hand exchange and consumption, to re-examine whether such activities can provide any basis for a progressive politics of consumption, and to signal the importance of these sites for future research trajectories.

Part I

Spatialities of Exchange

In this first set of interrelated chapters our concern is with the spatialities of second-hand exchange. The three chapters take three distinctive 'cuts' at this question. First, in Chapter 2 we consider the *geographies of location*. Entailing both physical and symbolic properties, these geographies are concerned with how and why particular versions of second-hand exchange come to be located where, yet reveal too the centrality of 'first hand' retail locations in this process. Here space, in the form of symbolic distance and proximity, is shown to be central in shaping just where in absolute terms second-hand exchange occurs. Secondly, in Chapter 3 we explore the *production of* car-boot sales, retro shops and charity shops as *spaces* that encode particular principles and premises about second-hand exchange. By contrast, both retro shops and charity shops are demonstrated to be associated with particular regimes of representation that seek to regulate second-hand exchange in ways that elevate specific, often singular, premises. Thirdly, in Chapter 4 we examine how these spaces are *made sense of* through shopping as *practised*. We are concerned here with how consumers constitute shopping geographies involving second-hand sites; with the modes of being and relations of looking (and buying) shoppers reveal; and with how these connect with particular subject positions.

A core thread running through the three chapters is the way in which all three spatialities are underpinned by an oppositional understanding of the relation between first and second-hand exchange. In the case of location this is displayed through the pervasiveness of a centre-margin metaphor; where the distance that this creates is used to confer both symbolic distance and proximity for different second-hand sites. Similarly with the production of space: second-hand retail spaces are shown

17

to use the same oppositional imaginary to suggest both disassociation with first hand exchange and to attempt to collapse this distinction. And with shopping as practised, regardless of subject position, we see how the first/second-hand opposition is mapped into practice; how shoppers use this to suggest vastly different but consistently oppositional notions of what second-hand exchange is considered to be about. In all these cases what is construed as 'centre' is clearly the spaces and the practices of first hand retailing. Loathed and revered, desired as well as shunned by those involved in second-hand exchange, their practices of exchange and their products figure as the constant against which and in relation to which second-hand exchange is constituted. And therein lies a problem: for these spaces and practices of the first cycle do not stand still. Instead, they encroach and emulate, as well as disregard what goes on within second-hand sites. What we see in practice, then, is a rather more fuzzy relation than the certainties suggested by the centre-margin metaphor, in which the first/second-hand distinction is increasingly being called into question – for example by 'mainstream' retailers selling second-hand goods, and by juxtapositions of 'the copy' with the authentic within second-hand spaces. Nonetheless, as we go on to argue, while (second-hand) retailers might be moving in certain directions, shoppers' practices continue to value the first/second-hand distinction, to the extent that this distinction is argued to provide the conditions within which value itself emerges within second-hand exchange.

t w o

Geographies of 'Location'

As we indicated in Chapter 1, one of the characteristics of second-hand worlds in the UK over the past twenty years or so has been their proliferation. So, from a situation in which the predominant forms of such exchange comprised locally organized jumble sales and the circulation of goods within familial and social networks, we now find a far more complex pattern encompassing multiple forms of second-hand exchange, characterized by diverse social relations, from car-boot sales to charity shops, retro shops and dress agencies, nearly new sales and the 'classifieds', auction clearances and antique fairs, as well as jumble sales. At the same time, the proliferation in forms of second-hand exchange has been accompanied by their growth numerically. Although notoriously hard to quantify, in that many forms of second-hand exchange are temporary and transient, numerical growth raises several key questions. Some of these concern issues of supply: with so many potential outlets for second-hand goods, traders are competing among themselves for stock and, for those trading within more conventional retail settings (shops, with regular rental payments), regular stock flow has become increasingly critical to survival. However, growth has also brought to a head questions of space, particularly: where second-hand exchange can occur; what appropriate spaces for various forms of second-hand exchange might be; and the relation between 'first hand' and 'second-hand' spaces of exchange. In a very real sense, then, the proliferation and growth in second-hand worlds has been about constituting geographies, about establishing appropriate locations for exchange – in some cases, as with car-boot sales, literally from scratch.

It is these concerns that provide our focus in this chapter. We begin by saying something more about proliferation and growth, particularly with respect to our case-study sites. Then, using three depth studies, we show how each of these entails highly distinctive negotiations with existing retail geographies to produce, in turn, particular geographies

19

of 'location'. The first, pertaining to car-boot sales in the mid-1990s, is a study in regulatory power. We show here how car-boot sales are located on the margins of, indeed often beyond, conventional under-standings of retail space, and that they are placed there through the workings of regulatory power – a power that in this case is about pro-tecting existing, often monopolistic, market environments through processes that both seek to 'other' car-boot sales and constrict the spaces in which they might operate. Our second instance is very different. Here we show how retro retailers invoke the notion of 'the alternative', counterposed to an imagined 'mainstream' that itself is identified with the high street, to produce geographies of location that are continually about symbolic positioning – for example, in particular cities and not others, within particular neighbourhoods and not others – and that, as a consequence, can be relatively transient, at least by the standards of conventional retailing. Thirdly, and finally, we show how other forms of second-hand exchange – charity shops – are increasingly being located in the interstices of existing 'first hand' retail space, literally on the high street and in small shopping centres, as well as in spaces identified with 'the alternative'. The coincidence between the project of charity retailing and particular tendencies within 'first hand' retail geographies has meant that it has become both desirable and possible for certain elements of the charity-shop sector to constitute the high street as an appropriate space of second-hand exchange. Rather than work-ing against the high street, then – as retro retail does – charity retailers are attempting to erase the very same distinctions that retro retailers valorize, and to constitute themselves in terms of the Same. At the same time, however, at least some charity retailers are positioning certain of their shops within particular cultural quarters, in the heart of the spaces of retro retailing. Although demonstrating the ubiquity of second-hand exchange – that this can occur literally anywhere – we argue that this is interpreted more accurately as highlighting the inappropriateness of certain forms of second-hand exchange in particular retail spaces. The study works therefore to show how geography matters in constit-uting limits to the possibilities for particular versions of second-hand exchange. Where this takes us is to a set of more general arguments about the spatialized practices of second-hand exchange, their relation to the varying premises of second-hand exchange and their connection to first hand retail geographies. These we discuss in the final section of the chapter.

Proliferation and Growth

The proliferation in second-hand sites of exchange in the UK, particularly from the 1970s onward, is something that was commented on
by most of the participants in this research. Moreover, it is demonstrably
ubiquitous, in that – aside from in the remotest areas – the spectrum
of car-boot sales, charity shops and the classifieds, as well as auction
clearances and the occasional jumble sale, are taken-for-granted facets
of social and economic life. Along with household tips, dustbins and
skips, they are sites (and events) that are assumed to punctuate everyday life. At the same time, however, proliferation has occurred in other
sites of second-hand exchange, which clearly mark out social difference
and inscribe it geographically. Indeed, in their different ways dress
agencies, retro shops, antiquarian and second-hand book and record
shops and antique fairs are all indicative of a burgeoning second-hand
market constituted in relation to middle-class sensibilities, values and
taste markers.

Seen at its simplest and most reductionist, proliferation can be equated
with consumerism, with the rise of multiple forms of second-hand
exchange being linked clearly to disposal practices that enable further
bouts of purchase, themselves fuelled by the product design cycle and
fashion imperatives. To see things entirely thus, however, is to deny
the complexities of these sites and their differences from each other. For
us, then, the importance of proliferation lies not only in its connections
to consumerism but in what it has to say too about the development
of the second-hand market in the UK. As we show now in relation to
our three sites, this has been a story of growth, and in some cases agglomeration – at least through the 1990s.

The numerical growth in particular versions of second-hand exchange
became a key area of debate throughout the 1990s, with negative press
being received by both car-boot sales and charity shops (see for example
Burns Howell, 1993; Keating, 1998; Rawlinson, 1992; Revell, 1998).
Invariably, much of this 'debate' came down to, and in some cases got
bogged-down in 'the numbers game', with car-boot sales providing the
most intractable set of measurement problems. Given their temporary
nature, not to mention the vagaries of the British weather and highly
variable regulatory contexts, measuring the number of car-boot sales
occurring per annum even in one region, let alone nationally, would be
a massive, highly labour-intensive undertaking. Certainly it was something that was beyond our research budget and resources. Moreover, it
is instructive to note that even those with the resources to contemplate

such an undertaking – local authorities and market research organizations – have been content to infer growth rather than measure it, relying instead on mass-participation claims to make the point (LACOTS, 1993). The launch of the 'alternative market place' listings guide *The Car Boot and Market Calendar* in July 2001, which aims to be the definitive guide to events, may make future numerical estimation somewhat easier. However, at present this is heavily biased toward car-boot sales occurring in the South and South-east, with listings for Sundays through July and August routinely recording approximately 130 such events. In our view, though, however well developed they might become, listings of car-boot sales will be at best indicative rather than definitive. Part of the attraction of car-boot sales is their location within detailed local knowledge – about which events are 'good' or 'better than' others. And, as even those behind listings acknowledge, this is likely to mean that some events will continue to remain less widely publicized than others.

By contrast, the expansion in the numbers of charity shops, particularly through the 1990s, is well documented (Horne, 2000; Mintel, 1997; NGO Finance, 1999; Parsons, 2000). So, for example, while the number of charity shops in 1990 was approximately 3200, by 1999 this had doubled to 6500, with shop income increasing from an estimate of around £130m in 1990 to £350m in 1999. Associated with the activities of the major charity retailers, including Oxfam (2001: 829 shops), British Heart Foundation (435 shops) and Imperial Research Cancer Fund (420 shops),[11] in the sector this expansion is widely considered to have 'peaked'. Indeed, the 2001 Charity Finance Report presents a picture of a 'shrinking sector', with more shops being closed than opened[12] and a marginal growth in profit of 0.6 per cent following the 1999 fall of 11 per cent and an 8.7 per cent decline in 2000.[13] Following a period of stasis, evaluation and consolidation consequent upon difficulties in sourcing, staffing and uncertainties over the business context for second-hand trading,[14] it is likely that the future for the charity shop sector will be 'leaner' and 'meaner'.

Growth too has been a characteristic of retro trading, and is in part connected to 1960s, 1970s and, latterly, 1980s design, fashion and interiors revivals (Alexander, 1999, 2000; Armstrong, 2000, 2001; Barkham, 1991; Bret, 2001; Gold, 2001; Homer, 2001; Polan, 1999; Rickey, 2001; Saunders, 2001; Spindler, 1994; Watson, 2001; Webb, 1998). It is important to note, however, that in comparison to the extensive commercial strategies of either charity retailers or car-boot sale promoters, this is small-scale and indicative of a specialist rather than mass market in second-hand goods. Growth here, though, is much harder to document than with charity shops, and not just because many retro traders continue either to trade from market stalls or to occupy short-term, end-of-lease units and consequently are frequently transient figures in the retail landscape. Indeed, even relatively established retro retailers are largely invisible in terms of conventional business directories and store listings. This we can see using the case of one of our retro case study cities, Nottingham. If one were to try to identify retro retail outlets from standard sources such as business directories, the Thompson Guide, Yellow Pages and so on, one would be under the impression that either there were no such outlets in Nottingham or that there were very few. Only one directory lists second-hand shops (Thompson) and even here only two retro or vintage clothes shops are listed (Daphne's Handbag and Revival). Further scrutiny of these directories locates other retro clothing shops in mis- or poorly classified places: Celia's is, for example hidden away under the fancy dress section, while Baklash is listed among the first-cycle menswear shops such as Burton and Cruise Flannels. Based on official sources, then, there would be very little evidence for the growth of retro retailing in Nottingham. Yet, if one abandons conventional directory listings and relies instead on localized, micro-geographical knowledge of the city, it is possible in time to identify at least 14 retro and/or vintage shops, some of which have been there in excess of 15 years (Celia's and Baklash), some of which have expanded their operations through the 1990s – Atomic, for example, had just one store in Nottingham in the late 1980s and now has three – and others which were new entrants in the late 1990s (Acrylic Afternoons, for instance).

A similar picture characterizes our other retro case-study cities. In Bristol, for example, the Nottingham story of invisibility masking growth repeats itself. Looking through the Yellow Pages and Business Directories again sheds little light on the extent or distribution of retro shops: there are no listings under second-hand clothes shops, nor under retro, nor under fancy dress. Indeed, the only headings that relate to second-hand are second-hand furniture dealers and house clearances. As with Nottingham, relatively long-established retro shops – Repsycho on Gloucester Road and Uncle Sam's on Park Street – are hidden away among the listings for first-cycle menswear, and appear in the Yellow Pages alongside ubiquitous mass-market retailers such as Top Man and Next. Again, then, without detailed local knowledge one might assume that there are only two retro shops in the entire city, when there are at least eight, the majority of which are clustered in and around the University streets of Park Street and Gloucester Road.

Our third retro case-study city is London – a reflection of its quantitative and qualitative significance in terms of (second-hand) fashion, as well as in avant-garde design, subcultures and streetstyle. Here though, our lack of detailed local knowledge makes the documentation of retro trading's growth difficult, if not impossible. Nonetheless, even the use of dedicated guides such as *Time Out*'s Shopping Guide (1999) and the *London Fashion Guide* reveal that London's retro scene has a long history, that it is temporally transient, and that – like Bristol and Nottingham – expansion has been accompanied by agglomeration tendencies, and increasing niche marketing. There are then over 50 retro and vintage clothing stores in the inner London area. Some of these are in stand-alone and isolated (in retro terms) areas of the city – for example, Hippy Chick in Uxbridge, which sells a range from black dresses to glam and glitter; Cornucopia in Victoria, which sells relatively cheap, often theatrical second-hand clothes; and Virginia in Holland Park, which is at the upper end of the vintage clothes market, and sells primarily to designers, collectors and models. By comparison, elsewhere there are marked clusters of retro and vintage stores, notably in the Notting Hill, Portobello and Ladbroke Grove area (including Still, The Antique Clothing Shop, Sheila Cook, Dolly Diamond, Ember, The Crazy Clothes Collection, One of a Kind, Rellick, Retro Man/Woman, Vent and 295). Complicated by transience, in that many of the stalls on Portobello Market also sell retro fashion (on Fridays and Saturdays only), this agglomeration is mirrored on a smaller scale in other areas of the city – for instance Covent Garden and Greenwich.

Growth as we have discussed it here, then, is clearly linked to the developing market in second-hand goods, as is agglomeration and specialization. Involving the exchange of mass and specialist goods, growth is indicative of the extent to which second-hand sites are not simply reducible to issues of disposal and consumerism but are about market differentiation and consolidation too. At the same time the debate over growth is itself instructive, and principally for the way in which it highlights concern over commercialization. So, whereas specialist second-hand sites – retro shops for example, although antique fairs would be another instance – are often talked-up as style markers in the fashion press and weekend supplements, it is the rise of the commercial mass second-hand market that is construed negatively, consistently. Witness how 'charity' car-boot sales are seen as acceptable whereas their commercial counterparts are not; how pre-packaged retro is seen as a stylistic cop-out; and how the debate over the image of the charity shop inspires considerable negative media attention. What this is about, in part, is threat and competition – that a fully developed second-hand market has the potential at least to raise question marks about some of the basic principles of contemporary consumption (as well as production and distribution), not least the identification of consumption with first-cycle purchase/s. But what it is also about, fundamentally, is questions of geography and space – that second-hand sites of exchange have to be located somewhere. In the following three case studies we explore in depth the constitution of three of these geographies of 'location'.

Constituting Geographies of Second-hand Exchange from Scratch: Car-boot Sales and the Workings of Regulatory Power

Located primarily, although not exclusively, in fields, car parks and/or open spaces on the urban fringe, car-boot sales' proliferation and expansion has been accompanied by periodic, yet extensive, debate over their regulation.[15] As we show here, using the debate of the early-to-mid 1990s as our example, the issues raised by such debate are profoundly geographical; they are about excluding car-boot sales from particular areas – typically those that come under the jurisdiction of local

Plate 2.1 Car boot sale, South-east England, September 2001

Plate 2.2 Car boot advertisement: Nottinghamshire, September 2001

authority market areas – and about precisely which sorts of spaces may become sites for second-hand exchange. Addressed head-on by commercial car-boot sale operators, frequently working in partnership with various landowners, and seeking to expand the frequency and geographical reach of their operations, these tendencies have brought commercial operators and particular local authorities into direct conflict. Correspondingly, what we see here is a situation in which, on the one hand, car-boot sale operators attempt to work around – and on occasion challenge – existing geographies of exclusion, while on the other, various regulatory bodies come together simultaneously to reinscribe existing spaces of exchange and to 'other' the car-boot sale phenomenon.[16]

The case of two commercial car-boot sale promoters provides clear examples of how geography matters to the development of their operations. Take 'Aladdin's Cave Fairs' (pseudonym). Set up in 1992, at the time of our research, Aladdin's Cave Fairs ran six boot sales in the North Nottinghamshire and North Derbyshire area. These took place in Chesterfield (Wednesday), Bolsover (Thursday), Pleasley (Friday), Skegby (Saturday) and Dinnington and Sherwood Forest Farm, Edwinstowe near Mansfield (Sunday). As the interview with the promoter of Aladdin's Cave Fairs revealed – notwithstanding the importance of intensifying the temporal and spatial reach of their business – it was the different approaches of particular local authorities that were critical to the location of these sales:

> North-east Derbyshire have been very hard, where I've been anyway. I think it often depends on the attitude of the landowners as well. You know we had a lot of hassle over the indoor one at Botany Commercial Park (Mansfield), but because we weren't going to give in, both me and the owner of the property, you can put up a really good case really... I was a little bit concerned about going into Mansfield, so near to the centre really. I mean, ideally if you can be outside of six and two-thirds of a market and near to a village or a reasonably built-up area and you've got facilities, then I think you're ok... But yeah, I would be very sceptical of setting up in the middle of Sheffield for example. You think you would be up against it there.

Certain local authorities in this area, then, notably Sheffield and Rotherham in South Yorkshire, and certain of the north-east Derbyshire authorities, were at the time taking a particularly hard line in relation to car-boot sale operations, going so far as to ensure that commercial operators such as Aladdin's Cave Fairs were actively excluded from their areas of regulatory control. And, in achieving this, as the testimony of this boot sale promoter revealed, it is the possession of market franchise rights that frequently proved critical.

Similar comments were made by the promoter of 'Funtime Promotions' (pseudonym): established in 1988, and based primarily in the North-east, Funtime Promotions at the time was the largest car-boot sale operator in Northern England, with nineteen venues then open per week – ranging from Wetherby in West Yorkshire to Carlisle in the West and Ashington, Northumberland in the North-east. A handful of these ventures were run in association with certain local authorities, but the majority were joint ventures involving Funtime and a private sector developer. However, just as Aladdin's Cave Fairs found certain of the South Yorkshire and north-east Derbyshire authorities to be 'very difficult', so Funtime ran into problems with Newcastle City Council and their proactive use of market franchise rights to protect the Sunday Market on the Quayside. But, unlike Aladdin's Cave Fairs, Funtime chose to take the local authority on, in several ways. So, rather than accept exclusion, the promoter chose to contest this – albeit unsuccessfully – by transgressing the 14-day rule, going to appeal and attempting to establish a site as a permanent boot sale; by suggesting partnership agreements and by offering the local authority a substantial sum by way of an annual car-boot licence fee.

Both these instances point to one of the key rationales behind the exclusion of car-boot sale operations from certain areas: the protection of monopolistic market environments by key metropolitan authorities, and the importance of the possession of market franchise rights in this. At the same time as taking on particular operators however, the same authorities played a key role in the anti-car-boot-sale lobby of the mid-1990s. As we show now, car-boot sales were here represented as the antithesis of 'quality', local-authority controlled markets and as sites of exchange in which goods, dealers and sellers are in flagrant contravention of exchange conventions. Therefore they figure clearly as 'the other' to conventional market spaces of exchange.

Through the mid-1990s car-boot sale regulation was repeatedly called for by a loose coalition of interest groups including: a small cross-party group of MPs, as well as local authority trading standards officers and their representative body, the Local Authorities Co-ordinating Body on Food and Trading Standards (LACOTS),[17] the National Association of British Market Authorities (NABMA),[18] the Association of Metropolitan Authorities (AMA), the Association of District Councils (ADC), the Federation of Small Businesses (FSB), the Chamber of Commerce and the police. This came to a head in 1994 with the debate over the DCO legislation,[19] and is interesting not simply in terms of its specifics but for its representation of car-boot sales as an enterprise culture out of control; as a phenomenon that existing legislation could not control; and, correspondingly, as a phenomenon that was in dire need of tighter regulation. Three themes underpinned this: the allegedly dubious nature of the goods for sale at car-boot sales (and their sellers) – stolen, counterfeit, peddled by 'criminals' and 'rogues'; the 'unfair competition' which car-boot sales were deemed to provide for conventional market and high-street traders; and the escalation story – that car-boot sales were literally out of control.

The 'dodgy goods, dodgy dealers' image of car-boot sales is one that featured repeatedly throughout the 1990s debate, and is indeed the 'story' that prevailed in the press coverage of the time. For example, in one article the journalist drew explicit parallels between car boot sale traders and the characters of Del Boy and Rodders in *Only Fools and Horses*,[20] highlighting car-boot sales as venues for the sale of counterfeit jewellery, clothing and perfume, as well as illegal copies of audio tapes, videos and computer games (and see too Allen, 1994; Boggan, 1994; Burns Howell, 1993; Constant, 1993; Lavelle, 1995a, 1995b; Waundby, 1995; *Which?* 1994; Young, 1993). Nonetheless, this view is one that connects most strongly with the trading standards remit of local authorities, and – as such – it was LACOTS that proved particularly proactive in disseminating this particular representation of car-boot sales. Indeed, in their 1993 discussion paper on car boot sales, LACOTS presented a picture of car-boot sales that, while acknowledging their popularity, depicted these events as populated by 'wheeler-dealers' of the 'Arthur Daley' style,[21] peddling unsafe, stolen and counterfeit goods on to an unsuspecting and naïve public:

> Most boot sales feature at least some trading disguised as private sales. The rogues engaged in such deception take considerable steps to avoid being detected. One example . . . involved vehicle licensing plates being obscured, or more enterprisingly, replaced with false plates. Another favourite trick, particularly by those selling counterfeits, is to display two or three items at a time. When these are sold an accomplice waiting some distance away with the majority of the stock will then supply further copies . . . without doubt car boot sales have become a major outlet for stolen goods . . . the spoils from a great deal of petty crime are ending up at a boot fair, the pickings from cars and garden sheds seemingly most popular. (LACOTS, 1993, sections 2.3, 6.3)

Similar representations spilled over into the interventions of MPs, and informed the pro-regulation stance of many involved in debate over the DCO legislation:

> I have been struggling to find an explanation for why the government have been inactive in addressing the very real problem of car boot sales which have been burgeoning and mushrooming during recent year. We know that they are breeding grounds for crime . . . at car boot sales deals are done in cash and stolen goods are here today and gone the next. They are run by fly by night operators. (Prentice, Pendle, *Hansard* 1994, column 568)

Although continuing to represent car-boot sales as perpetrators of noise, nuisance and disturbance, and as characterized by the exchange of stolen and/or counterfeit goods, other agencies involved in pressure to regulate car-boot sales in the mid-1990s promoted a slightly different image. For the FSB, the NABMA, the ADC and the AMA for instance, car-boot sales represented a form of 'unfair' competition for established businesses – notably market traders. Here, for example, is the view of Dr Bernard Juby, the then FSB spokesperson on trade and industry:

> Professional car boot sales and itinerant markets are creating a major problem for legitimate local traders and licensed market traders who are being undercut and undermined by unlicensed, unregulated, untaxed and often unregistered or non-VATable business. (quoted by Harris, 1994)

Similar sentiments were expressed both by the NABMA and by the ADC in response to the proposed abolition of market franchise rights under the DCO Bill (ADC, 1993, 1994; NABMA, 1994; and also ACC, 1994). So in their responses to this bill, both agencies represented car-boot sales as posing a direct threat to existing markets and market traders, and made some very clear links between car-boot sales and the then intense debate over town-centre versus out-of-town developments. Indeed, as the following extracts (in reply to DoE 1993) testify, permanent markets are argued to be bearers of tradition and heritage, and to be vital components within town-centre retailing, whereas car-boot sales are seen as their antithesis:

> Local authority markets provide an important focal point for retailing in town centres . . . the likely implication of relaxation of market rights would be the development of a number of small markets and car boot sales on the outskirts of towns which would operate in direct competition for the limited amount of trade that exists. The beneficial spin off effect which currently exists for permanent shop keepers would be lost, potentially undermining commercial viability of town centres and reducing the opportunity for local enterprise. (ADC, 1994, paragraph 2.1)

> Local authorities have successfully operated markets for many years. These markets are part of the country's heritage and tradition. Local authority markets make a vital contribution to the commercial viability of many town and city centres. The abolition of market rights will not only threaten markets but other town centre trading activities . . . Local authorities use their market rights responsibly . . . The vast increase in

car boot sales has caused problems for enforcement agencies . . . These events, which in recent years have proliferated, have caused many problems, particularly with respect to noise, nuisance, disturbance, stolen and counterfeit goods and public health concerns. (NABMA, 1994, pp 1–2)

In identifying car-boot sales as 'unfair competition' for local markets and local-market traders, such bodies highlight a local-authority role supplementary to that of trading-standards enforcement, namely that of enforcing a particular operating environment for exchange – one which enables existing businesses to continue to trade successfully and one in which the aim is to prohibit non-conventional activities. Throughout these texts, quality markets are equated with local-authority-operated events and are seen as sites of exchange where consumers have the right of redress, where goods for sale and traders have to conform with existing trading legislation, and where the site itself is run in accordance with environmental health regulations. In contrast, car boot sales are portrayed as the antithesis of such markets, as in complete contravention of exchange legislation, and as epitomizing a deregulatory market environment.

As well as portraying car-boot sales as 'unfair competition' and as dominated by 'fly-by-night' traders, a final strand in the anti-car-boot-sale lobby's representation of the mid-1990s was to present it as spiralling out of control. Promoted strongly by NABMA, and voiced by many of the local authorities responding to our survey, the following annotation to one of our questionnaire returns is typical of these sentiments:

> A few years ago car boot sales were low key with little problems. However, several began to be operated on a professional basis, including large numbers of professional traders. The scale of the boot sales increased dramatically, and with it a commensurate increase in noise, disturbance and traffic. Certainly there is a clear sense in which local authorities feel powerless to intervene and seek a stronger regulatory framework from central government and/or greater local authority power. (Northern local authority)

Unregulated and uncontrollable, highly successful and undermining of permanent markets and town centres, and characterized by a plethora of Arthur Daleys and Del Boys unloading mountains of dodgy gear onto the unsuspecting masses – such was the representation of car-boot sales in the 1990s, both in policy circles and within the mass media.

As we argued at the time, the above representation of car-boot sales was connected intimately to the protection of a set of interests and geographies of exchange that were disrupted, challenged even, by car-boot sales and their popularity.[22] But as well as being about existing geographies of exchange, the proliferation of car-boot sales raised profound questions about the temporalities and spatialities of exchange. Excluded from particular sorts of spaces by the existing regulatory framework, car-boot-sale operators turned to other landowners – often farmers on the urban fringe, racecourse executives and so forth – to establish sites. And the spectre that this introduced was 'matter out of place'. Bouncy castles, the pervasive smell of hot dogs and onions, a vista of fields and verge sides crammed full of thousands of cars stretching to the horizon, traffic jams at 5.30 am, throngs of people for the most part dressed in scruffy clothing, mountains of second-hand goods and litter: all combined to threaten the codes of English suburban-fringe Sunday-morning respectability and sensibilities. In transforming fields into boot sales then, promoters and developers were literally disrupting – visually, aurally and olfactorily – many of the taken-for-granted practices associated with the rhythms of weekly life among a particular fragment of the English middle classes. They were literally constituting

Plate 2.3 Sunday morning juxtapostions: middle-class suburbia and the boot sale

a 'inappropriate' form of exchange in an 'inappropriate' location, often at a time – Sunday morning – that was possibly the most inappropriate, at least by suburban conventions. Yet – and this is potentially the greatest irony geographically – in doing this, at least on no more than 14 occasions on any one site per annum, promoters and developers were working within the terms of the existing regulatory framework. In protecting their 'quality' markets then, local authorities simultaneously have displaced car-boot sales elsewhere – to the margins and beyond in retail terms – and facilitated the constitution from scratch of new geographies of second-hand exchange.

Constituting 'Difference' through Location: the Symbolic Geographies of Retro Retailing

In comparison to the situation with car-boot sales, the geographies of retro retailing have little to do with exclusion and regulatory power and a very great deal to do instead with the symbolic positioning of exchange. Here then, rather than being prohibited from particular trading spaces, it is the negotiation of the retail landscape that matters: for retro retailers, trading in one particular location and not in others matters critically to sustaining a particular positioning within and understanding of 'the alternative' that remains at the heart of their business – although, as we shall see, what this actually means in practice is hotly contested. This aside, inscriptions of the 'alternative' in the retail landscape – particularly when constituted in opposition to a 'mainstream' – are inherently unstable geographically. Continually vulnerable to the processes of property (re)valorization and gentrification (Smith, 1979, 1996; Smith and Williams, 1986),[23] attempts to 'fix' the 'alternative' in discrete bounded spaces invariably flounder, and result in transient geographies of location as yet more marginal spaces are sought out by those looking to escape the incursions of 'the mainstream' (Cooper 2000; Dyson 1998; Fletcher 2000; McConnell 1999; Rickey 1999). For retro retailers, as we show, this poses a dilemma: either they can become increasingly commercial, 'move up', and risk becoming incorporated within 'the mainstream', or they can 'move with' the flight of 'the alternative' and relocate, or indeed they can 'move out' of the business altogether. As such, their current geographies of location are argued to reveal much about, be dependent on, and sustain particular understandings of 'retro' within 'the alternative'.

Retro Retailing (as alternative)	Conventional retailing (the mainstream)
Products	
One-off; unique	Mass-produced; ubiquitous
Real; authentic	Manufactured; copies
Aesthetic; symbolic goods	Value as economic
Retailers and consumers	
Creative, scene-setters	Following 'fashion'
Individual	Corporate
Knowing (elite)	Unknowing (the masses)
Work practices	
Drifting	Planned (career)
Intuitive	Trained
Work as fun	Work as business
Work as creative	Work as dull, boring, routine
Spatialities	
Self-styled 'alternative' Quarters	High streets/out-of-town malls
In stylish cities	Everywhere

Figure 2.1 The oppositional imaginings of retro retailers

Figure 2.1 displays the core tenets underpinning retro retailers' talk about the business of retro retailing, its location within 'the alternative' and its reliance on an oppositional imaginary in which the high street and the mainstream are seen to represent the antithesis of what this particular take on second-hand is considered to be about.

Figure 2.1 also begins to uncover one of the central paradoxes of the business of retro retailing: that at the same time as mobilizing discourses of the creative industries, retro retailing rests on the exchange of previously commodified, often mass-produced goods – goods that typically were located in the mainstream during their first cycle of exchange and consumption. As well as marking out the differences between retro retailers and others working in the creative industries, whose businesses are often built on the commercial application of their own creativity (Leadbeater and Oakley, 1999), this paradox points to the critical

Plate 2.4 Nottingham, Lace Market

importance of space for retro retailers. Indeed, to sell this type of second-hand good – through distinction and discernment – requires that exchange itself be located within retail spaces that themselves are constituted through such meanings; typically in the cultural-industry quarters of key cities that are associated with a specific nexus of fashion, music and design tendencies (Manchester's Northern Quarter, Nottingham's Lace Market, Bristol's Park Street, Sheffield's Devonshire Quarter, for example, as well as London's Notting Hill and Hoxton). This we can see from the following comments by retro retailers we interviewed about Bristol's Park Street and Nottingham's Lace Market respectively:

> We came to Park Street because Park Street's more of a fashion street. There's a lot of shops in Park Street which are more interesting than going into the centre. The centre's more bland, more for family appeal. It's like, this is not, urm, more, fashion's come more into Bristol this year then, you know it's not like a small, not Carnaby Street, Kings Road, it's you know, it's just itself. (Kevin: Bristol retailer)

> I do like Nottingham . . . the student population certainly helps in creating a healthy retro fashion scene. But I think the types of courses

and students makes a difference. Loughborough is all sports students. But the fashion, arts and media people at Trent are very aware of style. They're much more concerned about their image . . . they tend to be much more creative about their style. (Elaine: Nottingham retailer)

Immediately we see how Kevin inscribes 'the alternative' into location: Park Street is counterposed to 'the centre'; it is represented as at the cutting edge of fashion, in comparison to the 'blandness' of the centre; and it is seen as distinctively different – not Carnaby Street, not the King's Road, just itself. Moreover, we can see too how Park Street is constituted as an individualistic space – definitely not for families – and that Bristol is being represented here as on the cusp, as a trendy, happening, buzzing city. Similarly with Elaine: particular cities for her equate with definite sorts of clientele, some of which (for example, Nottingham) are far more discerning, style-conscious and image-centred than others (here, Loughborough). Retro retailing, then, is clearly dependent on being located in particular quarters within particular cities; and as well as attracting the 'right sort' of clientele, it is this that sustains the notion of being part of 'the alternative'.

Moreover, it is not just that particular locations confer symbolic value. They work too in ways that confer competitive advantage through situated knowledge. Indeed, the latter is argued to enable trends to be identified before they take off and to enhance stocks of cultural capital through proximity to allied businesses, innovative pioneers and so forth. Furthermore, all these locations are talked about as the locus for particular 'scenes' grounded in business networks that are simultaneously social and friendship networks. And these, in turn, constitute communities of practice that shape 'what's in' and what's not, as well as 'who's in' and which places (clubs, bars and restaurants) matter to be seen in.

For retro retailers, however, the difficulty is that the increasing popularity and visibility of these same areas through the 1990s has meant that once-marginal retail locations have become increasingly subject to economic regeneration and gentrification. Inevitably, this has posed considerable problems. Indeed, as Michael – a Manchester retailer – relates, one of the consequences of spiralling property prices and rents has been the 'failure' of many of these, and related, businesses:

It's what happens in regeneration areas in towns and cities . . . particularly in this area of Manchester . . . they tend to be occupied by creative industries. You get a gap basically. The Arndale Centre left this area vacated, so you've got a lot of experimental businesses and artists moving in . . . until eventually there's enough critical mass for other people to start getting interested. And what happened there was that Afflecks Palace was one of the earliest businesses actually, and then people like me who started there moved out of it and open up other places [which] promotes the area. You start attracting more people which keeps you going and that starts expanding and then eventually people's rents get assessed and people start going out of business. It's a fantastic spiral, but it's what happens. (Michael: Manchester retailer)

The problems of gentrification however, are not just about the economics of trading, for a core characteristic of this process is that it brings with it key cultural changes, notably the incursion of particular chains that are seen to define 'the mainstream', tourists and the media circus. Portobello (London) is possibly the most recent and widely documented such instance, but the comments of Sophie – a trader in Notting Hill – have their echoes in Manchester's Northern Quarter and Nottingham's Lace Market:

Louise: Have you noticed the area changing from when you first started doing the markets?
Sophie: The markets changed a lot, and I don't think particularly for the better unfortunately. It's more commercialized and touristy which is a shame because it was somewhere that was always renowned for having character and new ideas.
Louise: How has it changed? Is it since the film? (*Notting Hill*)
Sophie: Yes, very much so. I curse the day that film was made. It's a real shame. It's brought the wrong sort of people, the wrong sort of money injected into the area and its ousting out a lot of people. Rates are going up so small businesses can't survive. All the chains are coming in. It's just defying the whole point. It's hideous. Absolutely hideous with Starbucks and Café Rouge . . .

Gentrification, then, disrupts the straightforward mapping of the 'mainstream'–'alternative' binary into discrete, bounded retail spaces, by juxtaposing both within the same retail areas. Moreover, it brings too an 'inappropriate' clientele – the 'wrong sorts' of people (illuminatingly referred to as 'average Jo(e)s' by some of those we interviewed), tourists and journalists, who come to look and not to buy, maybe even to laugh, and whose styles are discordant with those of the 'scene'. For a form of exchange dependent on being able to draw strong unproblematic associations between space and 'the alternative' this is critical. And it has been further problematized by various design trends too. Indeed, one of the tendencies of the 1990s – as retro became not just an increasingly common influence on the catwalk and high street (Gregson, Brooks and Crewe, 2001; Palmer 1999; Rickey 2001), and expanded to encompass household goods and cars – was for 'retro' to be undermined, blurred and destabilized by repro-retro.

We maintain that these tendencies, taken together, have necessitated the renegotiation of the retail landscape by retro retailers, one that continues to entwine understandings of 'retro' with space but in more complex ways than previously. What we are seeing currently within retro retailing is the emergence of two distinctive locational strategies. So, for those who continue to define 'retro' in terms of purity, authenticity and uniqueness, the encroachment of 'the mainstream' into the 1970s (and 1980s) has meant either a retreat historically – into vintage – or total disillusionment, to the point of getting out altogether:

> Once everything becomes mainstream you've already lost it. Manufacturers are manufacturing bad versions of originals which completely devalues the original item . . . and that's very much what's happened now really; everything's become a mish-mash of the fifties, sixties and seventies, in a nasty kind of retro . . . I'm getting out of it now, I don't want to do it anymore . . . (Michael, Manchester retailer)

And this historical retreat is often paralleled by, and symbolized through, a relocation to yet more marginal retail spaces. This is a strategy, then, that continues to constitute appropriate spaces for retro exchange through a mapping of the mainstream-alternative binary into retail space. It is, however, a strategy of 'flight' that can only be a temporary respite – witness the turn to vintage on the catwalk as we write.[24] For others though, the mainstream copy – repro-retro – is something to be played off, refracted against:

> [it's] not the thing. It's just doing kind of reinventions of it. The design quality, the quality of the products is poor and doesn't last. It's got quite a short lifespan, hence it's cheap. And I think the quality of the design is poor, and usually I can see what makes a watered down version and the lines aren't quite right and the colours aren't quite right . . . They're all imitations . . . so I'm a bit snobby about it and don't rate that kind of stuff at all. (Simon, Nottingham retailer)

Or, as in this case, something that 'tests' discerning, elite knowledge to the limits:

> God, you have to be really careful when you're buying now because you think you're buying but it's an exact copy of a 60s, 50s or 60s lamp, cos Ikea have introduced quite a few things like those lamps I've got with resin, the chunky sort of yellow glass ones, they're reproducing that. We bought an aluminium dish once – thought it was a 50s one, turned out to be Ikea!. (Paul, Bristol retailer)

Moreover, in this play of parody and authenticity, 'location' works to mirror the tendencies within 'retro', with juxtaposition being mobilized to sell both 'the copy' and 'the real thing' – literally to expand the business of retro retailing:

> you move with the scene, like with the army trousers, the sort of combat thing which came in obviously from Spice Girls . . . you can reflect it back to quite a lot of fashion . . . we do a lot of 60s as well . . . which is nowadays you find in Top Shop . . . you know basically they're still copying. We do trousers and things that's 80s 'old skool'; they're [Top Shop] still pumping that out as new in the 90s . . . [*Kate*: So do you do some new stuff as well?] Yeah, we do new stuff as well, which goes well with the 70s stuff, 60s stuff – we do some nice T-shirts, we do all the flared trousers and flared jeans. (Keith, Bristol retailer)

> . . . It's based on a kind of 70s look but sort of brought forward to the 90s. So you've got like a different kind of fit. The cut's different but like the essence of the shape is very similar. The 70s aspect would be the fact that they are flares but the different 90s aspect is that the cut at the top is very, like the cut of the jeans and the trousers themselves is very different. It's a little bit wider, a little bit. It's not quite as tight as it was in the 70s . . . (Tina, Manchester retailer)

Rather than reposition the alternative–mainstream binary in space, then, certain retro retailers have acknowledged its untenability and have chosen to remain in locations that allow them both to expand their businesses and, simultaneously, to comment critically through juxtaposition, parody and hybridity, on the mainstream.[25]

Symbolic positioning, then, remains critical to constituting appropriate spaces for retro exchange, and particular interpretations of second-

hand goods are critical to whether retro exchange occurs in either marginal or increasingly popular retail locations. Nonetheless, as well as
indicating the complexities of contemporary geographies of retro
retailing, the significance of this case study is that – in complete contrast
to the situation with car-boot sales – it reveals how spaces of second-
hand exchange can be located within and in juxtaposition to first hand
retailing; indeed, that first hand retailing can be attracted to (as well
as reshaping) such spaces – that when second-hand sells, as in this case,
the divisions and distinctions between first and second-hand break
down. In our final case study we look at a similar instance of juxtaposition, but this time where the movement is of second-hand exchange
onto the high street.

Desperately Seeking Location: the (In)appropriate Locational Strategies of Charity Retail

The past decade or so has witnessed a transformation in the charity-
shop sector, with the instigation and intensification of the charity retail
project (Gregson, Brooks and Crewe, 2002; Horne, 2000; Parsons, 2001).
Legitimated as a means to enhance fund-raising for specific charitable

Plates 2.5 Charity shops on the high street

Plate 2.6 Charity shops on the high street

concerns, this is widely talked about within the sector in terms of 'professionalization', and encompasses the adoption of standardized practices of retail display and sale. Correspondingly, many charity-shop organizations have been recast as chains, staffed by former retail employees (from executive level down to individual shop managers), and subjected to comprehensive retail 'makeovers' (with lighting, display strategies and pricing all coming in for attention). At the same time, this recasting has entailed major changes in the geographies of location. So, while certain charity shops continue to be sited in off-the-beaten-track marginal retail spaces, others – particularly those within the major charities' chains – are to be found increasingly in the high street or even city-centre locations.[26] As we show here, much as with the retro-retailing case study, this is about attempting to work with the symbolic qualities of location – in this case, to constitute 'proper shops' through proper, appropriate locations.

There are various ways in which this move to the high street works in practice. For some charity retail organizations, for example – Sue Ryder Shops would be a good instance – the policy has been to occupy short-term end-of-lease units, a situation that can result in highly temporary transient occupation. For others, however, particularly those with 'sunk costs' – who have made considerable investments in stores and in interior 'makeovers' – locational decisions are being taken in ways that replicate completely the practices of first-cycle retailers. So, pedestrian-flow counts, rents, length of lease and proximate unit occupation all figure in favouring particular locations and potential units over others. Part of this, and not a small part of course, is about the economics of trading, and selecting the likely most-profitable site from a range of possibilities, but it is also – as the following testimonies make clear – about engaging in proper practice, doing what the success stories of retailing are known to do.

The aspirations of many charity retailers re location are articulated clearly by the Shops and Marketing Manager of one major UK charity retailer, who in this extract begins by outlining the negative press accorded generally to charity shops, certainly prior to their 'professionalization', and the extent to which the latter is considered vital to both moves toward and acceptance within particular retail spaces:

> . . . you can work very hard at negotiating an image – parts of the country we are never going to get into [*Nicky*: Is that because of complete resistance on their part?] Complete resistance to having any charity in here, no way. We take umbrage against that, obviously, but at the moment there's nothing we can do about that, but there is certain places, certain towns that say we degrade their shopping centres. We all say, 'well that's a load of rubbish, come and visit our shops and you'll see, but the image is there, you see, the old image in their heads . . . I mean a lot of our shops are very big – a lot of charities don't do that, smaller units, just off the high street, tucked round the sides. We don't. We're quite brash. We want to be next to Marks and Spencers . . . [*Nicky*: And M&S don't have a problem with that? That's interesting] Yes, that shows we've been accepted . . .

That Marks and Spencer is highlighted here, notwithstanding its long-standing and well-documented trading difficulties (Hyman, 1999a, 1999b; see also Crewe, 2002), is not insignificant. Still taken to be at the forefront of high-street retailing, to be located next door is highly symbolic; it is an uncontestable visible mark of arrival. More generally, the locational strategies of charity retailers are themselves indicative of the degree to which charity retailers imagine themselves as first-cycle retailers and enact their practices accordingly. Here, for example, are two Heads of Trading for different charity retail chains talking about their locational strategies:

. . . there [are] certain criteria, like it's got to have a certain amount of pedestrians walking outside between the hours of 11 and 3. If it's something in the region of 500 per hour, and if not that, we do this on two different visits, two separate days to check the first wasn't just a fluke, so we do it twice, if it passes, OK, fine, then we look at car parks, bus stations and so on, nearness to post office, what competition there is, and not just charity shops, it could be market stalls . . . how close to another one of our shops, in terms of collections would we get enough stock into the area, and we look at things like unemployment. If every shop is advertising for staff in the window then we'd have a problem recruiting volunteers . . . there are certain towns we wouldn't go near, particularly villages cos you wouldn't get the pedestrian flow. But there are villages where there is a charity shop, and they've been there for years and they're very good. A lot of our shops which we've had a long time, their pedestrian flow is zilch, nothing goes through but the shop is fine cos everybody knows about it, the manager knows everybody by Christian name, and has watched the town grow up, and she's got a list of people who want to work in the shop, and she never advertises for volunteers – why can't we have 300 shops like that [*laughter*] I could put my feet up in the afternoon. Ideal world! . . .

. . . if you analyse successful charity shops they never fit into particular categories. What you're always told is that 'This is quite a unique business'. It is very, very influenced by the person running it, so our most profitable shop – I won't tell you where it is – in the South east of England, but it's in the most appalling trading position; it hardly has any pedestrian flow at all. But it has a devoted, dedicated, hard working manager, loved by the community, everybody brings her their stuff . . . a very wise ex M&S manager once said to me In you business [name] you should look for a manager and then find them a shop to run' . . . [but] really where we are is dictated by pedestrian flow, the rental, and we'd be happy to be situated in any part of town. We're not concerned about competition because the competition can actually bring you extra footfall . . .

What we find intriguing here is how, notwithstanding their acknowledgement that charity retailing is a unique business' where successful location remains something of a mystery, it is the standard practices of retail-site evaluation and comparison that remain the basis for their locational practice/s. For us, this is indicative of the extent of charity retailers' commitment to 'proper' practice, and this is further confirmed by their positioning of particular first-cycle retailers at the cutting edge of retail practice:

... the newer type fashion houses – Oasis for example, they have some good ideas about using vinyl in the window. We use vinyl, but this is exterior vinyl on the window and it doesn't get peeled off, it doesn't get damaged. So I tend to look at things like that. But you need to look at the basic shops too – Mark One, New Look ...

As well as looking to monitor their competitors within the charity retail sector, then, charity retailers are continually evaluating and attempting, where possible, to emulate practices in the first-cycle. In so doing, so we maintain, charity retailers seek simultaneously to constitute their shops as examples of 'proper shops' and to erase the spatial distinctions between first-and second-cycle retailing that both retro retailing and, in a very different way, car-boot sales for example rest on. They are therefore contesting one of the key premises shaping the constitution of other spaces of second-hand exchange, that second hand goods matter in ways that require their separation from, if not necessarily exclusion from, the spaces of first-hand exchange.

How successful this is, however, is open to question. Indeed, as we show now, the symbolic value invested in the very locations now characterized by charity shops can be a very long way from the 'proper shop' connotations articulated by charity retailers. When we look at the types of locations that charity retail chains have been able to move into, then, they are typically spaces of declining profitability; the very spaces deserted in the UK from the 1980s onward by key retail organizations as a result of the development of new agglomerations of retail space – malls, regional centres, out-of-town retail parks, and latterly through e-commerce.[27] These appropriate spaces then turn out to be primarily either secondary retail centres or declining high streets and city centres, where the proximity of alternative, more profitable locations (Meadowhall, Merry Hill and so on) has created a surfeit of cheap vacant units. Far from being characterized by the chains of positive association (Oasis, Next, even Marks and Spencer), then, these locations tend to be occupied by others seeking out similar cheap yet symbolic locations, for example discount shops, other second-hand shops and 24-hour convenience stores. Consequently, and in a twist that has considerable echoes with the othering of car-boot sales, we find charity shops cast – at least within the media – as the sign for the terminal decline of the high street. But more than this, we find charity shops being undercut by discounters, through price.[28] For us this constitutes a significant challenge to the project of charity retailing, for the question this raises is 'why buy second-hand when new is cheaper?' Discounters then focus attention back on the first hand/second-hand distinction that charity retailers have sought to erase. Moreover, they epitomize the reconstitution of the high street through value and appeals to the 'bargain basement' in ways that only discount shops within charity retail chains can match. Ultimately then, the problem faced by many charity retailers is that in seeing the high street as the space for a certain understanding of 'proper shops', they misread both tendencies to relocation within first-cycle retail space and the growing complexities of 'proper shops'. Indeed, in attempting to capture greater revenues through raising the price of second-hand goods sold on the high street, charity retailers are potentially attempting to constitute spaces of (second-hand) exchange that run counter to the value imperative of the high street itself. Maybe these are inappropriate retail spaces, then, for the type of exchange that charity retail is attempting to constitute.

To a degree at least it would appear that this is beginning to be acknowledged by some of the larger charity retail chains, for whom the development of specialization and segmentation strategies around key goods – notably books and retro – has led to a partial re-evaluation of location decisions.[29] So, one of the most significant recent tendencies within charity retail has been for particular shops within at least some organizations to be located not in the high street but in the heart of self-stylized 'alternative' quarters, for instance in Manchester's Oldham Street and in London's Covent Garden.[30] High risk – in that, as we have already seen, such areas command increasingly high rentals – these moves are too recent to be evaluated conclusively. However, it is our view that 'success' is likely to be muted, even questionable, for reasons that link back to the previous case study. There we saw how such areas are invested with meanings that locate them, and those who trade there, as 'alternative' in ways that clearly embed them within the creative industries. The problem for charity retailers, then, is that they are manifestly not part of this 'scene'; even if they might be able to find staff (volunteers and managers) who are, the difficulty is the organizational basis for trading – one that runs counter to the independent and individualistic ethos of retro retailing (see Figure 2.1). Moreover, we can see too how – having come from the high street and declining city centres – retro retailers might read this particular incursion. Not surprisingly then, charity-retro forays were identified by retro retailers as 'emulators', as problematic and as inappropriate in their practices as mainstream repro-retro, in short as 'not doing it (meaning 'retro') properly'. Where this leaves such forays is hard to say at present, but it is our view that attempting to undercut retro retailers in self-stylized

Plate 2.7 Charity shops meet 'the alternative': Manchester, Oldham Street

'alternative' locations, while it might appear a sound business proposition, is a risky strategy. Not only is it heavily reliant on regular quality stock-flow and on charismatic staff – in itself a 'big ask' – but, possibly even more significantly, in bringing the value imperative into retail spaces constituted through 'difference', distinction and discernment, it risks constituting a form of exchange that in its premises is out-of-place.

When we look at charity retailers' attempts to constitute appropriate spaces for exchange, then, we find a far messier and inconsistent picture than with our two previous case studies. In comparison to these, the practices of charity retailers appear chameleon-like and suggest, at least at first sight, that it is possible to do anything with second-hand goods and that they can be sold literally anywhere. While this is the case to a degree, a rather closer reading shows that the expansion and proliferation of charity shops has frequently failed to acknowledge the ways in which geography matters to constituting the premises for exchange, particularly that specific retail spaces are invested with meanings that render certain imperatives more important than others – 'value' rather than fund-raising on the high street, discernment rather than 'value' in cultural quarters, for instance. It is this, we maintain, and not just concerns over supply chains, that ought to figure in discussions about overcapacity and declining shop income in the sector (Charity Finance Report, 2001). For us, then, notwithstanding their visibility within second-hand exchange and importance within the charity-shop sector, charity retailers are still struggling to find the most appropriate spaces for exchange. And the fact that they are reflects the difficulties of con- stituting spaces of exchange where the core principle is fund-raising, to maximize charitable income through the sale of second hand goods. Not only does this attempt to erase price distinctions between first and second-hand goods but in substituting fund-raising for profit, it goes against the core principles of retailing itself. It is our view then that rather than looking to the practices of 'proper shops', charity retailers ought to be looking to the locational strategies of another strand of the charity-shop sector – hospice shops – for more appropriate visions of how to constitute spaces for cause-related (second-hand) exchange. Situated for the most part in small retail parades within definable city neighbourhoods, these shops have the advantage of being able to mirror their local/regional cause through location, but what they point to as well through their continued financial success relative to the major charity retailers (Charity Finance Report, 2001, p 45) is the potency of 'the local' in shaping charitable practice/s – be this donation or purch- ase. Correspondingly, we maintain that it is these forms of retail space – low-cost, off-centre and away from the retail conglomerates – that offer the greatest scope for constituting spaces of exchange through the fund-raising imperative.

Conclusions

More generally, the three preceding case studies enable us to develop a broader set of arguments about spaces of second-hand exchange.

First, the studies – albeit in very different ways – highlight that the principles of second-hand exchange rest on establishing appropriate spaces for particular forms of second-hand exchange. Sometimes, as the case studies of both car-boot sales and retro retailing show, these spaces are established, literally from scratch, by mobilizing and inscribing in space the first hand/second-hand distinction. Moreover, although the cases are very different – in that one is the result of exclusion and the other part of a deliberate distancing from 'the mainstream' – both show conclusively that the success of these sites, at least initially, has been bound up with their distinctiveness and separation from other, more conventional, retail spaces. Space, then, has been critical to their constitution. And in a sense its importance is further borne out by the charity-retail case study, which documented the attempt to constitute a different exchange imperative (fund-raising) in spaces constituted by very different premises of exchange – value and difference. The relative failure of the charity-retail project then, while it can be attributed to a number of other precipient causes, is in part about the failure to recognize how (retail) space is itself invested with particular imperatives that constitute limits, as well as possibilities, for particular versions of second-hand exchange in particular locations.

Secondly, and following on from this, we can see how these limits and possibilities connect to the landscapes of power produced and regulated by retail capital. This works both literally, in terms of absolute space, and symbolically. Indeed, we can see from the foregoing how the complex mosaic of space dedicated to first hand retail – encompassing malls, shopping centres, out-of-town retail parks, factory outlet centres, high streets, local shopping 'parades' and markets, not to mention railway stations, airports, mail order and on-line – works as a landscape of power, through which and in relation to which geographies of second-hand location have to be constituted. At one level this power is all one way: as two of our studies show, dedicated second-hand trading of whatever form is consistently excluded from prime retail sites – sometimes transparently, as in the case of car boot sales where the wielding of regulatory frameworks provides a clear instance of protection, and sometimes indirectly, as with charity shops, where although particular trading locations might be desired they remain off-limits for economic reasons. Moreover, and as our retro retailing study showed, this power can also be incorporative, in that when retro sells its spaces become attractive to first hand retailers. Yet this is an enabling power too; one that permits dedicated second-hand exchange to occur in secondary retail locations – notably particular high streets and self-stylized 'alternative' retail spaces – or to be located elsewhere, beyond conventional retail space – in places like church halls, school playgrounds and hospital car parks. This is critical. Indeed, we would argue that it is precisely this zone of 'the possible' that second-hand traders of whatever form have to work with to constitute 'location'. How they do so, though, necessitates an engagement with the symbolic, with the relation between first and second-hand goods. When constituted oppositionally – as with retro retailing (or, for that matter, jumble sales and nearly-new sales) – this works to position appropriate locations for exchange at a distance from the 'norm' that is 'first hand'. It becomes imperative, then, to signify cultural distance through physical distance.

By contrast, when the relation is contested – as with charity shops and certain forms of car-boot-sale trading (or dress agencies for that matter) – physical proximity to the desired assumes significance. The specific geographies of location associated with particular forms of second-hand exchange, then, are the product of both absolute possibilities and a symbolic imaginary working within, and sometimes against, the possibilities constituted by the landscapes of power produced and regulated by retail capital.

Thirdly, we would point to an issue that is of growing concern for those trading with second-hand goods, that the various spaces of second-hand exchange that we are concerned with here work with very similar types of second-hand goods – mass-produced (and consumed) items of clothing, household goods and so forth. Indeed, in the case of charity shops and car-boot sales there is considerable overlap; the same goods could equally be for sale in both sorts of site. And, to the untutored eye at least, much of the clothing sold in retro outlets could appear identical to that available in charity shops. This degree of interchange-ability, apparent and actual, attests to the importance of constituting differences between second-hand traders and retailers. And here too the symbolic importance of 'location' turns out to be critical. So, for example, while a pair of branded jeans might be sold for around £5–7 at a car-boot sale, the symbolic value imparted by a particular location within 'the alternative' would enable a sale at considerably more than this. Here it is symbolic location that is being used to inscribe distinc-tions in price between particular spaces of second-hand exchange – a practice that, in its principles, is no different to the differentiations drawn by first hand retailers, but which is different in the way it relies on generic symbolic location, and not a specific retail name, to achieve its effects.

In turn, this point about the importance of generic types of second-hand space allows us to open up a final issue: that geography matters, fundamentally, to the constitution of second-hand worlds, and not just to their relation to first hand exchange. Thus, both the proliferation in (and expansion of) second-hand sites and the degree of interchange-ability of goods between sites mean that inscribing difference between these sites – in principles, in premises and in practices – has become imperative. In part this can be achieved through location, absolute and symbolic. But it is also constituted by and through the production of distinctive types of 'interior' selling spaces: spaces that attempt to spatialize and routinize particular practices around the sale of second-hand goods. The following chapter examines these issues in depth.

three

Constituting Difference

As we show in this chapter, the differences between forms of second-hand exchange are articulated not only through location but by working with the principles of exchange itself, that is by working against conventional relations of buying and selling to constitute spaces of exchange that are, in their practices, distinctively different to standard first-cycle conventions. But, as we show too, differences can also be forged through the constitution of selling spaces. A second objective of this chapter therefore is to show how the development of relatively 'fixed' sites of second-hand exchange – typically in shop units – has been accompanied by practices that seek to shape shop interiors in ways that encode particular premises about second-hand goods. Although highly variable, these practices all use shop interiors – particularly strategies of display – to encode visually specific readings of second-hand goods and to encourage particular relations of looking (and buying). In short, then, they attempt to spatialize particular premises, to constitute specific regimes of representation around second-hand goods (Nixon, 1996). Nonetheless, and as we go on to show, certain of these regimes are unable to regulate out relations of looking (and buying) that are grounded in other premises. Indicative of the multiplicity of readings inscribed by consumers in second-hand goods, these 'moments of rupture' are argued to be highly significant. Not only do they point to the limitations of certain spatialized practices of selling in the second-hand arena, but they signal too how looking (and buying) is connected intrinsically to practices of consumption.

As with the previous chapter, this chapter is organized primarily around three case studies pertaining to our three sites, and again as before, while the studies can stand alone they also display a strong degree of contrast and comparability. We begin this chapter as previously with the car-boot sale example. We argue here that car-boot sales in many ways represent a continuation of practices established in relation to second-hand sites with a longer historical trajectory in the UK, notably jumble sales and more recently nearly-new sales. Here, then, in these spaces, the emphasis is very much on establishing and reproducing particular principles of exchange: principles that literally are about working out how to sell and how to buy, and how to construct the transaction. It is this, we argue, that constitutes car-boot sales as spaces of exchange distinctive from other second-hand sites and from exchange as enacted in the first cycle. In contrast, our other two forms of second-hand exchange take place in shop settings – that is, in units in dedicated retail space of one form or another. Furthermore, both assume that the principles of exchange established in the first cycle will transfer unproblematically to these spaces. Both charity shops and retro shops, then, are taken to be spaces where sellers and buyers come together as retailers and consumers respectively, where goods that are preselected and displayed by retailers are exchanged through money, and where prices are determined by retailers and are non-negotiable. Beyond this, however, and as we show, both attempt to inscribe very different premises of exchange into retail space.

In our second study, then, we show how retro retailing works with, and is constituted in terms of, four sets of spatialized premises. Two of these are shaped through relations to goods that are about celebrating 'the authentic', recontextualizing and revalorizing second-hand goods and appreciating them aesthetically. But, while one encodes this in interiors and relations of looking (and buying) that owe their inspiration to the gallery and the exhibition, the other takes its cues from wardrobes and attics to produce interiors that are literally crammed full and that necessitate relations of looking that are about rummaging rather than dislocated appreciation. By contrast, a further two sets of premises are associated with the commercialization of retro. One is the dressing up/fancy dress mode, where selling spaces become spaces for fun, play and amusement and are constituted primarily through irony, kitsch and the celebration of trash. The other is all about 'the mass', where serial rows of core retro 'staples' – typically jeans, jackets and shirts – are offered up for easy shopping, in a manner associated with the conventions of the core high-street retailers. As we go on to argue, the difficulty for many retro retailers is the coexistence of these contrasting premises: while retailers themselves might be entirely clear about the premises they are attempting to spatialize through the apparently bounded interiors of their shops, customers frequently contest these, with the result that various premises come into juxtaposition, even conflict, within particular shop interiors – a juxtaposition that in turn may lead retro retailers to question the very principles of exchange itself.

Although less complex, the third study displays considerable parallels with certain facets of retro retailing. We see here, then, how charity retail has mirrored its move to the high street through restructuring interiors in ways that are about retail 'makeovers'. Interiors have become standardized, categorized, blocked-out and mapped out for the customer, in ways that reflect one of the core premises of this version of second-hand exchange – the erasure of the first hand/second-hand distinction. Moreover, the spatial divisions within these shops, particularly the separation between front-shop and back-shop, are shown to be critical to enabling this premise, with the latter being associated with various divestment and decontextualization practices – washing, cleaning, steaming and ironing for instance. Much as with retro retailing, however, although these selling strategies are clearly designed to suggest particular relations of looking (and buying) they are unable to regulate out other readings and other practices grounded in very different premises about second-hand exchange. In this case, the instabilities are associated primarily with two issues. One issue concerns the critical effects of the discourse of 'charity': although charity retailing is grounded in a principle of exchange that is substituting fund-raising for profit, its key difficulty is argued to be the way in which other readings of 'charity' enter shop space/s and disrupt the spatialization of the fund-raising imperative. A second issue pertains to the regimes of representation associated with other forms of charity shop: the charity-shop parallel to the wardrobe/attic regime of representation of retro; these are valued by certain charity shoppers precisely because they enable particular modes of (charity) shopping that are written out by the charity-retail project.

We end the chapter by reflecting more broadly on the limitations of strategies that attempt to regulate relations of looking (and buying) second hand goods. Although clearly designed to inscribe specific meanings in second hand goods, to control these through particular singular regimes of representation and to encode differences between certain second-hand sites, the diverse dispositions of consumers toward second hand goods means that such strategies will always be open to subversion and contestation through counter practices associated with counter premises. We argue, then, that the most appropriate regimes of representation for second-hand goods are those that maximize the possible in terms of creating the conditions for value determination – rather than those that try to minimize these. Successful second-hand regimes of representation, then, are those that appear to allow consumers to do the work of looking and to find things for themselves, and that enable goods to suggest themselves to them, rather than those that would appear to be overly prescriptive. With their connections to wardrobes, junkyards and attics, such regimes are to be found in car-boot sales, certain charity shops and some retro shops, and much of their success is argued to be located in their distinctions from the overtly mapped-out spatialities associated with first-cycle retail space. They therefore encode the first/second-hand distinction as one that matters both representationally and spatially, in selling strategies as well as in geographies of location. Furthermore, in their appeal to various storage sites and spaces, these regimes are argued to signal the importance of previous consumption histories and practices to the meanings inscribed in second-hand goods.

Re-learning Exchange in the Space of the Car-boot Sale

Devoid of the fixtures and trappings of permanent forms of retailing – display stands, racks, mannequins, lighting and so forth – and reliant on altogether more impromptu domestic paraphernalia such as decorating tables, suitcases, tablecloths, plastic sheeting and cardboard boxes, not to mention the car itself (its boot, bonnet, doors and interior), the presentation of goods 'for sale' at car-boot sales reveals the extent to which this particular version of second-hand exchange is constituted from scratch, its links with domestic consumption, and its connections to other forms of second-hand exchange, notably jumble sales (see Plate 3.1). Moreover, these styles of selling are at some remove from those that we discuss in the subsequent two sections, where the representational strategies of selling constitute relations of looking (and buying) which appeal to those associated with other retail and/or visual locations, notably the high street, the designer boutique and the gallery, rather than to the jumble sale. Already, then, we can begin to see how particular sites of second-hand exchange come to be associated with specific styles and practices of selling. In the case of car-boot sales however, the paraphernalia of selling is just one facet among several to signify difference, albeit the most visual. As we show in this section, participation in car-boot sales is, for both buyers and sellers, about establishing the principles of exchange and reproducing them. It is literally about working out how to buy, how to sell and how to constitute the transaction both generally and personally, and in the process about constituting a space of exchange that is distinctively different – from other forms of <u>second-hand</u> exchange and from the retail spaces of the first cycle.

Plate 3.1 Car boot sales: selling paraphernalia

The imperative of exchange principles and their particularity to car-boot sales is something that all those we spoke with articulated, often through retrospective talk. Many, for example, looked back on their first attempts at selling as 'naive' and 'green', even 'terrifying', describing how they had highlighted to all their 'novice' status – for instance by turning up at the advertised start time and by displaying everything at once:

> As soon as we got there all the other sellers came round and as soon as we were getting the stuff out of the car they were buying it. They were buying it as soon as we got it on the table! You know we were stood there and it was hands everywhere – 'what do you want for this?' 'what do you want for that?' They were stuffing things in great big plastic bags. (Ruth, 40-something trader)

And we can see the same thing going on in our field diaries: for example, where women – usually driving expensive cars and smartly attired – were instantly 'mobbed' by buyers and sellers alike, literally as they drove onto the site.

Others – mostly buyers – talked about purchasing 'mistakes' or being 'tricked' – typically through buying things that either failed to work or that turned out to be not entirely what they expected – audiotapes and CDs that didn't correspond to the cover, books with missing pages, 'bleach' that turned out not to be and so on.

In according with what seemed to them at the time to be appropriate practice, at least by the conventions learnt from participation in other retail environments, these initial forays in buying and selling reveal that car-boot sales work differently; that there are different principles of exchange at work here. And they show too how these principles are learnt, through practical accumulated knowledge, grounded in partic- ipation. Sellers, then, have to learn how to sell and buyers how to buy and – as we show now through some detailed examples – this is, in many ways, about working out these general principles and shaping them individually to determine the premises shaping their participation.

To take sellers first: Daphne and Phil are in their late 60s and have been selling at car-boot sales now for around ten years. They describe themselves as 'dabblers', in that they only 'do' three or four boot sales a year, primarily 'for fun' – although an important part of this 'fun' is making money. Beginning initially from household clear-outs, they have subsequently moved on to 'buy to sell', exclusively from car-boot sales. For them, as for more serious 'traders' whom we talked with, the core premises of car-boot-sale exchange are: to know value and to know how to attract buyers to their 'pitch'. Daphne and Phil place a high premium on knowing what is 'collectable' and what is not; on knowing which type of goods are worth buying, and which not – because they are appropriate goods to sell in these spaces; and they acknowledge too the importance of the geographical mediation of value – not just that particular goods are worth more in certain areas and neighbour- hoods than in others, but that different value regimes constitute the same goods differently in different places. In addition, like many other committed 'traders' they know the standard retail (first hand) price of many of the items they sell.[31] Rather than accord with the types of myth we discussed in Chapter 2, therefore, Daphne and Phil are dismissive of attempts to sell the (high-value) collectable at car-boot sales, and are much more interested in buying goods that they know will sell well within particular highly localized geographical neighbourhoods. Given this, knowing how to price becomes a critical practice, and indeed Daphne and Phil get as much pleasure from 'making' 50 pence on an item bought for under £1 as they do from selling something obviously more collectable and priced accordingly. Why? Because the sale is a

Plate 3.2 Phil and 'the stall'

manifestation of their learnt and embedded knowledge/s, not imposed by an external value regime. At the same time they talk at length about the importance of 'the pitch' – of being located at the right point on the site (not next to 'traders' or 'commercials', not near 'novices'), and of the skill involved in 'slotting-in' in the queue to get on the site to be adjacent to appropriate rather than inappropriate vendors; and of laying out their goods in ways that ensure people will stop and look and not just wander on past (see Plate 3.2). In their case this is about having a central display object – something unusual, that is probably unlikely to sell immediately – for its curiosity value. At the time we spoke with them this was an ornamental bird with flapping wings. Described as 'a ghastly thing', its predecessor had been a pair of collapsing sunglasses:

. . . They were good because you could spend a lot of time taking them apart and showing them to people . . . and they had a little black leather case that zipped up – that's the thing, you need to have a 'lead' item in the centre of your stall. People come and look at it. (Phil, car-boot sale 'dabbler')[32]

For others though, stopping 'the punter'[3] is an altogether more theatrical performance still:

> *Two major performers here, with a major line in patter. 'This is the coat Prince Charles wore on his bachelor night! Oh, it's got a label inside. What's this say 'M. Shinwell'! You sir – to a man with a large beer belly – you look like the fitness type! A squash racquet' – flourishes racquet above head. Punter replies, 'the only fitness I do involves a pint glass!' 'Glasses – 10 pence'! A man buys the proffered pint glass! The pair jest 'You've got to keep ahead in this game'! And the crowd grows, drawn by the entertainment* (Nicky, field notes)

Involving repartee and banter, and with clear resonances with both pantomime and the fairground, the above is akin to an impromptu comedy act where the goods are props, and 'buyers' the audience but where the performance is used to work the sale.

For buyers as for sellers, value is a core premise, one fundamental to the determination of what to buy and even whether to buy. But so too is 'risk'. Colin exemplifies the importance of both. In his mid-50s, Colin has been going to car-boot sales as a regular Sunday morning pastime for years and – much to the annoyance of his (female) partner – returns each time, usually with something described initially to her as 'a bargain'. That he returns with what is constituted as 'a bargain' first, and only secondarily as a specific object, is critical. Indeed, it is this – as for the majority of participants that we spoke with – that shapes his patterns of purchasing, for Colin will not buy anything unless the transaction allows him to capture value. This, as we see now, shapes his entire practice/s of participation. To begin with, then, Colin's participation is all about identifying potential sites of maximum value – stalls and 'pitches' that might enable him to capture value. So he surveys the site methodically, going up and down the rows, ignoring obvious traders (where value by definition is going to be limited) and concentrating on the range of 'amateurs' and 'dabblers' (where greater value is potentially to be found). He might make enquiries, in a very half-hearted kind of way. But he never buys. Rather he moves on, 'finishes' his reconnaissance and makes his decisions over 'targets' while having a cup of tea.

At this juncture, he dons his purchasing signifier and 'disguise' – his baseball cap – and returns to attempt the purchase/s.[34] At this point too, 'risk' enters the equation. Risk for Colin is a central element of exchange within car boot sales, and he has clear rules that he works with here. Some goods – high-price electricals for example: TV sets and so on – are deemed 'too risky – because you know that they are not going to work'. Others, though, are constituted as desirable, precisely because *if* they work they will be more of 'a bargain'. If they turn out not to, though, that's acceptable risk – because this is part of the game. Exchange here, then, is construed as a gamble, as a bet. Sometimes Colin wins, sometimes he doesn't, but this is all understood and a core part of the fascination and the attraction. We see all this encapsulated in the following field-diary extract:

> *After about an hour we bumped into Colin again . . . He'd already got himself what he classified as 'the bargain of the century if it works' – a Walkman and a good make for £3 . . . He'd also seen a* Forrest Gump *CD at a stall two rows behind . . . which he said was £16.99 in the shops and the bloke seemed to want £5 for it. Colin was unsure as to whether to go back and bargain for it. Could he get it for less? In the end and after much dithering and consultation, he decided 'yes'. On went the baseball cap . . . but when he went back the CD had gone! (Nicky, field diary)*

Others, while they may be less prepared to gamble with risk than Colin, more than attest to the importance of capturing value, or attempting to:

> *I was standing looking at quite a large pitch – the goods were displayed on a blanket on the ground as well as on the standard table – when a woman beside me makes a clear decision (communicated to partner, and to me (!) but not audible to the vendors) that she's going after a checked shirt, and also a pair of Levi jeans, though importantly she doesn't reveal this to the vendors immediately. Her first salvo is 'How much for the shirt?'. The booter replies £5. She replies, "I'll give you £3". Female vendor consults with partner – 'OK'. She gets out a fiver and as she is handing over the cash reveals her interest in the Levis – offers £4 for both and secures both the jeans and the shirt for £4 . . . She almost certainly had primarily targeted the Levis but had completely outmanoeuvred the vendor by homing in apparently on the shirt, and by waiting to the very moment of exchange to go for the jeans too (Nicky, field diary)*

> . . . For instance, I saw this really nice pair of jeans. She'd marked them up at £5 and I think I got them for £2. They were Chipie jeans and they'd

probably cost £40 and she hadn't worn them much. So I was getting almost a brand new pair of jeans, but I didn't necessarily know that they were going to fit me, so I didn't want to pay £5. So in the end I said 'Look, I'll give you £2 for them'. It did take a while and she was quite reluctant. I left it for a bit and then went back near the end, when it was obvious that she wasn't going to sell them. And sometimes I'm a bit devious, and I'll make out that I've only got £1.50 on me. And they'll go 'Oh go on!' And I'll get things that way! (Rehmana – 20-something).

Just down and across from that stall sat a . . . student on a deckchair, and what do I see in her books' box but one copy of Global Shift. Aha! An ideal item to wield as an example of 'what you can find at a boot sale'! So off I go into bargaining routine. And I was feeling really mean this morning. So I started off at £2. She wanted at least £5 for it – no chance! I got her down to £3 but wouldn't pay any more than £2.50 . . . She wouldn't play ball, saying 'the real price is on the back' . . . Ho ho, no sale! And when I left the site I went to check – yes, Global Shift was still sitting there. (Nicky, field diary)

Typical of the encounters that take place within car boot sales, all three of these instances demonstrate the impromptu that characterizes this version of exchange – that goods are being responded to as potential, and not pre-planned purchases, and that capturing value is more important here than the goods themselves, to the extent that – as in the last instance – this overrides purchasing. What they point to as well, however, is the intensity and rapidity of some acts of purchase. All three of these extracts then show how the moment of potential transaction can be a highly competitive encounter in haggling, literally acts (of purchase) where cash – if exchanged – is more the signifier of the buyer's acknowledgement of value's capture than of the seller's realization of 'profit'.

Although what we describe above is the normative mode of partic-ipation in car-boot sales, it is important to note that not all car-boot-sale transactions take this form. Some are much more straightforward – purchasing 'cut price' from 'commercial' traders for example. The bulk buying of 'cheap' household goods such as toilet rolls, washing-up liquids and detergent that occurs on some more commercial sites would be a good instance of this. Here exchange is little different to the practices of purchasing associated with discount retailers, and is a quick, largely unnegotiated transaction. Others by contrast are far more pro-tracted. Richard, for example – 30-something – recounted how he spent approximately 20 minutes discussing the purchasing of a welding solder with a (male) vendor. After much deliberation, during which the current fault with the item was fully explained by the vendor, Richard decided that, with the assistance of a friend, he would be able to repair the solder. Both men then agreed the price – £16 – that was mutually satisfactory: for Richard it represented a massive saving on what he would need to have spent in a shop, whereas for the vendor it was £16 for something which for him – without the networks to repair it – was 'useless, mate'. Another instance, this time observed, was where a group of men discussed at length whether an electrically operated bicycle could be cannibalized for its battery, with the subject of deliberation being the battery size – 6 volt or 12. Finally, yet others talked about how they talked with vendors about the history of particular goods – suits that had sat in wardrobes never worn, suitcases that had been around the world, children's cloth-ing . . .

For us the important facets of these latter transactions is that they are all about not just the exchange of money but about the exchange of knowledge too. Two of these instances are about practical knowledge/ s. In both cases the object of the transaction doesn't currently work, and in the instance where it is being bought for repair much of the discussion is about just what is 'the problem'. Where cannibalization is going to occur 'the chat' is all about who might be able to assist in this. More broadly, however, both encounters establish that there is a commitment here to use values: that what matters here is not captur-ing value and risk, but whether these restored and/or modified goods will actually work. By comparison, the third set of transactions show the emphasis that can be placed in this arena on knowing about goods' biographies and geographies, their histories of consumption. Exchange here, through its juxtaposition of buyers with sellers who are con-sumers, is as much about acquiring these details as it is about the exchange of money.

The foregoing has demonstrated that car-boot sales are a site of second-hand exchange that require participants both to work out the principles of exchange that operate in and shape these sites and to work with these. And, particularly in its normative conventions, we can see how exchange is being constituted here as a game between buyers and sellers, as fun and as something that people take pleasure in. Which, of course, requires that they are able to participate in these ways and to read these codes,[35] and that there are other spaces of exchange where things can be taken for granted, will be reliable and so on. Car-boot sales, then, provide a space for the theatrical and the carnivalesque – a stage on which people can (if they wish) assume different personas through exchange and a stage where the conventions of retail purchase in the first cycle are suspended, and a venue where the standard relations associated with the high street, the shopping centre, the mall, mail order or online shopping, are subverted – wherein those who normally just buy are allowed to both buy and sell, and where buyers can contest the power of the seller to determine value, through money and through the exchange of knowledge/s too. That they permit all this, and encode it in their principles, is for us a key factor in accounting for car-boot sales' popularity. Yet all this is also at a considerable distance from what takes place within our other two sites of second-hand exchange, where the relations of retail are used to constitute two possible positions of exchange – 'retailer' and 'customer' – and where the power of the retailer to determine pricing, and therefore restrict the conditions for capturing value, is re-established at least in principle. Rather than constituting difference through the principles of exchange, then, as we show now both retro retailing and charity retailing work more with the premises of exchange to constitute different versions of second-hand exchange.

From Aesthetic Appreciation to 'the Staple': Spatializing the Premises of Retro Retailing

Retro retailers frequently have long histories of involvement and investments in design and/or fashion. Some are graduates of various fashion/design degree courses around the country, and typically have spent a period of time working in the industry (as designers or buyers for particular retailers) before gravitating to self-employment. Others began on the markets, selling a combination of their own work and sourced goods (McRobbie, 1998), before moving up to trade in a shop setting. Their ways of talking about the things they sell, then, are highly distinctive, as the following examples testify:

> *Sophie*: It's about beautiful things. Eclectic beautiful things that are there for style, cut, quality and fabric . . .
>
> *Simon*: You buy things because you like them, not because you think there's loads of money it . . . I'll buy if I see something I like, I don't really care if it's sat in my front room – I'll be quite happy anyway . . . things designed by Olivetti, Braun – that kind of thing. A few people do know about it, but you're average Jo/e doesn't, and those are the things that you really do well on. Because to most people it would be like an old typewriter, old calculator, old phone, whereas there are certain people who know what it once was, what it was. It's something specialized . . .

Plate 3.3 Atomic 1

Michael: I was a design student originally and I became quite interested in the social history of the twentieth century related to products; so quite a high-brow academic interest. I started a few years ago collecting icons of their day; design icons whether they were hairdryers or vacuum cleaners or whatever . . . so I decided perhaps I could make a living out of buying and selling design items . . .

Beauty, style, location within design and fashion histories, the details of construction/production and of consumption in the first cycle are all characteristic markers in their talk, as is the importance of aesthetic appreciation and collecting. Indeed, all three of the above retailers point to how the meanings invested in their shops are not simply confined to exchange but extend to see the shop as a space in which to display their personal collections of things. As we show now this can have some profound effects on the constitution of shop interiors.

Plate 3.3 shows Simon's most recent retail venture in Nottingham. Framed by strong, clean minimalist black, the windows here work to isolate, highlight and 'showcase' key pieces of furniture and lighting. Here objects are displayed in a manner that takes its cues transparently

Plate 3.4 Atomic – interior 1

Plate 3.5 Atomic – interior 2

from the art exhibition and the gallery. We are clearly being positioned here to look and to admire; to see these goods not just as goods for sale but as design icons, as things that are to be valued for their aesthetic qualities and place in design history. Inside the same premises prevail (see Plates 3.4–3.6). White walls and shelving are used to enable goods to be displayed as exhibits. Straight out of the gallery, these strategies of display are supplemented by others that equally celebrate the aesthetic: lighting is used to throw other objects into relief (notably ceramics and glassware); chairs are positioned in ways that invite look-ing, but not sitting; walls are hung with occasional pieces of modernist art (that are also for sale); and there is even that marker of museum/ gallery reverence – the de-humidifier – in the corner, to preserve and conserve.

Plate 3.6 Atomic – interior 3

We see similar tendencies at work in another Nottingham retro shop, Luna (see Plate 3.7). Here, in the window, a diverse range of toys, glass, lighting, radios and ceramics is displayed individually on dedicated shelving but in a manner that takes its inspiration from the display case. Inside, pieces of furniture – typically tables – double as both shop fittings/fixtures and items for sale, while the other categories of goods are displayed in ways that take their cues from the auction catalogue, with each item being accompanied by information as to date, design(er)/ make and price. Constituted through a regime that values and celebrates the aesthetic, this is a space that manifestly takes its visual inspirations from the gallery – where people are encouraged to linger and look, and to admire the pre-selected. Similarly with Sophie's shop:

> This is a really beautiful shop just off Portobello Road. Has a boutique feel and sells a beautiful, careful and very stylish array of clothing – cashmere cardigans, a beautiful 50s dress and jacket and a 50s grey wool suit. Some nice accessories and beautiful antique silk nightwear. All in very beautiful fabrics . . . the shop is minimalist and quite scary in a small boutique kind of way. (Louise: field notes)

Plate 3.7 Luna – the window

Although the goods here are clothes rather than design-interiors, the aim here – much as with Simon – is to inscribe in space notions of aesthetic appreciation. Goods are displayed in ways that facilitate looking; individually highlighted, often through back and spot lighting, they invite scrutiny and often distant admiration in ways that clearly take their inspiration from the gallery and the designer boutique. By contrast, Michael has moved in directions that allow him to display his 'collections' while simultaneously making money from other forms of retail – notably cafés and specialist clothing boutiques:

> . . . there are electrical goods in the cafés, like coffee machines through the ages, which you just think are nice and shiny but as a matter of fact they're a specifically put together collection of the history of design, so they relate to all eras of the twentieth century. You can look at them in any way you like; think they're shiny or weird, or ignore them, or think they're really interesting because they're influenced by Nazi Bauhaus functionalism.

Part gallery, part personalized collection, these 'shops' are temples to style and design, where things are revered both for what they are and for the knowledges encoded in their production and recovery. There is a sense here, then, in which the selection of goods for sale is construed as an artistic creative endeavour, and as a materialization of retailers' own tastes and knowledges as well as their skills in restoration and repair. Further confirmed by temporary tactics that make connections with other artistic forms – Eve, a Nottingham retailer, for example occasionally turns her wall space into a gallery space for local artists – this version of retro retailing is constituting a selling space where the core premise is aesthetic appreciation.

By comparison, although they continue to talk about the things they sell in the same aesthetic and knowledge-rich ways, other retro retailers constitute interiors in ways that are the converse of minimalism. Here space is literally crammed full, in an appeal to the wardrobe and the attic:

> . . . *just off the main market, this is so crammed full with stuff that me and the two other people in there make it a real squash. This is packed full – of vintage stuff, some 70s, some 50s . . . linen dresses, 60s beaded numbers, snakeskin-looking shoes . . .* (Kate: field notes)

> . . . *Old coats, leather etc hanging up outside, window crammed full of jackets and lots of guitars . . . a small dark cavernous cubby-hole of a shop, again crammed with 70s stuff.* (Louise: field notes)

Encoding strong notions of the personal and the domestic, these regimes of representation clearly invite relations of looking that are about browsing and rummaging. Moreover, and unlike their minimalist counterparts, they positively encourage touch. Rather than constituting notions of dislocated admiration, these regimes encourage those who enter these spaces to make their own 'finds' in the wardrobe-cum-attic. Although pre-selected by retailers in a manner that is no different to 'the gallery' regime, this – to us – less intimidating regime of representation is a selling strategy that we found to be particularly common among women clothing retailers. With its nods in the direction of relations of buying in other second-hand sites (car-boot sales, jumble sales and nearly-new sales for instance), as well as its play on domestic storage spaces, this is perhaps not entirely surprising. Furthermore, it is significant for what it suggests about the core premises shaping these selling spaces: that, as well as being about aesthetic appreciation, this form of second-hand exchange is about relations of discovery and uncovering, of actively using knowledges in the practices of shopping to make discoveries. Rather than have goods packaged and displayed in a manner that is obviously pre-selected, this type of interior values and constitutes as pleasurable the effort – work even – that has to go into looking (and buying).

Plate 3.8 Fun, play and laughter 1

At the other end of the retro retailing spectrum are those shops dedicated either to supplying the commercial retro scene – clubs, 60s and 70s club nites and parties – or to classic retro 'staples' – Levi 501s, needle cords, leathers, shirts and so on. The first – typically – is about glitter, glitz and glam. Wigs, boas, outrageous platform boots and hot pants and so on prevail in such spaces, spaces which consequently take on the aura of the 'prop room' and dressing-up box and which invite relations of looking (and buying) that are about laughter, fun and play (see Plates 3.8 and 3.9). Worlds away from the previous premises, aesthetic appreciation is here supplanted by a relation to goods that is a celebration of the superficial, of the outrageous and of excess, which mobilizes irony and kitsch to select the 'trash' of previous decades for playful purchase. The following constitutes just one example of this tendency, in Nottingham:

Plate 3.9 Fun, play and laughter 2

This is real 1970s heaven – like a time warp. The outside of the shop has lots of hippy dresses (fringing, cheesecloth etc) hanging up outside and the window is emblazoned with fluorescent flowery 70s writing arguing that this has 'the biggest selection of flares this side of 1972'. Inside it's actually two shops knocked into one, and is a haven of bad taste – joss stickey type aromas, fluorescent Afro wigs, huge huge platform boots á la Sweet or T Rex . . . long vinyl boots, long gloves, stick on sideburns . . . Glitter and glam is very big . . . awful pictures of discomen strutting their stuff in white flared suits, framed Robin and Sirdar knitting patterns. There is a clear and very apparent sense of fun and irony here – a sign greets you as you walk in saying 'no bags – but handbags are welcome'. (Louise: field notes)

Plate 3.10 Regulation 70s

By contrast, retro shops dedicated to retro 'staples' display few differences in their selling strategies to those of the mass-market high street.
Here goods are ordered by category, colour and size; standardized and
mapped out for 'easy' shopping (see Plate 3.10), the premise here is
clearly that second-hand exchange can be conducted in ways that replicate certain strategies within the first cycle:

> . . . *as you go in, the coats and jackets – racks and racks of them – are to the*
> *left, piles of leather and suede . . . moving right, the jeans area – largely denim,*
> *largely flared but not loon. Mostly Wrangler, Lee and Levi, some Falmer. Further*
> *right again – men's shirts, including Fred Perry and Lacoste. Then women's shirts,*
> *tops and blouses . . . [then] a rail labeled 'Fancy Dress'.* (Nicky: field notes)

Resting on the accurate identification of which goods (will) constitute
'staples' and dependent, indeed reliant, on regular, reliable supply
chains, these versions of retro exchange are – in the face of increasing
supply difficulties – among the riskiest economic forms of second-hand
exchange that we encountered in our research.

When we examine the constitution of retro shop interiors, then, we
find that they encode a range of premises about second-hand exchange
that encompass the elite, aesthetic appreciation of goods and the
relations of the mass market, that both valorize the distinction between
first and second-hand exchange and question this. And, at least to a
degree, we find that these premises work, in that they attract the 'right
sort of customer' who shares the same values. So, we find retailers for
whom the aesthetic matters talking positively and approvingly about
certain of their core clients, applauding their style, taste and knowledge:

> . . . Johnny and Lucy have a house in X, and they've kitted it out with
> all second-hand stuff. They keep going to charity and second-hand shops
> and coming back with these like really great little containers and things.
> And that comes from the music. They're really into the Beatles and David
> Bowie . . . Lucy's got this fantastic jumper and then she found the cardigan
> to match much later in another charity shop . . . they know so much,
> they're just so smart. (Elaine)

And we find those shopping for fun and trash talking in ways that
clearly appreciate the 'wildness' and 'wackiness' of the fancy-dress style
interior, where the goods available appeal to codes of dress that emphasize loudness and outrage and are transparently about 'dressing-up':

Dominic:	You make a conscious effort to make it big and wild
Louise:	What's that all about?
Dominic:	Standing out in the crowd . . .
Sarah:	Yeah definitely
Dominic:	and having a good laugh. It's basically when you go out on a night people enjoy getting ready and that's half the night out
Sarah:	Everyone loves dressing up for whatever, and 70s is just another excuse to dress up

But, while retro retailers and certain of their core customers might themselves be clear about the premises inscribed in particular shop interiors, others are not. And the difficulty that many retro retailers face, particularly those for whom aesthetic appreciation matters, is that their shops are not bounded spaces. So, rather than being able to regulate out particular 'inappropriate' relations of looking (and buying), these spaces turn out to be ones open to counter-readings located in contrasting premises. Here, for example, is Elaine – a Nottingham retailer – lamenting having to sell to those who do not appreciate her clothes:

> . . . A lot of people go out with their friends to 70s clubs, but you'll find they don't want to wear the real clothes of the 70s. They just want to wear flares and halter necks and you show them a dress that actually comes from the 70s which is down to the floor and huge and smocked, and they won't wear it . . . whereas people who do wear second hand clothes and wear them all the time are delighted to wear smock dresses. They'll say 'Wow, look at the fabric of this' and they're wearing it because they adore the clothes, not because they're following a club trend . . . the people who are just going out 70s clubbing will buy very sparkly, glittery things for a laugh and they won't wear it again. They'll come into the shop and they'll say 'Oh my god, this is hideous' and 'I'm only going to wear it once' . . . it's just so disappointing when you sell to people and they think it's hideous and you know they're only going to wear it once. I'd much rather sell to – well I'm happy to sell stuff to anyone, but I'd much rather sell stuff to people who appreciate it.

Similarly, Michael talks about the frustrations of people not appreciating 'the point' of his shop-cum-gallery:

> It was really, really popular but not for buying; really really popular for people to come and look at weird and wonderful things . . . you only

tended to get fanatics or lunatics who played valve radios who knew every valve ever made; gay men who are mainstay customers because they seem to be the only ones with any kind of taste whatsoever . . . and prop hire and things like that, which was TV companies, and usually Christmas people looking for wacky present ideas . . . my shop was tiny but often full of people just looking like a free museum type thing. So I thought if I opened a café then I could put loads of things in the café of my own . . . and people would come in and eat and drink and at least I'd be making some money.

In both cases what we see is the power of the heavily commercialized premises of retro exchange – fun, laughter, 'trash' and surface – to destabilize the premises of distinction and discernment, and in the first case too we see how the imperative of making 'the sale' wins out over the aesthetic. Elaine may wish to sell to discerning clients who share her values, but she has to make money too. So, while certain of her transactions are about exchanging aesthetic appreciation, others are reduced purely to money, in a manner that reveals the limits to certain premises of retro exchange. For Michael, however, the sale was not even an option – people simply came to look and laugh. Not surprisingly he got frustrated and fed up, to the point where he talks about the commercial unviability of this form of retro (pure, authentic and located exclusively in design history) and moved into café-cum-collection options.

The limitations and inevitable compromises of the aesthetic as an exchange premise is something that has led other retro retailers to work in more complex ways with interiors, stock and even the very principles of retro exchange. Take Celia for example – another Nottingham retailer. At the same time as retailing her primary interest, vintage clothing – Victorian, 20s, 30s and 40s goods – she stocks clothing from the 1950s, 60s, 70s and 80s, including staples such as flares, catsuits and safari suits. Although steering clear of glitz, glamour and sportswear, the more commercial end of retro has been admitted here, in a way that acknowledges the importance of diversity, rather than singularity, to commercial success. Furthermore, Celia – like a number of other clothing specialists – operates with a dual pricing strategy, one for purchase and the other for hire. Targeted at the 'inappropriate' market, hiring not only allows Celia to maximize the exchange value of certain goods – 60s and 70s goods being particularly lucrative in this respect – but also enables her to hold on to goods which she constitutes through aesthetic appreciation until they find an appropriate purchaser.[36] Rather than being caught in the bind articulated by Elaine of having to sell to the 'inappropriate', or of being unable to make her business a commercially viable concern like Michael's, Celia has found a way of moulding the principles of exchange to mirror – and not erase – the premises that shape her work.

Rather than ending this study of retro retailing with Celia, however, we want to go back to moments of rupture. While laughter and ridicule constitute transparent instances of these, there is another less visible critique of the premises of retro retailing, which makes its presence felt not through exchange but in its absence. Articulated by those we talked with who themselves are steeped in design and/or fashion histories and knowledge, and for whom rummaging, browsing and looking in various second-hand arenas has long been a key pleasure, this is a critique of the whole retro retailing project – as 'too easy', 'too selected', 'too prescribed'. Here, for example, is Steven – a 30-something artist:

> *Kate*:   And do you look in the kind of retro shops as well as the charity shops then?
>
> *Steven*:   Not so much, but that's out of arrogance really, cos it all immediately starts to be prescribed again then, that these things are deemed good taste and bad taste, and I don't want anybody doing that, that's the joy of it, declaring it good taste or bad taste yourself, as soon as it's in a retro shop somebody's already made that selection; it feels like you're being told what to wear.

For individuals such as Steven, then, the pleasures of second-hand spaces of exchange are about making 'the find' for themselves, to identify it among the mass of goods, and to capture it from the unknowing in a way that conjoins symbolic and exchange value, economic and cultural capital. The development of dedicated retro shops, however – be they constituted through aesthetic appreciation, trash or even easy shopping – is widely identified here as foreclosing these possibilities, as removing the scope to make 'the find', and as reducing the potential to capture value. In this way, then, retro retailing is seen to be indicative of the commercialization of second-hand exchange, and the means to its contamination and ruination as exchange becomes increasingly constituted through the market. Somewhat ironically, then, the attempts of retro retailers to constitute spaces where the premises of exchange run counter to the commercial mainstream are themselves both read and condemned by others as indicative of the very same tendency.

Just Like New: Doing Things 'Properly' in the Charity Shop

As we showed in Chapter 2, the movement of charity shops to the high street has been constructed as 'professionalization' and, in what amounts to a direct attempt at copying certain practices of retail, has been accompanied by a widespread 'makeover' of the sector. Charity retail chains have thus seen the introduction of both new logos and new colour schemes, in transparent attempts at branding and increasing visibility on the high street (see Plates 3.11 and 3.12). Furthermore, 'makeovers' have extended to encompass shop interiors. Correspondingly, stock display has become increasingly standardized, with goods differentiated on the shop floor by category and price and by colour-blocking. Not only are these practices ones that facilitate the accurate monitoring of sales figures (and targets), but they have rapidly become part of normative display conventions across the sector. In short, they have played an integral part in the professionalization project, and are widely seen to legitimate claims to being 'proper shops'.

At the same time however, these standardized interiors are productive of particular regimes of representation. Here goods are presented in a

Plate 3.11 Charity shop logos

Plate 3.12 Charity shop logos

manner that is highly regulated. Sorted by volunteers through particular criteria imposed from Head Offices that elevate price bands, the general stock category (women's – differentiated, men's and children's clothing, books, vinyl, etc.) and colour, this regime is constituted around and striated by the mass market and mass consumption. Moreover, it is intrinsically about 'easy', quick, value-based looking (and buying), where the core motivations of the customer are assumed to be 'the bargain' and time. The parallel to the 'easy' retro-shopping instance, the importance of this regime lies in the way that it removes the work of looking: here those who enter into these spaces are encouraged to follow what is mapped out for them by the constitution of the interior – to look methodically and select (or not) from the 'choice' provided by pre-sorted categories. It is, then, an intensely regulated constitution of retail space, and one that appears to regulate customer possibilities entirely. But, what it also encodes is some of the core premises shaping this particular version of second-hand exchange: that (first-cycle) retailing provides stocks of knowledge/s and practices relating to selling that can be transplanted into the second-hand arena; that second hand goods can be sold in ways that are identical to these; and that the first/second-hand distinction can be erased through representational strategies.

We have already expressed our doubts about some of these premises elsewhere (Gregson, Brooks and Crewe, 2002). In part these rest on the disjuncture between charity retailers and their supply chains. Unable to control production runs as mass-market retailers do, and dependent on highly unpredictable flows of second hand goods, questions can be raised as to the appropriateness of mass-market, mass-consumption representational strategies for this particular form of exchange. Indeed, unlike with the retro equivalent – where similar strategies are at least deployed around core 'staples' – it seems to us that charity retailing ought to be looking toward the representational strategies developed in relation to other commodities in the first cycle, where individuality and uniqueness matter. This aside, the point that interests us here concerns the sheer amount of effort that goes on behind the scenes in charity shops to sustaining the premise that the first/second-hand distinction can be erased. So, and in a situation that is the converse of retro retailing, here teams of volunteers across thousands of shops engage in routine ironing, steaming, washing even – literally to divest garments of traces of previous consumption and of their consumers, and to attempt to rekindle something of their original value. Rather than, as in retro retailing, being worked on through creative restoration or sympathetic alteration – that is, in ways that value age and authenticity – these goods are being exhumed, in an attempt to make them as good as new and to make them acceptable for the shop floor. This we can see articulated in the following extract from an interview with one charity-shop manager in Sheffield:

Sue: . . . generally we get all sorts – absolute rubbish which is no good to anyone

Nicky: So do you have quite stringent criteria on what actually goes out?

Sue: Yes, I'm quite strict about what goes out; I have full control [laughter] – when I have a day off . . . the first thing I do is get in that room and look at what they've lined up and I don't want some of it, so it's 'I'm not putting that out'. So, if it's not sort of black bag-able – real rubbish – then I put it in a green bag for another shop – I'm not putting it out but they might. So I do that, I don't want old-fashioned stuff with a hole in.

Nicky: So it's got to be clean and tidy?

Sue: Yes, stuff that we can wash and dry – we have that – but it's got to be worth washing and drying – we can't wash everything. Most of the stuff that comes in, a lot of it is alright; it's fine – and we have a steamer that gets all the creases out which is fine – and

some of the stuff which comes in it's all crumpled, but that
steamer gets all of that out, it's fantastic.

Motivated by the desire to constitute charity shop goods as equivalent
to 'the new', these practices – through their very significance – work to
reinscribe the importance of second-hand as a distinction that matters.
In working to make these goods seem identical to those of 'proper
shops', charity shops reveal that these goods are not the same at all.

Putting our reservations regarding premises to one side, the issue that
we focus on in the remainder of this section is the one that connects it
most strongly to the retro study; that much like certain retro retailers,
charity retailers are unable to constitute bounded spaces of exchange.
So, much as before, we see here how the regime of representation associated with the charity retail project is unable to regulate out counter-
readings of charity shops grounded in counter-premises. This time,
however, the space for counter-readings is provided by charity retailers
themselves; by their positioning as *charity* retailers as well as by the existence of contrasting regimes within other parts of the sector.

As we argued in the previous chapter, one of if not the key principle/
s of this form of second-hand exchange is its substitution of 'fund-
raising' for profit: 'the cause' here is the reason for being for the shops,
the transplantation of retail sales strategies a means of maximizing
income generation. 'Charity' however, has a range of other meanings
and – as we see now – it is precisely these associations that enable
counter-readings to enter into and disrupt both charity retail's principles
and premises and the increasingly normative regime of representation.

Instances of alternative readings of 'charity' to the 'fund-raising'/
charitable-cause imperative were recurrent features of our year's participant observation work in charity-retail organizations, but the following
provide classic examples:

> . . . *Later on a very drunk trampish looking man comes in and spends a long
> time looking at everything . . . I think as we are en route to the DSS we get people
> who come in just to pass the time and/or for a warm knowing that it's OK to
> browse in Oxfam in a way that would cause problems in a 'proper shop' given
> the way they look/act etc.* (Kate: field notes)

> . . . *Sheila comes through from the front . . . with a youngish bloke who wants
> 'to ask something which is a bit embarrassing really'. I am standing on the
> step ladder [sorting] the books. Sheila asks if he minds me being there (I later
> learn that she feels a bit uneasy about him) – No – It turns out that he has to*

dress up as the character he labels as Elsie Tanner from Coronation Street and
so has to get dragged-up. Poor Lad has No Idea. He works as a Care Assistant
and this is to be done to raise money for charity. Sheila and I are wheeled into
action as style consultants . . . Sheila finds a matching imitation two-piece . . .
then she finds one of those 80s black jumpers with shiny bits all over it, together
with a short black skirt . . . far more suitable if combined with a pair of black
tights. He's not so sure and goes out into the back room (ie the toilet!) to try it
all on. Sheila goes back out the front and I'm left to advise on all this. I suggest
that he's going to have to find a pair of stillies from somewhere – looks of intense
worry, where does one find a pair of size 11 stillies? Also he needs to DEAL
with his legs – black tights won't cover that degree of hair! We then get onto
the inevitable question of deficiencies in certain bodily areas. I suggest
(ironically) a pair of implants. Sheila comes in and I raise the question of
bras . . . Oxfam is not supposed to sell these, but we do have one enormous DD
black effort . . . Eventually he gets all of this for the knock down price of a tenner.
(Nicky: field notes)

In both instances we see how individuals – who would, without question, be excluded from first-cycle retail space by shop security – construe charity shop spaces as spaces that ought to be accommodating of them. Both individuals then are drawing on readings of 'charity' that are about acting charitably – in the first case toward a self-styled charitable case, and in the second (allegedly) in support of another charitable cause. So, 'tramps', the homeless and so on come into these spaces, not to look in the manner suggested by charity retail's representational strategies, but to keep warm, to ask for clothing and to talk to others – volunteers, customers. And others, as in the 'Elsie Tanner' example, avoid the racks altogether and end up in back-shop space, and leave with ensembles that have cost them next to nothing. Rather than accord with specific fund-raising imperatives and charity retail's core premise that these are 'proper shops', certain individuals at least engage in a series of practices that suggest that charity shops are a long way indeed from their models, and – both implicitly and explicitly – invoke counter-readings of 'charity' to legitimate their actions.

To suggest that all, or even the majority, of charity shoppers engage in these types of practice, however, would be misplaced. Although 'disruptive' practices are far from uncommon – and would include too instances such as groups of students trying on clothes for fun on the shop floor and children being allowed to play with stock that is for sale – others, at least superficially, would appear to be comporting themselves in ways that accord with desired practice: looking methodically and buying. As we show now, using two diametrically opposed examples, this is not necessarily the case.

Christina is early 30s, a single parent with a young pre-school-age son. At the time we spoke with her she had been on income support for around four years and described herself as 'poor'. Charity shops provide one of her primary outlets for clothing both herself and her son, and she devotes a large amount of time each week working routinely through shops, comparing prices and available quality and, occasionally, buying. In practice, then, her actions look like ones coincident entirely with charity retail's regimes of representation, but as we see from what she says she is in fact highly critical of both the charity-retail project and its premises:

> . . . pricing wise there seems to be a big difference between charity shops. Some of them seem to have started pricing their children's clothes more than others . . . they're sort of pushing up . . . but some things are ridiculously priced. You can certainly get them new from cheaper shops. They [meaning charity shops] have a certain responsibility to the poorer people in this country who have always relied on things like jumble sales, and whether they like it or not charity shops have actually taken away those goods from jumble sales – kind of taking away a resource for people who are poor, and although I think it's good that charity shops are raising money you know, and I'm all for recycling clothes, I also think that they ought to bear in mind that most people I see in [area of Sheffield] are people with children who are shopping in them because they have to and not because they have choice . . . I think they actually don't care who the charity is.

For Christina, then, charity shops are primarily resources that ought to be there for poor people first and foremost, and not a means of fundraising. And it is instructive too how she makes clear links between charity shops and other second-hand sites, notably jumble sales, which she regards as having a similar moral purpose. Rather than accepting charity retail's attempt to erase the first/second-hand distinction she is reinserting it, insisting on its importance even to enabling household provisioning for those in disadvantaged circumstances.

By contrast, Judy is early 60s, a housewife – her term – and a grandmother. She has been shopping in charity shops for over 35 years now, initially from necessity but now because this is an integral, pleasurable part of her weekly shopping practice. This is how she describes her charity-shopping practices:

I first of all do tops which is what I'm usually looking for, like jumpers or skirts. Then I usually look at trousers, then jackets of course. Jackets are my weakness I think. Occasionally I find a really good Windsmoor. I've got upstairs a pure linen Windsmoor. It's really nice for weddings – £1.50 on the sale rail! So excited about that!

Apparently, then, Judy is working through the goods in exactly the same manner prescribed by the regime of representation – by category, by price – looking for 'the bargain'. But, as she later reveals, her ideal charity shop is one where she can spend much more time, a shop that is packed full and that requires her to 'rummage', to use her skills of looking and selection to the full. Judy, then, like many other charity shoppers, is critical of the 'makeover' project. Talking about previous regimes of representation, she says:

[they were] more jumbly, more like jumble sales really, you had to hunt and get underneath piles, they didn't have proper rails and things like they have now. But somehow it was more exciting, cos you thought you'd find something you liked. But I think some of the shops are a bit too organized now, aren't they . . .

For her, and for many others, this has not only made charity shops look like high-street shops, but it has taken away some of her pleasures in looking:

Margi: . . . you go round to the Red Cross Society Shop, which is slightly off the main drag, when you go there, that's more like what charity shops used to be – things are more jumbled around a bit – they've still got all their shirts together and their skirts together – but it's not as regulated, whereas now it's when you walk in it's the yellow shirts and the red shirts you know, and I just find that

Trish: It defeats the object of charity shopping.

Margi: Yeah – you're losing that – you haven't got that rooting around – 'Oh that's nice!' 'Can you take that off that'. Now I feel like you're walking into Top Shop or something . . .

Grounded in regimes that take us back to the wardrobe and the attic metaphor, we can see once more how potent this spatialization is for those shopping in the second-hand arena. It encodes these goods as second-hand, it makes clear their linkages to previous consumption practices, and it connects to practices associated with other second-hand spaces of exchange – jumble sales, nearly-new sales, car-boot sales and certain versions of retro. Moreover, and critically, it positions 'shoppers' in relations that require them to make selections for themselves, rather than have these presented to them. It is our view, then that, in attempting to write out such premises through the representational strategies of particular versions of first-cycle retail, it is just possible that charity retailers might have constituted an inappropriate spatialization for the goods it primarily sells.

As both our charity-shop and retro-shop case studies show, at least certain forms of second-hand exchange in the UK are now located within shop settings. In turning away from the temporary retail spaces associated with forms of second-hand exchange with longer histories – jumble sales – as well as those utilized by car-boot sales, these forms of second-hand exchange have been constituted in ways that accord entirely with the conventions of standard exchange relations. Here then, as in the first cycle, retailers do all the work of sourcing and selling; they pre-select goods, display them and offer them at pre-determined prices to 'customers', who are positioned to look, desire, choose and buy (or not). As we have seen, though, the ways in which they constitute these shop interiors reveal very different sets of premises about second-hand goods – from aesthetic appreciation to being just as new, from fun and trash to the bargain basement. Moreover, we have seen too how encoding these premises in particular regimes of representation can be problematic; that certain of these regimes prove to be open to contestation and rupture, in ways that simply do not happen in first-cycle exchange. In the final section of this chapter we reflect on why this occurs.

Conclusions

When we look across the retro- and charity-shop case studies we can see that the two regimes most vulnerable to critique and rupture are those of 'the collection'/exhibition and the charity-retail project. For us this is no coincidence. Although vastly different, in that one appeals to elite taste and the other to the mass, both are highly regulated regimes that leave consumers with little work of looking. Instead, 'customers' are mapped into interior retail space in ways that attempt to constitute specific relations and practices of looking – on the one hand dislocated admiration and on the other methodical working through. Categories of goods, racks, display stands and so on, then, work to funnel 'customers' toward and through particular goods, in ways that mirror what occurs in units on the high street and in shopping centres, or indeed in many exhibitions. Having over the course of this research talked with many who frequent second-hand sites, we have little doubt in our minds that it is these associations that are being railed against, at least in part. Part of this resistance is about an insistence that the goods being sold in these spaces are second-hand, and that this ought to make a radical difference to (strategies of) selling. So, rather than find attractive the evidently pre-selected, regulated and ordered offerings of certain charity and retro shops, many of those who use these spaces take pleasure in the work of selection, seeing what they choose to buy as a realization of their skills of seeing and looking and not those of the retailer. They therefore actively prefer regimes that appeal to rediscovery. Equally, others – for whom second-hand provisioning is a long way from pleasurable and a routine practice – connect the pre-selected regimes of charity retail with price rises and see the high-street copy as a means of their legitimation. For them, while such regimes might enable 'easy' shopping, they are simultaneously a means to erasing the value that they see as an integral, defining and normative feature of 'second-hand'. Given this, we can begin to see why regimes of representation that appeal to the wardrobe, junkyard and attic remain popular: they are seen to encode the distinction between the first and second cycle and to enable the consumer (and not the retailer) to identify, select and determine value. Resonant with the conventions associated with the full spectrum of second-hand sites from jumble sales at one end through to elite auction houses at the other, the latter is a clear principle of second-hand exchange. For us, then, some of the most recent attempts to constitute distinctive spaces of second-hand exchange go against these principles by attempting to locate the identification, selection and definition of value as the exclusive preserve of retailers. Moreover, they are still struggling to find appropriate representational regimes to encode the goods that they sell. And, in attempting to regulate positions and relations of looking so intensely, they could even be eliminating the possibilities for value creation by consumers – witness the situation in certain retro shops or the critique of colour-blocking in charity retail, both of which appear more to preclude than to encourage exchange for some.

If we are to draw any general conclusions about our various sites of second-hand exchange, then, it would be to emphasize the centrality of space to their successful constitution. The spaces that 'work', then – ones that are both popular and a commercial success – are those that manage to combine different principles of exchange with creating the conditions for value creation, to create distinctive spaces through distinctive practices. They are those spaces, then, where the principles of exchange differ from standard conventions – where for example 'price' is negotiated or where hiring occurs – and where regimes of representation allow consumers to (appear to) do the work of selection – where the practices of looking and buying conjoin in ways that run counter to, suspend and possibly even subvert those of elsewhere. Occurring in car-boot sales, in some charity shops (but not charity retail) and in some but by no means all, retro shops, this regime transcends the specifics of particular trading settings, encompassing everything from fields, church halls, junkyards, market pitches and shop units. It is one that insists that second hand goods make a radical difference to the representational strategies of selling and that encodes connections to the biographies of goods and their consumption histories. Moreover, it connects the more recent versions of second-hand exchange that we have considered to others with a longer trajectory and history. If we are to account for this regime's continued contemporary potency however, it is not to history but to current consumption practices that we need to look. Correspondingly, it is to these that we turn in subsequent chapters. In the following chapter, however, we move to explore in depth how those shopping second-hand practice (second-hand) shopping.

Spaces of Shopping Practice

The previous two chapters have established the degree to which spaces of second-hand exchange are constituted as distinctively different from the spaces associated with first hand retail sales and from each other, and the extent to which these encodings rest on entwining particular understandings of 'second-hand' within specific spatializations. Thus far, however, we have devoted rather more attention to how second-hand spaces have been 'produced' – by retailers, by promoters and by those who participate in acts of exchange. And we have been concerned with these spaces in the singular, as discrete, differentiated albeit related spaces of exchange. In part indicative of the effects of proliferation, in part a consequence of our initial focus on the variable principles and premises of second-hand exchange, the differentiation between second-hand sites is something that starts to break down when we look at how those who frequent these spaces combine them and weave them together in practice. Correspondingly, this chapter focuses on precisely this issue, our objective here being to examine the ways in which second-hand spaces of exchange are incorporated into shopping practices.

Leaving aside the undoubtedly numerous instances of those who do not frequent these, or any other, sites of second-hand exchange, and who shop exclusively in first hand arenas,[37] the argument we forward here is that, for the majority, second-hand spaces are all about juxtaposition and combination, with the spaces of 'the new'. Second-hand sites, then, tend to be woven together in practice in ways that both blur their differentiations from each other and seek to maximize their distance from the spaces and practices of the first cycle. Equally, however, both first and second-hand spaces are shown to exist in a situation of relational interdependence. The exception to this general pattern is where second-hand spaces are constituted oppositionally, as a direct critique of the practices associated with shopping first hand. We identify three sets of shopping practice where second and first hand spaces are articulated through interdependence. The first of these is where second-hand spaces provide the primary means for satisfying certain forms of household provisioning, and where the spaces of the first cycle work both as desired and as an occasional release from the hard work of shopping second-hand. Associated principally with those on limited incomes, this is the reverse of the second practice, where second-hand spaces provide a temporary suspension – from the ordinary work of everyday household provisioning and from the working day. Here, where shopping can – but critically does not have to – result in the purchase, second-hand worlds constitute a treat in themselves, and a space for the self. The third set of practices is very different: here, second-hand spaces provide key resources for particular discursive communities to enact both distinction and skill. Long associated with the dress of various subcultures (Becker 1963; Frith 1997; Gelder and Thornton, 1997; Hebdige, 1979; Muggleton, 2000; Redhead 1993; Thornton 1995; Young 1993) – from hippies to punk, the New Romantics to grunge – second-hand worlds are shown to be combined in shopping practices that are about ransacking the past to create distinctive 'knowing' looks, and where 'knowingness' is signified as much through the spaces and places of purchase as by the object purchased. At the same time, however, second-hand spaces are situated within other discursive communities – this time of women – to enact and subsequently display their shopping skills. Finally, we turn to consider the few instances we encountered where second-hand sites are mobilized in an oppositional sense, both to critique the consumerism of capitalism and its manifestation in first-cycle retail space and to constitute second-hand sites as providing the basis for all forms of household provisioning bar food. Enabled by the expansion and proliferation in second-hand sites, this critique is grounded in both anti-consumerist and pro-recycling rhetoric but is shown to be one that frequently breaks down in practice, with both 'the brand' and standard definitions of 'value' proving no less central to purchasing practices in the second cycle as in the first.

Having established the primary ways in which second-hand spaces are woven together in shopping as practised, we end the chapter by arguing that these practices are themselves both constitutive of particular shopping geographies and indicative of the premises shoppers inscribe in second-hand spaces. Four such premises are seen to be critical. One is to insist that second-hand spaces are a key part of a moral economy; that they are necessary facets of redistribution and should be embedded in local communities. Here 'shopping' is defined in terms of social reproduction, basic needs and core provisioning, and second-hand sites as a means of redistribution within communities. Strongly localized, this is at a considerable remove from a second, much more spatially extensive, premise. Here second-hand sites come to be seen as a way of knowing places and positioning and differentiating between place, literally as a means of encountering and making sense of place. Thirdly, second-hand sites are argued to be intrinsically about identity formation. Open to various permutations, they can be mobilized to constitute 'difference', or work as a space for enabling other identities to be temporarily reasserted, but equally and much more negatively, they can be spaces that mark out and reinscribe social exclusion. Finally, at least in part, our research provides some evidence for the development of premises that locate second-hand spaces in resistant shopping practices. Second-hand sites are seen here to provide at least the conditions for practices that contest the imperatives of the first cycle. At the same time, however, there are clear limits to these practices. We close the chapter therefore by reflecting on why second-hand worlds are only limited spaces of resistance. Taking us back to our core concern in this section with the principles and premises of second-hand exchange, this allows us to draw some more general conclusions to this section. To begin the chapter, however, we want to say a little more about the weaving together in practice of second-hand sites.

Blurring Difference, Maximizing Distance: the Complex Strategies of Combination

As we showed in Chapter 3, certain of the participants in car-boot sales as well as those shopping in and frequenting charity shops and retro shops are well aware of the distinctions between these sites and spaces. Nonetheless, although clearly articulated in both talk and practice, another feature – at least of talk – is the way in which these distinctions frequently break down. Apparently paradoxical, even seemingly contradictory, these elisions provided us with some of what seemed at the time to be among our 'most frustrating "interview moments"' – for example, as when individuals appeared to run together charity shops and retro shops, and to drift from talking about charity shopping to car-boot sales and jumble sales, almost at whim. As ever, though, while we were preoccupied with distinctive spaces, their principles and premises, those we talked with were signalling something critical – in this case, that practice can simultaneously acknowledge difference and blur this, in this instance to produce second-hand worlds that are continually articulated with and understood in relation to spaces associated with and identified with 'the new'.

To give some flavour of the elision and slippage we encountered, we begin this section with three notable examples. All drawn from instances we introduced initially in the context of Chapter 3, these are isolated again here both to emphasize the apparent contradiction in individuals' talk and to open up some of the analytical distinctions we make later on in the section:

Louise:	Where do you get your clothes?
Sarah:	Charity shops
Dominic:	Charity shops
Louise:	Which ones in Nottingham would you be going to?
Dominic:	Golden Cage is very good for hiring, but not so good for buying. Celia's you can buy from, but they're quite expensive . . . there's one up in an attic somewhere, I can't remember what it's called
Louise:	Baklash
Dominic:	Yeah – that's the one . . .

Nicky:	. . . So if we talk a bit then about how you actually go through them [charity shops] then
Margi:	Our actual shopping technique!
Nicky:	Yeah – [*laughter*]
Trish:	Well I've found that over the past few years charity shops have very much changed their layout – I don't know so much about here, but in London definitely [*talk over*] and articles – they have all their skirts together, and all colours together – and obviously someone's got in there with a bit of marketing
Nicky:	Which bits of London do you hang out in then?
Trish:	North London – Hampstead
Nicky:	Camden?
Trish:	Camden's a bit steep actually on the charity-shop front – laughter – you know, it's because all those people up there at the weekends and they'll pay money for anything. So generally Camden High Street is a little bit steep – I'll tend to go more to Kilburn where they have you know whole racks at 50p – your best bet is still the church-hall jumble sale though. Fight with the grannies for 20p!! – [*laughter*]
Nicky:	And that's what gives you a buzz then?

Trish:	Yeah – the whole thing of 'I deserve this just as much as you do', and 'I got here just as early'! – [*laughter*]
Margi:	Yeah – jumble sales, if you're not there in the first hour forget it
Trish:	I haven't been to jumble sales actually for quite a while [. . . *explains why*. . .] but you have to buy quickly, you haven't got time to – it's trestle tables [*indicates arm-wrestling technique*] and you might find that one person behind the counter is charging a bit more than somebody else, so you have to suss that out – it's all detection!
Nicky:	And would you go to boot sales as well – though this is Central London
Trish:	Well they do have boots but I find that the boot sales down there aren't as good on the clothes front and I don't really need nick nacks and I don't really need anything for the house – so car boots yeah they do have them but often they have the traders – the other thing I've noticed with charity shops is that a lot of them aren't prepared to barter . . .
Christina:	. . . I'm inclined to think that they [charity shops] have a certain responsibility to the poorer people in this country who have always relied on things like jumble sales, and whether they like it or not, certain charity shops and other second-hand shops that have sprung up have actually taken away those goods from jumble sales, so although there are jumble sales around, they're not so frequent, they're not so local and they're harder to hear about. You get a lot of people who are selling clothes on who are going in and buying up in bulk, whereas they used to be very selective in them.
Kate:	You mean like second-hand shop people?
Christina:	Yeah, oh yeah. They're infiltrated by them. You go in there and you either have to – I mean with a small child, you have to be selective to get things that you like, you can't do it really. It's very very stressful. I mean people are just grabbing armfuls of things and buying them cheap because they they can, because they're selling them on the market on second-hand markets.

In the first instance the interviewer – in this case Louise[38] – is concerned to articulate the distinctions between retro shops and charity shops but Dominic and Sarah are clearly comfortable with running the two together, for 'The Golden Cage', Celia's and Baklash are not charity shops but some of Nottingham's dedicated retro shops. Initially when we interpreted this transcript we were unclear what to make of this; was this what it appeared to be on first reading – an inaccurate mis-interpretation of second-hand spaces? Or was its elision of what we saw as distinctive saying something more profound about practice? Our inclination now is to opt for the second interpretation: to see Dominic and Sarah's second-hand shopping practices as about weaving together and blurring retro and charity shops through a practice that is a cele-bration of fun, laughter, play and bad taste.

By contrast, in the second lengthier extract we see the interviewer – in this instance Nicky – changing the interview 'track' to charity-shop interiors and practices of shopping, but how the talk drifts and slips in a relatively short space of time to open up the space for comparisons between spaces to be articulated – initially from charity shops to jumble sales, and then – following prompting – to car-boot sales, before drifting back immediately to charity shops. Again this is indicative of the effects of practice. Both Margi and Trish engage in complex practices of second-hand shopping that, unlike Dominic and Sarah's, utilize the full range of second-hand spaces. To try to talk about any one of these spaces in isolation, then, is both an impossibility and a disruption of their prac-tice/s.

The third instance – that of Christina, this time interviewed by Kate – is another example of relational slippage, where charity shops are again compared directly and juxtaposed immediately in talk with jumble sales. Here, though, we can see the emergence of a strong degree of critical talk. Charity shops and jumble sales are not being compared here, as before, in terms of what they might enable but as spaces of moral exchange, and in terms of redistributional practices. Here then second-hand spaces are understood through shopping practices that weave together sites as resources for those on restricted incomes, and as resources that ought to be – but increasingly are not – equivalent.

All three of these extracts demonstrate conclusively that second-hand spaces are conjoined in practice to produce particular practices of second-hand shopping that are reflected in different patterns of talk. Moreover, they begin to open up that these practices have very different motivations, ones that span the full gamut from fun and laughter at one end through to need at the other. In the remainder of this section we examine these practices and their motivations in depth, and argue that these are all located in understandings that seek to counterpose second-hand worlds (and practices of shopping) with those identified with the first cycle.[39]

Hard Work and 'the Binge': the Work (and the Limits) of Provisioning through Second-hand

Christina, the single parent whom we met initially in Chapter 3, exemplifies the practices of shopping second-hand through necessity. Previously a nurse and degree-educated, she has been on income support since the birth of her son (pre-school age when we talked with her). Christina's meshing together of second-hand spaces is primarily a survival strategy; something that she literally has to do to clothe both herself and – more importantly (to her) – her son. The following is indicative of how she talks about this practice:

> . . . I've now actually got to a stage where I can't actually afford to go into proper shops to shop and I arrived at that about a year and a half ago, and it then dawned on me that when I had an inadequate number of clothes that I'd actually have to make a point of doing shopping trips round all the charity shops that were suitable for trousers and things, and so I've actually been going on tours of particular charity shops to find clothes that I can use . . . most of the people I see in [area of Sheffield] are people with children who are shopping in them because they have to and not because they have the choice. You know it's just not a fun thing to do.

Christina's talk, then, is explicitly of poverty, of 'being poor' as she terms it, and of its effects on household, and particularly clothing, provisioning – in her case exclusion from 'proper shops' and reliance on second-hand sites and second-hand goods. But it is also as we saw previously about how hard she has to work in order to accomplish this. So, as we saw in the preceding extract, we can see how she talks about the sheer effort and stress of going to jumble sales with a young child in tow (literally on her back). And the same degree of time and effort also characterizes her charity-shopping trips – although, like a number of others it is important to note that she talks about charity shopping with a young child as less stressful than ordinary shopping.[40] As she explains, the work of charity shopping is not just about traipsing from shop to shop on a regular basis, but about thoroughly assessing and evaluating the respectability, wear and price of (children's) clothing:

> . . . they have to be in reasonable condition . . . most of the things I buy in charity shops, I tend to, I think they have a certain amount of quality about them. They're not things that I would have thrown away in that state . . . I've noticed that whereas before if I wasn't quite sure about an

item of clothing – whether I really needed it – I'd have probably bought it and thought about it later, whereas now I don't. I actually will only buy something if I, I'll actually go away and think about it before I buy, even if it's only £3 or £4 for a pair of trousers – when you're living on £40 a week and that's your budget for food and everything, transport, you don't want to make mistakes . . . I always look at children's clothes because he's growing all the time and he obviously gets through more and more clothes you know. Even if things are too big for him I can buy them and put them by . . . you can buy things in advance for a child . . .

When she talks about her practices of second-hand shopping, then, Christina shows how she is continually thinking about budgeting, thinking (and purchasing) ahead, and being vigilant; for her it is critical not to make mistakes. And similarly, the same patterns of routine, careful, thorough and intensely comparative practices characterized other single parents that we spoke with, like Jane and Tom. However, as Jane's testimony reveals, while these practices are hard enough work for those with a pre-school-age child, the transition to school frequently makes this even harder, virtually impossible:

. . . income didn't get a lot more, but the need for [daughter's name] at the time, to go out not in clothes that were obviously from a charity shop, I wanted her to go to school looking nice, and if I'd bought the clothes in proper shops I felt that she looked nice, and if I'd got them from a charity shop then I kind of felt that it wasn't quite right.

Jane is struggling here with her own materialization through clothing of appropriate mothering strategies. She is arguing that somehow, while previously appropriate enough, second-hand is inappropriate here, at school, because of its potential effects. Although tacit here, we would identify these as marking out her daughter as 'different' and therefore vulnerable to bullying and in peer-group friendship formation, and exposing herself to potential social censure as an inadequate mother. So, while Jane could (and would) be working very hard at being 'the good mother' through continuing to use second-hand sites, devoting massive amounts of time and investment into clothing her child, we can see from this that second-hand sites have clear limits in her mind. Indeed, that they are seen to be at or even beyond the limits of social acceptability for clothing a school-age child. Charity shops (and jumble sales) at this juncture are just not good enough, or even appropriate, spaces for clothing this child.[41]

Now, although these transcripts and others like them are character-ized primarily by this type of talk, they are simultaneously interspersed with references to the shopping spaces of the first cycle in ways that make clear that, while these spaces can be subjected to critique, they are at the same time desired, for what they offer in terms of shopping practices. So, while Tom, Jane and Christina all articulate some of the anti-consumerist, pro-recycling critique that we discuss later, they talk simultaneously about the attractions and the seductions of buying 'the new' in 'ordinary shops'. For Christina, who literally has not got the money to do this, and without access to credit facilities, this is largely talked about as unsatisfied desire, as what 'it would be nice to do':

> . . . I would like occasionally to be able to buy myself something new, particularly say something special to go out in, if I ever got the chance to go out – laughs – I'd like to be able to buy something like that occas-ionally maybe. And the other thing which would be nice, certainly with children's clothes, is if your child needed something to be able to go out and buy something from a shop without actually having to worry if you've got enough money to pay for it or not . . .

Encompassing significantly 'special' clothing for herself and specialist children's clothing – tellingly she goes on to mention children's sports kits immediately after this extract – these wished-for goods are seen to be easily purchased in the spaces of the first cycle, compared to the 'days or weeks of hunting through charity shops'. Moreover, they contrast markedly with the only items of clothing that she continues to buy new – underwear, 'his pants, underwear and socks – they're cheap enough to buy you know. I can just about stretch to buying pants – laughs'. By contrast, Tom – who still has credit facilities – talked at length about temporary 'binges', occasional phases of 'going mad with the credit card' (and then 'regretting it') during which he bought both for himself and for his son. Concentrated in periods when he was relatively 'flush' – the result of living on a graduate-student grant rather than on income support – it is the spaces of the first cycle that work here as a release from the day-to-day hard work and effort of second-hand provisioning.

As both these instances make clear, for those forced through financial necessity to weave together various second-hand sites as resources for certain forms of basic household provisioning – notably clothing – the routine practices of shopping work to constitute second-hand worlds as spaces where shopping is work – hard, routine, repetitive and often unrewarding, in that purchasing itself can take, as Christina says, literally days and weeks of hunting. By contrast, the spaces of the first cycle work as their relational counterpart. Seen to offer quick, 'easy' shopping, where 'needs' and desires are seen to be instantly satisfied and immediately satisfiable, their power lies in their connections to shopping as practiced. For, when shopping is work there is a clear imperative for it to be, in certain times and places at least, otherwise. This we see from the following set of shopping practises, where second-hand spaces figure this time as the counterpoint to everyday routine shopping practice/s and everyday working routines.

The Treat, Time Out and Space for the Self

At first sight the practices of Judy, the 'housewife' whom we met initially in Chapter 3, look much like those of Christina. Judy then engages in charity shopping as part of her weekly shopping routine; she has a planned, mapped-out route, starting at one end of the West Country town where she lives and ending up at the other; and she is extremely thorough and methodical in her practices of looking – working through specific clothing categories, tops, jackets, skirts and now, since she is grandmother to a couple of young babies, baby clothes. Furthermore, she weaves this together with visits to second-hand and junk shops – accompanied on these occasions by her husband, who also works in the second-hand trade. When we examine Judy's talk, however, it is transparent that these practices are a very long way from routine, repetitive hard work. Instead, her pattern of talk is littered with markers of how pleasurable she finds this shopping practice; it is described as 'exciting' – not a word used by Christina for example – and as something that enables her to buy in bulk. Indeed, Judy describes one of the chief attractions of charity shopping as coming away with armfuls of plastic bags! Importantly too, though, charity shopping allows her to spend time alone, doing something that she enjoys and taking her time doing this.

Undeniably, a lot of Judy's pleasure here is connected to one of her primary motivations, capturing 'the bargain'. However, as important to our minds is the way in which she sees second-hand spaces as pleasurable spaces to spend time in, as pleasurable in themselves. Connected to the ways in which she – unlike Christina, Tom or Jane – does not have to make the purchase, this pleasure is further attested to when Judy reveals that much of the time spent accompanying her husband on his 'business trips' is actually spent charity shopping. For Judy then, charity shopping is both a routine practice and – critically – a way of spending her leisure time; it works as 'a treat'. And others talk similarly. Margi, for instance, talks here about the pleasures of both popping-in to certain charity shops and of spending a couple of hours rummaging through a particular type of charity shop:

> . . . I go to Help the Aged probably twice a week and I go into the Red Cross probably once a week, or once every two weeks . . . normally I keep them as a bit of a treat . . . there's this one in [village in Derbyshire] and it's like somebody's just shoved it all in . . . you walk in and there's a two by five area where you can stand and then there's the counter and there's just stuff up to the roof and it's just brilliant. It's only ever open between 1 and 4.30 on Tuesdays – one of those funny ones – but I've only done what I'd call a small graze into it, but to me it would be a solid two hours to do that shop . . .

Likewise, she and many others talk of the ways in which a day spent dedicated charity shopping – or a day out at a car-boot sale – is in itself intrinsically pleasurable, in ways that make clear that the pleasure lies as much in the practice as in the purchase.

For all these women, the practices of second-hand shopping and the spaces that comprise these are constituted, at least in part, as a treat. Correspondingly, to engage in these practices and to shape them through the treat requires that time and space be set aside specifically for them. Sometimes, as some of our respondents made clear, this is 'window time', usually framed by and within the parameters of the standard working day. So we see Val for example, a secretary, devoting many of her lunchtimes to charity shopping, and Margi 'popping in' to charity shops while ostensibly doing something else, typically visiting the bank. Yet others, however, talk about meshing together second-hand sites as a weekend 'treat'. Karen, for instance, often spends one day of the weekend touring the charity shops of Greenwich, in conjunction with a visit to the market and the occasional pop into a retro shop. Similarly, Tom (a different Tom to the one in the previous section) construes charity shopping as a Saturday afternoon treat. For others however, without the constraints of the rhythms of the conventional working day and week, second-hand shopping is a planned 'treating' activity: for instance as a reward to celebrate finishing an essay (a classic student response), as part of the routine associated with collecting the pension, or to give oneself a 'day off' (a graduate-student strategy). Treating here, then, is not just about purchasing for self (and others), but about an activity that centres the self through the space it allocates through practice to the (consuming) self.

That second-hand spaces can be woven together in these ways is highly instructive as well as suggestive. For some, then, and here we are thinking primarily of our older and/or middle-aged female respondents, there is a strong sense in which these second-hand shopping practices are about doing something that is not about the significant men in their lives. Both Val and Judy for instance consciously do not go charity shopping with their respective husbands; neither do they buy (or even look) for them in second-hand arenas:

> *Nicky*:   . . . And would you ever look at the men's? For your husband?
> *Val*:   No!! No way!! He doesn't buy very many clothes at all, but if he
>   does he buys smart things at proper shops. I don't know but I
>   don't think that men's clothes are as good in charity shops . . .

Instead, and here we do not think that we are overexaggerating the case, they are engaging in a set of practices that, in centring looking (and buying) for themselves and doing shopping differently, are about the partial, temporary subversion of other practices that require them to buy for and attend to the 'needs' of significant others. Charity shopping for these women then is, in our view, a form of resistance – a way of making space and reasserting the self within relationships that con-stitute Woman as carer and homemaker through the modification of a practice – shopping – that is taken for granted by them to be highly gendered.[42] It is, then, a practice that makes sense when seen in relation to what goes on elsewhere in these women's lives – where they take primary responsibility for household provisioning. By comparison, the younger women with whom we spoke– who clearly constituted their relationships in very different ways – use the practice of second-hand shopping both to treat themselves and frequently to treat significant others. Margi, for example, talks about buying for herself and for her partner, and for a few close friends in a way that emphasizes that a key part of this treat is the gifting of her time and skill. At the same time, however, these younger women also see second-hand shopping prac-tices as activities that they might do with their (women) friends. Again talked about as intensely pleasurable – in that these practices are represented as characterized by much laughter – such shopping exped-itions can nonetheless be highly problematic. As Penny reveals, they can be extremely competitive and stretching of friendship ties, and are best conducted between friends of different body sizes and shapes, where the self is not under threat from others:

. . . It's more fun because you laugh more, you know if you're shopping on your own, I mean sometimes if you see something really funny you'll laugh out loud when your on your own, but on the whole you're just chuckling inside. But when you're with friends it's just so much fun you know. Finding things, finding things for each other as well . . . I think it's quite important to shop with someone who doesn't take the same clothing size . . . cos you know at the end of the day you're not going to fight over something because it either fits one of you or it fits the other. You know, they're either a lot taller or a lot thinner or whatever, so it's alright. If I went shopping with someone who was my size it would be – it can get nasty. I remember shopping with a friend years ago and finding this absolutely beautiful old hat box, a bit like a vanity case but it was actually a hat box, absolutely gorgeous, and I found it, I saw it on the shelf and I pulled it down and said 'Oh look at this, it's so beautiful'. But she had a hat that needed a box, but I'd found it. And we stood there for about ten minutes in this shop pulling, like physically pulling at this box, from side to side . . .

The connections between the practices of shopping in second-hand spaces and the treat, however, are not just significant to the constitution of relationships with significant others. Indeed, they are as important for what they have to reveal about the spaces of the first cycle. And here the key issue for us is why 'the treat' comes to be associated with the practices of second-hand shopping. In the following extract Val provides us with some of the answers:

. . . I'd have to be fairly desperate to go to a shop like Marks and Spencers [*Nicky: Really?*] Oh yes [*Nicky: Why's that?*] Well it's all the same! And all these big shops, they all have, you know, it's either the white short sleeved jackets or it's the black something else you know, you can't get anything, you can't set your mind on something and go and get it – I know you can't get it in a charity shop either – like when I was looking for the jacket for the wedding I went in every single shop in Sheffield looking and couldn't find one that I liked, none of them had one that I wanted, and it's just so tiring walking round looking at the same stuff . . .

Her disparaging comments about the high street, and about Marks and Spencer in particular, are telling here. Certain of the spaces of the first-cycle, then, are seen to be too repetitive, too pre-selected and in many senses too easy for her to construe them as pleasurable spaces to spend time in. Moreover, they are seen to be too restrictive in the choices that they appear to offer – she recounts for instance how she spent some time looking in these spaces for a black jacket to wear to a wedding, only to find something far more suitable eventually in a charity shop. So, when Val does use the spaces of the first cycle it is not surprising that she turns to small independent clothing retailers to supplement her charity-shopping practices:

> . . . if I want something fresh to wear then I go up there [independent boutique] . . . because there's a limited number of things and I know that there will be clothes there some of which I'll like . . .

For her, then, both the regimes of representation of many first-cycle retail outlets and their connection to mass production-mass consumption constitute severe limits to the practices of shopping. Rather than allowing her to constitute shopping as pleasurable (a core motivation for her) and enabling her to prescribe goods to herself, they are seen to define her through the mass. Consequently, here it is the practices of the high street that serve to place 'treating' as a shopping practice reserved for the second cycle. Here then we have a situation which is the exact counterpoint to that articulated in the previous section: when shopping is seen to be (and can be) at least in part about pleasure and a treating practice, many of the spaces of the first cycle are considered to fall short, precisely because their practices are seen to be too easy, too routinized and to offer too much of the same.

As well as being the converse of each other the two sets of second-hand shopping practices discussed above share another point of contact, their location primarily in practice. Rarely talked about, at least explicitly, these practices – like those discussed by Miller (1998) – were considered largely unremarkable by many of those we talked with, as activities that they simply got on with as unexceptional parts of their everyday lives. By contrast, a third practice that articulates the spaces of second and first hand exchange through interdependence is one that is situated within and helps to define particular discursive communities. These shopping practices, then, are very much ones that are talked about.

Fun and 'the Boast', Taste and Display: Talking Second-hand Shopping in Discursive Communities

One of the clearest illustrations of the connection between the practices of second-hand shopping and discursive communities is provided by

Dominic and Sarah, the two students we met earlier in this chapter and in Chapter 3 shopping in retro shops and charity shops for wild, wacky 70s clothing. As they and others emphasized, the motivations for this are shaped by and through a shared sense of fun, play and laughter. And this, as we see now, frequently translates into shaping shopping practices. Indeed, in this extract Simon – another one of our student charity shoppers – recounts the fun that he and a group of friends had in one particular Sheffield charity shop:

> *Nicky*: . . . You said much earlier about how it's fun to go with some-
> body else. Can you describe a bit about why that's so much fun
>
> *Simon*: That's because most of the stuff in there's a joke!! It's just these
> huge pink frilly shirts, stuff that you would never dream of wear-
> ing even in your worst nightmare. So it's just fun to see the stuff,
> and it's never the same. It's like it's never as funny listening to a
> joke on your own, you can't look at the other people and catch
> their eye and see what they're thinking and play off one another
> . . . I was walking through [area of Sheffield] . . . and I encouraged
> two [friends] to come in . . . and it was really good fun. They had
> a pair of firemen's trousers. And I got one of them to try them
> on. So that was just like really good fun. It was totally ridic-
> ulous! . . .

Importantly, the fun is only constituted here through being together, to talk, laugh and mock, through shared assumptions and shared humour. Simon and his friends then comprise a classic instance of a discursive community, one that in this case views second-hand spaces as spaces to play, joke and lark about in through a mobilization of ironic laughter.

A very different example of second-hand shopping practices' location within discursive communities is provided by their positioning within 'subcultures' and within particular subcultural styles. And, not surprisingly, we met many such instances in the course of this research, from 'ageing hippies' with tales of afghan coats, through former punks, New Romantics and Goths, to ex-indie girls, who recounted shopping practices that conjoined charity shops and markets (McRobbie, 1989). But, while all talked at length about what they bought, as they all equally made clear, what mattered as much within these subcultures was where you bought it. Here, for instance, is Tom – the single parent we intro-duced previously – talking about shopping as a punk:

76, 77, 78 – punk rock – [*laughter*] and it would be go and get an old jacket and rip it up and put a Bay City Rollers badge on it, something like that. There were quite a few things that I was really pleased to get. Like old pin stripe suits for 25 pence, shirts for like 30 pence – things like that that were on the far side of bad taste. But also amongst friends, I mean there was great value, a great value of having got something, having picked up some clothes really cheap from somewhere. Stuff like 'I got this from the church bazaar' – [*laughter*] – you know, that you'd managed to pick up something which felt incredibly transgressive and subversive . . .

And similarly in the following extract, Penny, who dabbled to varying degrees in both the New Romantic and Goth scenes, talks about the imperatives of where things were purchased:

So everyone was wearing like shirts and sort of handkerchiefs, sort of New Romantics – flicked hair and burgundy leather box jackets, and Farrah trousers, and so I started to wear like a lot of evening wear, like men's evening suits and shirts, but then I'd put loads of diamante on them and things like that. And all of this stuff was picked up from junk shops and charity shops and sometimes I'd go to antique fairs and pick up bits of jewellery with bits of diamante missing and they'd sell them off for 50 pence or whatever but I didn't mind . . .

As both these extracts testify, these practices of shopping are ones that rest on the existence of specific discursive communities. These, however, are not just important to identity formation. Rather, standing and kudos even within these discursive communities is related to the skills of shopping itself. So, the more outlandish and obscure the site of purchase, the more symbolic value comes to be invested in particular purchases and the greater its 'boast' value within friendship networks.

Seen to encode knowingness and skill, these subcultural shopping practices are ones that clearly elevate cultural over economic capital. And as we see using the example of Sue, Mark and Maria, a group of friends formerly into the Goth scene, they continue to exert a major influence on later shopping practices. All now homeowners, for them knowingness and taste are critical to their constitution of home interiors, and – once more – it is a combination of second-hand sites that have proved critical here. So, charity shops, car-boot sales, junk yards and a variety of second-hand shops plus the occasional retro shop are all routinely visited and perused for items that might proclaim their self-declared taste:

Sue:	. . . most of the things came from car boot sales and not charity shops . . .
Mark:	This is organic isn't it, you can't just go and buy the lot together
Sue:	Some things are just attractive to you
Mark:	That's what makes something so attractive, something you have got to invest time into, it says a lot about you . . .
Maria:	It's also a bit scary though, when you come into a community that's into that sort of thing, and all their houses are such a reflection of their taste . . . it's terrifying actually. I think 'Oh my God, what if I haven't got any taste?!' How would I know? – [*laughter*] . . .
Sue:	That's the exciting thing, you know, the thing about charity shops is that it's like going to about 100 different shops all at once . . . you can look at those things and choose the one that attracts you instead of being bombarded by a hundred things that are all the same

Similarly with Steven, another 30-something but an artist who also lives in Bristol. His home contains 70s furnishings (mostly from his mother) juxtaposed with various self-selected pickings from an assortment of charity shops, car-boot sales, jumble sales and junk shops. Rather than being constituted in relation to subcultural identities and their discursive communities, it is the discursive communities of particular friendship groups that provide the audience for these domestic performances in taste and cultural capital.

While these transcripts and others like them are peppered with instances of talk that show how critical second-hand sites are to the maintenance of these discursive communities, they all reveal too how the spaces of the first cycle are considered. Sue, Mark and Maria, then, talk about 'Ikea or something like that, where there's not a big choice' and Habitat as an unrisky form of prescribed taste. Similarly, they refer to 'fashion shops' as spaces where things are 'presented to you' and for 'lazy shoppers'. Likewise, Tom – a 30-something part-time lecturer and painter – talking about charity shops says:

> . . . I think you possibly retain the choice you don't really have in the high street . . . I find it more of a pleasure to go into second-hand and charity shops than high-street shops. I resent it now. I mean the Trafford Centre outside of Manchester, it's a mecca to shopping, I won't be going.

Abhorred, loathed and universally avoided within this group of respondents, these spaces are despised for their prescriptive practices and regulation of taste. They figure, then, as the Other to those with the cultural capital to constitute taste with certitude and without anxiety.

Although most discussions of discursive communities emphasize connections to knowingness and taste – often ironic – we want to end this section with one instance that bucks this trend. Associated exclusively with women second-hand shoppers, this concerns what we refer to as 'bargain boasting'. Our research contains legions of examples of this, but the following provide an indicative flavour:

> *Judy*:   . . . Occasionally I find a really good, a Windsmoor I've got upstairs, a pure linen Windsmoor. It's really nice for weddings – £1.50 on the sale rail. So excited with that!
>
> *Nicola*:   My friend . . . she'll always have a nice top on. And I'll say 'Where did you get that from?' And she'll say – [*adopts boasting voice*] – 'Well in Miss Selfridge £20 but I got this in Shelter for £4!' And, coming onto my BIG bargain [*laughter*] the Ball is this Thursday, and I got my ball dress from Oxfam, and it's a dark blue velvet one – it was like in the retro section. But as well as in what they call the retro section, I think it's really quite classy. And that was what I'd call a real bargain – ten quid! (20-something, university student)

Now at one level what this is all about is clearly capturing 'the bargain', but what the practice of bargain-boasting reveals too is that it is important to be able to display these skills through talk to other women, who in this case constitute the discursive community. This is clearly understood and articulated by Judy, who – much to the chagrin of her husband and others – insists on telling everyone, but particularly other women, about the value that she has captured through her practices, and hence displays her skills as a clever shopper. This, then, is something that she definitely does not want to hide away:

> *Kate*:   It's not saying 'I'm only worth £5'
>
> *Judy*:   No, it's like saying 'I've been clever enough to find this, which is worth a lot more than £5 really!' X [husband] gets a bit cross with that if we're out somewhere and he says 'Don't tell everybody'. X [friend] down the road, she says 'Well don't, you mustn't say it . . . nobody would ever know'. And I think 'Well I want them to know!' . . . [so] . . . I'll say 'you know this was only £2 and this was £4 the skirt, and my whole outfit come to £6'. She says 'Don't tell people because it looks expensive!' And I think 'Well that's the

whole point'. You want to look expensive but to tell people it costs £6. That's an achievement to me . . .

And the fact that during the course of this research we were the recipients of many similar such tales is something that we take to be highly significant in terms of the assumptions being made about us by other women. This, then is something that we – as other women – were seen as being automatically interested in.[43]

Somewhat differently to those with large amounts of cultural capital, then, the relation of this set of practices to the spaces and practices of the first cycle is not one of distance and othering but of distancing through out-doing. Here, then, it is the very practices encouraged within certain of the spaces of the first cycle – thrifty, bargain-centred and saving-oriented shopping, the type of shopping practices where women are encouraged to work hard – that are transplanted to the second. And much of the pleasure to be found here for these women is that the spaces of second-hand allow these skills to be satisfied even more. Taken to its extreme, what we find, then, are instances such as Judy, where the spaces of 'the new' are visited only for certain clothing necessities (underwear again). Here, then, the first-cycle is subverted by 'the housewife' through the displacement in space to second-hand sites of the very skills, desires and seductions that it has encouraged.

In contrast to the three previous sections where second-hand sites are woven together through practices that relate them intrinsically to the practices of shopping in first-cycle retail space, our final set of second-hand shopping practices are about opposing and resisting the first cycle – in some cases virtually completely – and are located in understandings grounded in political economy. Articulated by only a minority of those we talked with,[44] these arguments were expressed exclusively by individuals with high degrees of cultural capital and/or by those who described themselves as 'alternatives' or at least outwith 'the mainstream'.

'Alternative' Practices?

As both Rehmana and Chris opined at various points in their interviews, the motivations for second-hand shopping can be beyond income and beyond identity politics. Indeed, they can be about economies and their reproduction through consumption: 'it's about fighting against the capitalist system. It's about not being drawn into consumerism' (Chris). Chris is particularly interesting here, for her move to this position is one that has developed through practice, rather than something that she has come to – like Rehmana – through higher education. Now in her 50s and with a Sociology degree (gained as a mature student), she is a social worker with three grown children. Her initial motivations for second-hand shopping, however, were much like Christina's – money, or the lack of it. Subsequently, this developed into the kind of price critique of the first cycle typically associated with the 'bargain-boasting' position discussed previously but, over the course of the next ten years or so, she moved to an increasingly 'green consumer' position, whereby recycling (clothes, paper, plastic, glass) and maximizing the use-values of objects constitutes a primary household motivation.[45] Indeed, it is now 20 years since Chris bought any items of clothing in a first-cycle shop and her only engagement with these spaces is through the supermarket. Instead, her clothing, that of her children and of her husband has come, and continues to come from a range of jumble sales, charity shops and car-boot sales – practices that at certain times of her life have clearly marked her out as 'different' from her neighbours:

> When we used to live in [white, middle-class, family-oriented neighbourhood in Sheffield] it was like important to have the Cole Brothers (John Lewis franchise) delivery van calling [*Nicky: mmm, like a status symbol that you'd arrived sort of thing?*] Not that I ever did [*Nicky: but that was what it was about?*] Yes [*Nicky: So how would they have made sense of what you were doing?*] Well I did get comments. Like I'd go to jumble sales and buy. I'd go to the Scouts' jumble sales and to the school jumble sales and I'd actually be buying things! – [*laughter*] – and they just wouldn't dream of doing so! They'd help out, but not buy. And I'd be going round with a sack full. And it was obvious they were thinking 'Why is SHE doing that'!

While Chris and Rehmana's critique of 'the system' is about consumerism, both Margi and Trish take this further to locate their practices of second-hand shopping within a critique of retailing, and particularly of the homogenizing tendencies of retail capital:

Nicky: . . . Would you ever go to say Meadow(hell)?
Margi: Oh no, Oh God no!
Trish: Meadow what?
Margi: A big like shopping centre
Trish: Oh right, I live just down the road from Brent Cross, and I've never been. Two tube stops away. And that's got every store you know, massive Boots, massive Baby this, but Brent Cross is madness. I've never been there. I'd hate it!

Margi: I went to Meadowhall once because WH Smiths had the Scrabble
         set that I wanted

Nicky: But if you tried to summarize this, what is it that you hate about
         it?

Margi: Oh just the consumerism!

Trish: Everything is so IN YOUR FACE!!!!!!! [*laughter*] and you're just
         thinking 'Oh God, that's on special' or whatever. And they just
         talk you into the fact that you need stuff which you don't really
         need!

Margi: Yeah, I just think about going to those sorts of places and I feel
         nauseous

Trish: In London like the Chinese and Indian shops are cheaper than
         the big supermarkets and the chains, and you get a bit of a laugh
         when you go in there. I go and do my veggie shop on a Monday
         morning at a streetmarket and OK I pay a little bit more that I
         would at a supermarket but I know it's all fresh – and it's really,
         really chilled out, it's a really nice experience – shopping shouldn't
         have to be a stressful thing

Margi: Yeah – as you walk into Meadowhall and you look at all the
         people and you see them, and all their shoulders look hunched
         up and you can just feel – if you had a stressometer you know
         [*indicates shoulders in air*] that's the thing, they're sort of driven
         to have to consume. And I like to think that I've lost that, that
         that drive button's been switched off with me . . . there's no hum-
         anity, to me that's really dehumanizing . . . if I can buy something
         on X [Derbyshire town] market or in a little electrical shop I'd
         rather do that than go off to Dixon's because I can save £1.99 –
         because the interaction is going to be probably a much nicer time,
         it's going to be 1000 per cent less stressful, and yeah – to me the
         whole of this conglomerate world – multinationals and things –
         is just so prevalent that I don't think that's a healthy way for the
         world to go – all individuality is being lost . . .

Second-hand shopping here, then, is enmeshed within practices of
other forms of provisioning that are about supporting small independent retailers (for what they represent rather than what they sell)
and using vegetable co-operatives and/or markets, and extend – as with
others like Tom (the ex-punk single parent) – to encompass wholefood
co-operatives and 'fair trade' products. Indicative of an ethical consumption position, and not just a pro-recycling disposition, this is clearly
about constituting practices of shopping that are both reflexive and

grounded in a materialist view of politics. As Margi says: 'we live in this world, we have to consume, that's it, but you can think about what that's about'.

As others have argued, both these positions and practices, as well as other practices like LETS (see for example: Lee, 1996; North, 1999; Thorne, 1996), are premised upon attempts to constitute 'alternative economies' that are either outwith capitalist exchange principles and social relations altogether, or that try to resist certain tendencies – globalization, homogenization, the concentration of retail power and its effects on manufacturing, the product cycle and so on. For us, however, one of the key question marks over the location of second-hand shopping within these practices is the degree to which this does actually constitute resistance in this sense. To what extent, then, is this set of shopping practices anti-consumerist? And to what extent is there evidence in practice for this set of spaces comprising part of an 'alternative economy'? Our response here is to be equivocal at best. So, for example, Chris is one of just a handful of individuals we met during the course of this research who seemed utterly impervious to the attractions of 'the brand' and 'the label', who was buying items of clothing purely for their use value (as just jeans, T shirts, shoes and so on). Instead, virtually everyone else – including those who articulated the anti-capitalist, anti-consumerist rhetoric – turned out, at least in part, to be buying 'the brand'. Rehmana for example recounts the case of the Chipie jeans, Margi a Jean Paul Gaultier T shirt, one of the Toms Peter England shirts . . . And they do so in ways that make clear that the attraction here is to get the brand cheaply. Moreover, plenty of others expressed the opinion that their consumerist tendencies were actually enhanced by second-hand shopping. Fuelled by the ability to get more for less (the value imperative again), in practice much of this second-hand purchasing to us seemed to be about expanding the content of wardrobes and homes and increasing the choice of what to wear – not reducing it.

At the same time we would argue that various of the tendencies discussed in both Chapters 3 and 4 raise question marks over individuals' attempts to locate second-hand shopping practices within 'alternative economies'. The charity-retail makeover is one obvious instance here, as too is the commercial expansion of retro and of car-boot sales. Indeed, it is hard for us to see anything 'alternative' at all in many examples of the latter two instances. With charity shops, the situation is rather more blurred. Seen by many to be part of the moral economy of redistribution and to exist in tension with their fund-raising imperatives, they were, however, read by others as ambivalent politically –

chiefly for their charitable associations. So 'charity' was regarded, at least by some, to be not outwith but as a 'stop-gap' for the failings of the capitalist system. And, consequently, the rhetoric of 'helping-out' through 'acting charitably' came to be questioned as in practice no more than both 'propping up' inequalities and as a substitute for the activities that were seen to rightfully be those of 'the state'.

The Progressive Potential of Second-hand Shopping Geographies

Rather than closing this chapter by casting conclusive doubt about the place of second-hand spaces within 'the alternative', we want to end here on a more positive note. Perhaps one of the most significant findings of this chapter has been to show conclusively that those shopping in second-hand arenas are neither heroes/ines nor dupes, but women and men who – in their shopping practices – demonstrate their agency through shopping. Second-hand shopping practices are not simply about constituting identities through goods, nor are they just about the materialization of social relations, nor are they prescribed as in the spaces of the first cycle. Instead they have to be forged, in ways that are fundamentally geographical – that require individuals to look around and explore the nooks and crannies of retail landscapes, to know the possibilities of place/s, and to be aware of where and when transient events like car-boot sales and jumble sales occur. And sites have to be woven together as personal shopping geographies, in ways that require shoppers to think hard – not just about what they might look at and/or what they might purchase, but about what shopping itself is about in these spaces. So, as we have seen, we find those who shop in these spaces thinking hard about exchange, about value, about consumerism, about use and need. And we see them too thinking hard about what shopping ought to be about, about the normative. Such reflexivity, however compromised it might turn out to be in practice, is for us a clear indication that these spaces offer the scope at least for critical praxis. Moreover, in that the practices of second-hand shopping are ones that are intended to insert a radical, albeit relational and for the most part interdependent, gap between the practices of first and second-hand shopping, we can see that this praxis has definite effects.

For us, insisting on the distinction between first and second-hand shopping worlds is the most important of these effects. But critical too is the way in which the various practices of second-hand shopping conjoin to suggest to shoppers some core premises associated with second-hand spaces. Although dependent on and mediated by particular subject positions, these premises are ones that we think transcend specific individuals, even if they might be talked about differently. They are, then, generally held sets of assumptions among second-hand shoppers about what second-hand spaces should enable and encompass. Within our diverse range of research respondents, four such premises seem central. First, and perhaps most significantly, these spaces continue to be located by many within a moral economy that is both seen to be a local resource and grounded in need. These sites, then, are considered to be resources not just for 'poor people' and people on restricted incomes, but situated resources, where the traffic in things that occurs in second-hand sites is about redistribution within areas, and not between areas. Sitting somewhat uncomfortably with this, at least in part, is a second premise; that second-hand worlds constitute a means of knowing place, being in place and encountering place. Reliant on the same identification between people, place and goods that lies behind the moral economy of redistribution arguments, the difficulty with this premise is that it runs together both subjects who are relatively mobile with those who live very much more constricted lives. For some, then, this premise is extremely extensive; it allows them literally to travel the country differentiating 'knowing' from 'unknowing' places. For others, however, knowing place through second-hand spaces can be more akin to being confined to spaces that in their traffic in goods reinforce social exclusion. A third premise is that second-hand spaces are enabling of multiple identities, and not identity in the singular. So, rather than encode particular visions of specific 'ideal' shoppers – as is routine practice in many first-cycle retail spaces – these sites are widely seen to be ones that enable and juxtapose various forms of purchasing by diverse groups of shoppers. They are, then, sites that are regarded – at least ideally – as spaces that can accommodate those shopping through particular taste communities through to those looking for value, those shopping for fun and those who are purchasing because they have to. Fourthly, and finally, another core premise is that these spaces provide scope for resistant practices of one form or another. Encompassing both identity politics – for example, 'subcultural' style and the partial resistances of 'the housewife' – and critiques of 'the system', second-hand sites continue to be widely regarded as distinctive from the high street and the mall or shopping centre, even if some of their associated practices might contest these assertions.

Looking across these premises, and at the shopping practices in which they are grounded, we are forced to end this chapter by returning to reconsider our foci in the previous two chapters. Indeed, confronted by practices that blur the distinctions between second-hand sites and maximize their difference from the first cycle, and by a very clear set of shopper premises, we are encouraged to raise question marks over many of the strategies that we discussed previously. So, in emphasizing the distinctions between second-hand sites, we can see that many second-hand retailers appear to be encoding in space the very opposite of what occurs in second-hand shopping practice, while in trying to minimize the differences between first and second-hand sites other second-hand retailers risk eliminating the very difference that constitutes the basis for the practices of second-hand shopping. We are compelled, then, to conclude this section on a note of caution: that when difference disappears and second-hand spaces of exchange become seen to be the same as first hand, then both their purpose and their potential is lost.

Part II

Practices of Second-hand Consumption

This second substantive section of the volume is about journeys. In all three chapters we are looking, in different ways, at the passages of commodities through time and space and about how things enter into and move through second-hand worlds, focusing specifically on key moments of commodity de- and revalorization. The focus is thus on the temporalities and spatialities of commodity journeys and particular object:person encounters. At a conceptual level we aim to do two things in this section. First, our focus is on both rethinking acts of purchase and moving beyond them, looking specifically here at questions of value(lessness) and worth(lessness). Secondly, it is about exploring rituals of disposal, sourcing, transformation, personalization and possession.

To take each of these issues in turn. First, then, our aim here is to disrupt the linearity of many conventional accounts of consumption which see either the act of purchase or the point of production as the key defining moment in a commodity's biography. Such accounts, we argue, either attempt to define and delimit the key moment of meaning and value creation by unveiling regimes of commodity production in order to expose the hidden material realities of a product, or try to elevate the site, space and moment of purchase to the position of explanatory variable within circuits of retail capital. Contra such accounts we are endeavouring to destabilize the linearity of such narratives and to see processes of purchase as (potentially) both the end *and* the start of a commodity's life; as both the beginning of one journey and the ending of another. So, rather than developing a linear narrative of meaning production that ends with the constitution of social relations and subjects through the purchase of a finished product, we are making an argument about the continuous and circuitous nature of meaning-creation. The significance of second-hand is that goods can be 'cast off' and 'cast out', but also that they are locked into endless cycles of re-enchantment. Value, under this conceptualisation, is not an inherent characteristic of commodities, but something that is open to constant relational and active negotiation, determined through the interplay of desire, demand, knowledge and supply, and shaped by personalization. Consumers and traders, as we go on to show, have considerable bearing on, and variable interpretations of, the value of particular commodities.

Secondly, and linked to the above, we acknowledge that commodities have histories and geographies which create and alter meaning and value. We will be looking at how and why commodities enter into and circulate through the second-hand arena and at how value(lessness) and worth(lessness) are subjectively assessed. Value is rarely (if ever) an inherent property of objects, but rather a judgement made about them by consumers and traders (Appadurai, 1986: 3). And it is these judge-ments about value that interest us here. Some commodities enter the second-hand arena through the practices of second-hand traders whose 'work' consists in part of sourcing goods to sell, and in turn whose skill in part depends on detailed geographical and commodity knowledges – about what products have a potential and as yet unrealized second-hand value; about which places will yield potentially profitable finds (jumble sales, obituary columns, house clearances and skips). Such knowledges in turn inform traders about the appropriate times and spaces in which to sell: there are both geographies and temporalities at work in the second-hand market and part of the skill of successful trading relies on being able to see and to unlock the imaginary potential of a commodity at a particular time and place where the consumer will 'see' its value. We are interested too in understanding the ways in which individuals discard commodities which have limited value to them but which they see as having value to another. In part such practices are bound up with questions of good housekeeping, and of monitoring and regulating domestic consumption levels. In this sense such domestic regulation is also a deeply gendered activity, performed predominantly by women as both a form of household maintenance and as a means of, quite literally, making space (in the wardrobe, the cupboards, the attic, the kitchen) for future acquisition. But critically too, such clearing-out practices depend on the constitution of 'deserving others' and are subject to practices of self-surveillance whereby only 'appropriate' commodities may be discarded, those which are suitably respectable and have residual life or value embedded within them. The process of casting out is, we argue, a practice which, ostensibly about good housekeeping and the moral economy of thrift, is in fact also associated with particular gendered and class-rooted subjectivities which, together, shape the range and availability of second-hand commodities. The final set of object-person encounters we consider in this section are practices of gifting, where the object comes to encode one's relationship to others, and collecting, where ownership is conventionally divorced from use in ways which determine and control a commodity's biography.

Redefining Rubbish: Commodity Disposal and Sourcing

Introduction: Determinations of Rubbish and Reverence

We are interested here to understand the processes and mechanisms through which commodities cross the putative boundaries between different categories of value, and in particular at how they move through different regimes of value. To date there has been little conceptual or theoretical work on the processes of rubbish transformation, exchange, circulation and consumption.[46] But in order to understand how the second-hand market comes to be, we need to explore the sequence of value transformations as commodities pass through different stages in their biographical journey. The relationship between rubbish and value is unclear, complex, convoluted; transfers and shifts occur between and across these cultural categories which are themselves fuzzy and striated: at one end is rubbish, at the other is high (commercial and aesthetic) value, but in between are a range of possible object:value relations, gradations which include junk, debris, trash and kitsch on the one hand, and heirloom, antique and treasure on the other. Quite how such socially and culturally malleable concepts come to be imparted onto particular commodities at particular times is one of the major aims of this chapter. And so in order to understand such transformations of value we explore the social and cultural practices and premises through which the definitional boundary dynamics between rubbish and value shift in time and space.

There are, we would argue, structural reasons for value transformations: the ending of a process of production can signal an upturn in value – examples here would include skilled corsetry-making and traditional garment-beading skills, both of which are now in short supply in the fashion industry and which give value to original, traditionally-constructed garments. Such technological shifts may give rise to revalorization based on reverance and nostalgia for a time that pre-dates mass fashion production. Some of our interviewees see 1960s fashions, for example, as valuable precisely because of the quality of their production and, as we go on to discuss in Chapter 6, the styles of the 1960s seem to be fixed in some consumer's imagination as more classic than those from the 1970s and 1980s, and are seen to embody qualities of craftsmanship, design and attention to detail which were lost with the turn to mass production and large retail capital in the 1970s and 1980s. Conversely, the development of new production processes can signal a downturn in commodity value, as (apparently) more efficient or effective means of production come on stream. Examples here would include the devalorization of hand-knitted and home-made clothing once mechanized industrial production methods were introduced into the clothing industry. Similarly, the spread of particular retail outlets can devalue the potency of a commodity through ubiquity and brand dilution, while the opening of new retail forms can act as a trigger for new modes of consumption. The spread of boutiques along the King's Road in early 1960s London in many ways heralded the emergence of a new era in British fashion consumption and made the department store appear archaic and uninspired. For the first time, and in part as a result of more sophisticated mass-production techniques, rapid fashion change became technically possible and stylistically desirable. The temporalities of taste speeded up, and expendability and built-in aesthetic obsolescence increased the pace at which commodities became devalorized. In a rather different way the closure of a particular means of distribution can increase the perceived (and real) value of a commodity – the closure of Mary Quant shops in the late 1970s is a potent example here. And in a rather different way the death of an artist or producer can also have a revalorization effect – the example of Versace's shooting and the value of Warhol's Pop Art are cases in point. And there are institutional reasons too for upward (and downward) value transformations – an art, interiors or fashion and costume exhibition can bring about an upturn in value and desirability – witness Paul and Simon's Whitefriar's glass examples below, the Armani retrospective in New York's Guggenheim Gallery in 2000 (Showalter, 2001) and the Biba exhibition at the Laing Gallery in Newcastle in 1993 (Tyne and Wear Museum, 1993; see too Brampton, 1999; Windsor, 1988). Prior to the launch of the Biba retrospective the Gallery ran a 'Bring out your Biba' campaign, to which more than 600 people responded with offers of loans or information about their shopping histories in the store. Clearly here we are seeing the ways in which original commodities which, in their first cycle were bought as cheap throwaway fashions, are revalorized through memory and time to become meaningful treasured items, ciphers for particular memories of particular times (and see too Thompson, 1979).[47]

Beyond such structural shifts in value that occur as a result of broad economic transformations such as the commodification of culture and production-process changes, however, are a range of more subjective, personalized evaluations of potential commodity worth. Some of these, notably the fortuitous finds, the owner who suddenly 'sees' the value of an object and the 'eccentric aesthetic valuations' of a small minority (Turner, 1979: 29), may well be responses to the broader market conditions identified above. But significant too are subjective evaluations about commodity devaluation, the determining moments at which value is seen to have ceased to exist, and the point at which a commodity can be cast out. It is to these perceived judgements about downturns in value – which are themselves shaped by knowledges about product life cycles, market conditions, fashion cycles, commodity quality, functionality and durability – that we turn in the following section.

Entering the Second-hand World

There are, we argue, a range of practices that determine which commodities come to enter the second-hand arena, when, and at which sites and spaces. Such strategies range from the more organized retro and car-boot trader sourcing strategies and charity sorting warehouses to the more personalized, fortuitous discarding strategies of individuals clearing out commodities to either donate to charity or retro shops or to sell on at a car-boot sale. It is important to think too, here, about temporalities of possession and disposal and the differences which exist in relation to this across different commodity groups. Some commodities are treasured, loved, never to be discarded. Others, mistakes for example, or unwanted gifts, have a very short temporality and are quickly put back into circulation. For analytical ease we will distinguish in what follows between traders' sourcing strategies which typically comprise detailed and ongoing searches for commodities to sell (i.e. akin to an occupation), and the more personalized, ad hoc casting-off and disposal strategies which individuals undertake in their homes and gardens as part of broader consumption practices.[48] Taken together, sourcing and disposal strategies determine when and how commodities enter and leave the second-hand world. In practice of course such analytical separation rarely holds up; the boundaries between sourcing and disposal are fuzzy, unclear and ruptured; many traders work in unplanned, unorganized ways, ways which are worlds apart from conventional buying and sourcing work undertaken in formal retail spaces; many 'good housekeeping' sorting and discarding strategies are themselves highly regulated, ordered and organized in ways which approximate hard work. Sourcing, sorting and disposal strategies vary, then, not only across and between the three case-study sites, but also in terms of the levels of investment which individuals make in such practices. The spatialities of supply are complex, circular and dynamic and reveal both the connections between our study sites and the variability across them. In the following two sections we try to capture the range and complexity of ways in which things come to be in second-hand worlds, focusing first on the disposal of commodities and their deposition by individuals in second-hand spaces, and secondly on the ways in which commodities are sourced for sale in the second-hand world. We identify three key disposal dispositions and two main sourcing models, although again, as we have been at pains to emphasize, these strategies are not mutually exclusive in either time or space, but rather may occur concurrently.

Disposal Dispositions

Throughout the course of our work we encountered a range of different investments in different kinds of disposal practices. These practices are in turn linked to the spatialities of disposal, as individuals make often quite complex judgements about not just how, but where, to dispose of their 'rubbish'. The spaces of disposal themselves map onto and parallel individual constructions of commodity value and judgements about appropriate disposal behaviours – that which is defined as rubbish or garbage at a particular moment in time is likely to be discarded to the bin, the skip, the tip or the landfill site. Junk, in contrast, is more likely to be hoarded, collected and, much later, either rediscovered and revalorized (by self or other), or given away, cleared out or sold, ending up in the recycling bin, the jumble sale, the car-boot sale or at the charity or retro shop. But again such valorization judgements are neither linear nor objective, but vary in time and space and are subjectively determined. There are, too, a number of evaluative layers at work here which makes it often difficult in practice to determine with any certainty the precise motivations underpinning disposal strategies. For example, while the dumping of a washing machine onto a skip might be read as the straightforward disposal of a non-functional (and therefore value-less) commodity, there is rarely, we would argue, a straightforward association between functionality and value. In the case of consumer durables, it may appear on first reading that functionality is the key determinant of value, but in fact, and as we go on to demonstrate below, such connections are far more complex and relate to a matrix of variables which include functionality but critically also involve design and aesthetic issues, so that apparently 'functional' commodities may be cast out not simply because they don't work, but because an owner's aesthetic principles have shifted – the casting out of formica units and Bakelite telephones are illustrative examples here of commodities which have been cast out (and devalorized) and subsequently refound and revalorized not simply by repair but by design shifts too. Again, this example illustrates the complex interplay between structural and market shifts on the one hand, and design history, aesthetic taste and subjective style judgements on the other in determining the practices and spaces through which disposal occurs.

Below we argue that disposal – as a means of making space – is the primary strategy through which individuals 'cast out' and the main way in which commodities enter the second-hand world. Quite which spaces commodities are cast out to, however, depends on both the nature of the commodity and, critically, on the disposal disposition of the subject, as we go on to discuss below. For conceptual ease we identify three main 'disposal dispositions' as a way in to tracking where commodities are cast out to.[49] These dispositions in turn have particular potency for particular commodities and particular gendered subject positions, and we thus use particular commodity groupings as lenses through which to uncover the range and variability in disposal motivations. These three dispositions we call *philanthropy*, *economic/political critique* and *money-making*. The three dispositions serve as an analytical framework to shape our discussion below but, again, such distinctions do not always hold up in practice: some consumers, as we go on to illustrate below, may display several disposal dispositions at different times for different commodities in different contexts. Consequently, the importance of subject position and the subject:object relation infuses the specificities of disposal strategies through time and space.

Good Housekeeping Practices: Disposal as Making Space

For all of our study sites, individuals disposing of commodities as a way of making space are the primary means by which goods enter the second-hand world. At face value such 'good housekeeping' strategies are motivated simply by the need to make space in the home. Val, for example, has an annual 'clear-out' of her clothes. And for Trish, the Australian woman we met previously, the need for freedom from baggage is particularly acute as she is currently saving up to continue her travels around the world and has no permanent space in which to amass commodities such as books:

> . . . I think I've come to a complete standstill – just because I'm trying to get rid of things from my life. I've come to the stage where I've got a lot of possessions and I either live with them and settle down or I have to keep myself movable and not have the possessions . . .

Tina too, a retro trader in Afflecks Palace, Manchester, reveals how stuff enters the second-hand arena in a variety of ways, many of which have to do with individuals no longer having sufficient space to store the things. We get stock, she says, 'from here, there and everywhere . . . people bring it in usually, they come with a bag . . . mostly donations. People come in and say 'oh, here you are. We don't want this anymore. It's just in our attic'. And for many amateur car-boot sellers the transition to becoming a vendor was no more than a simple loft-clearing/space-making exercise,

> We had a loft full of tosh . . . horrible glassware, sort of 'gifts from Morocco or Greece . . . those awful china cats . . . my dad's old shaver, the collapsing sunglasses. Now the collapsing sunglasses, they were great! They were my uncle Albert's'. [*much laughter*]. Full of bits and pieces we couldn't shift. When we got round here and saw the tosh that other people were selling you thought your tosh was that much better! (Phil, south-east London)

But more interesting to us than these simple space-making arguments are the ways in which such good housekeeping practices are both highly gendered and hinge too on notions of respectability. First, we see that it is invariably women who undertake the sorting, sifting and bagging up of household items which are no longer wanted, particularly women's, men's or children's clothes. Women, then, are the primary caretakers of many interior domestic storage spaces (wardrobes, cupboards, drawers) and determine when, and to where, an item will be donated or sold. In doing this, the women are both affirming their role as homemaker and reproducing assumptions about men's lack of interest in clothes, shopping and domestic provisioning more broadly. These notions are encapsulated in the following extract:

At another stall further on, a woman (and her husband/partner) are selling loads of clothes. She – and it is obviously she who is in charge here (he's sitting in the car, cold and bored!) – has arranged things into a mini-department store – kids, menswear and womenswear plus coats . . . She says to me she's trying to get rid of a suit (husbands) because it no longer fits, but that it's well nigh impossible to do so. We have a laugh about trying to find someone to fit it when the stall is surrounded by women, with no men in sight! (Nicky, field notes: Site E: North-East England)

Another interviewee recounts how, having moved into her partner's house, she finds a complete absence of any good housekeeping skills:

I'm desperate to find some space in the sodding wardrobes for my clothes. There is a huge dressing room with wall-to-wall wardrobes but they're all full of Ian's stuff. I don't think any of this has been touched for years. There are some unbelievably awful white shiny slip-on shoes (and retro man he is not), some hideous short-sleeved cheesecloth shirts, awful slacks. I bag the whole lot up in bin liners ready to chuck and find I have a whole wall of wardrobes free for my stuff. What I hadn't bargained on, though, was finding all this stuff back at the top of the wardrobe a few weeks later, having been salvaged from the wheelie bins. This is hoarding man in action. (Louise)

Here we see not just the distancing of male partners from the organization of domestic spaces, but also the workings of tacitly shared assumptions between women about men's lack of interest in clothing and their own superior skills of domestic management. Framed in terms of discourses of familialism and domestic responsibility, it is women here who oversee and undertake good housekeeping strategies, who see themselves as having the knowledges and skills to make appropriate decisions (and who are prepared to invest the time in doing so – based on judgements about taste, fashion, style as well as quality and fit) about when and where to dispose of commodities. Disposal, then, draws on, and is reconstitutive of, highly traditional conventions of gender.

But when it comes to women disposing of their own clothes, such apparently straightforward space-making strategies are often refracted by considerations of respectability and embodiment. Discarding of one's own clothes, as we go on to show, is potentially far more problematic than disposing of others', and invokes questions of bodily size and shape, the threat of bodily failure and/or bodily delusion being ever present. And it is here that the disposal space to which an item is destined becomes important. In the case of charity shops and retro shops, it is possible to discard anonymously, unidentified. Such anonymity is a common practice, particularly in relation to charity shops, where it is the norm either for male partners to drop off discards by car (in a manner that to us appears to have parallels with common practices at household disposal sites), or to dump bags outside when the charity shop is closed . . . even though the shops themselves request that this is not done (see Plate 5.1).

In the space of the car-boot sale, however, anonymity and distance is more difficult to achieve and the donating of second-hand clothes is consequently potentially more troubling. This is, we would argue, the riskiest of our three disposal spaces in that identities and commodities meet head on. For here, unwanted clothes are in the process of being sold to another who is able to see (rather than imagine) bodily presence. The process of selecting cast-offs for sale at a car-boot sale therefore becomes open to issues of respectability and embodiment. In those circumstances where clothes are being discarded for what might be termed positive reasons (for example as a result of a change in lifestyle such as retirement, or the disposal of maternity clothes) the disposal process is comparatively straightforward and can be mutually affirming.[50] So, when another woman purchases such an item the buyer is in a sense approving both the taste and the identity of the seller. By contrast, negative

Plate 5.1 Dumped outside Imperial Cancer – the donations in rubbish sacks

reasons for disposal are potentially far more fraught. An instance here
would be clothes that are too small. Here disposal requires the 'good
housekeeper' to negotiate either her initial self-delusion in making the
purchase in the first place (that is, with her seduction) or with her
changing body size and shape. She is exposing to scrutiny, then, either
her initial lack of skill in selecting a garment, or her inability to control
her body in order that her clothes fit. In short, she is exposing to others
her seduction with a particular item, and its hopelessness, its futility.
The alternative, of course, would be to keep the item in the wardrobe,
safe from public view, hidden away. But this is rarely a solution: not
only does the garment sit there, a daily reminder perhaps of failed body-
management attempts, but it also takes up space, space which could
be more productively used to store goods which endorse a woman's view
of herself as skilful, appropriate shopper.[51]

Within these broad space-making strategies, however, we see a
number of different dispositions and motivations that determine which
commodities will be cast out, why, and where they will be cast out to.
We identify three specific motivations here, but point again to the ways
in which individuals vary, interconnect and justify their disposal
practices at different times and for different commodities.

Philanthropy

The first rationale we explore is based around notions of philanthropy,
of casting out in order to help others deemed or imagined to be less
fortunate. For certain people, participation in second-hand consumption is not something that they would ever consider – to buy cast-offs
is simply not for them – but they are happy to donate their discarded
goods to 'deserving' others – often via charity shops.[52] This disposition
in part is described as about doing good through disposal. Sam provides
one example of this practice: a 20-something secretary, she recounts
how part of her good housekeeping space-making strategy is about
selecting clothing for people 'less fortunate' than herself. Moreover, she
is careful to ensure that this clothing is deposited at what for her are
appropriate charity shops – in her case 'the Cancer shop'. This disposition, however, is not confined to those who just donate. Val both donates
and purchases, and she provides one of the few instances among our
respondent group for whom fund-raising imperatives over-ride prag-
matism in shaping disposal practices. Indeed Val drives from one area
of Sheffield to the other side of the city to deposit her goods at a shop
dedicated to fund-raising for a local animal charity.

For others, casting out as philanthropy is triggered by key world events such as recent world crises in Rwanda, Kosovo and latterly, Afghanistan. Often linked to media reports and charitable appeals for donations to, for example, Romanian orphanages, this is about helping out others in distant places. Anna, for example, discusses how she prefers to give to a known cause when having a clear-out, telling how she has 'just given a whole bagful to Romania, to the orphans', while Nicky recently donated a bag destined initially for either the nearest charity shop or the next plastic-bag drop to a door-to-door collection for Kosovo. And closer to home still are the successful 'toys for Christmas' campaigns in the UK that again depend on the philanthropic conscience of potential donors.

What we see here is the moral imperative of disposal: not only is disposal constituted as an appropriate good housekeeping practice, but part of this good housekeeping is overlain with notions of casting out appropriately, in ways that depend clearly on the identification of the deserving other. Desperate, poor and needy, the other is here constituted unproblematically, as the assumed-to-be-grateful recipient – in short as the charitable case, defined by those who are in the position to act charitably (see too Gregson, Crewe and Brooks, 2002b).

Political and Economic Critique

This second disposition connects with the moral economy and political critique perspectives we discussed previously in Chapter 4. For some this political critique is a fairly straightforward rejection of the rampant commercialism and aggressive consumerism they see as typifying first-cycle consumption. We have already seen how, prompted in part by desires toward recycling and sustainability, at least some of our interviewees mobilize narratives around global equity in order to explain their desire to dispose of commodities into the second-hand arena. Margi and Trish are clear examples of this emergent sense of a critique of first-cycle consumption:

Yes, we need to be clothed and we need to feel good about how we look, but that doesn't mean we need to impose all of this bollocks onto the world – so in a way it's almost a protest against that in a way – you know, recycle to survive I think is a really good philosophy. (Margi, Derbyshire)

If you're a charity shopper, you know, everybody's junk is somebody else's treasure – you know, if I have a clear out, there might be some little nick nack, but I make the effort to go and get that bag just because I know that somewhere somebody is not going to be making money out of it . . . it's also about the world and recycling. (Trish, London)

More specifically, we would argue that disposal for reasons to do with political critique is particularly marked in the case of certain commodity groups. The case of children's clothing illustrates this disposal disposition particularly keenly, and it is here that we find the most developed sense of a critique of first-cycle exchange and consumption as well as the tentative stirrings of ethical consumption. Given the speed with which young children in particular outgrow clothing, individual items have a very limited temporality of individual use. And they are thus frequently disposed of to second-hand sites such as charity shops and car-boot sales in order that others might benefit (note the connections here to philanthropic dispositions). One of our interviewees, Daphne, whom we initially met in Chapter 3, is particularly instructive in articulating this version of ethical consumption. She expressed considerable disquiet at what she sees as the extortionate cost of children's clothes in the shops and argues that it is 'not right' to charge £40 for shoes that will last children six weeks or to charge £60 for a jumper for a five-year-old. Her disposal and sourcing strategies in respect of children's clothes are thus best interpreted as resistant strategies in a broader moral economy of household provisioning. And Anna too discusses the ways in which second hand clothes for babies and children circulate around friendship and kin groups 'Caroline brings her stuff from her daughters for Caroline E to check through, and Caroline E checks through it and then it's handed on to me and I check through it for my friend in York, and I parcel it all up . . . it's like this big thing going on, there's no money involved but there's all this exchange'. And so while the disposal (and indeed purchase) of second-hand clothing for children serves to reproduce gendered discourses about Woman as (style-conscious) mother, nurturer and carer, it also offers scope at least for a partial reworking of these discourses. In coming to recognize that the characteristics of newness and difference need not mean the same thing as never worn and currently in the shops, women put both a subtle twist on the style-conscious mother construction and provide themselves with the basis for a moral critique of the intensifying commodification of children on the high street and through the media. In short they are constituting second-hand arenas as a way of offering nearly new, often fashionable and very cheap clothing for children, and in so doing are invoking a prototypical version of ethical consumption, for and of mothers (see too Clarke 2000).

Although most clearly developed in relation to children's clothing, such strategies are also apparent around a few other commodities, specifically books and toys, which also have a residual life that transcends their use by their initial owner. Passing such goods on to others through the medium of second-hand sites such as charity shops and car-boot sales seems to us to approximate a consumer:object relation that is best viewed in terms of temporary possession rather than ownership. Charity shops, then, operate as a form of alternative library facility, from which books can be bought for a nominal sum and to which they can then be returned. Similarly with toys – Val for example, recounted how she put her initials on jigsaws that she had already bought/returned. Reducing the need for costly first-cycle purchase of such commodities, we argue more broadly that this form of political critique is often less about the recycling of matter and its associated environmental benefits, and rather more grounded in a narrative that desires to extend the useful life (i.e. use value) of commodities.

Money-making

Our third disposal disposition we call money-making. This disposition is distinctly about exchange values. For some this is about making money from used commodities; for others it is about supplementing low incomes. Again, this strategy varies both across and between destinations and is acutely differentiated in terms of product category. And again, like our other strategies it is variegated by gender, so that while both women and men dispose of goods in order to make money (often to buy more) this strategy is on the whole, we would argue, apparently far more masculine than our other two strategies, and is bound up more with functionalist discourses rather than questions of embodiment, respectability or political critique.[53] First, then, at one level there is evidence of a fairly straightforward selling-to-make-money approach demonstrated by both men and women. Sophie, for example, told us

> *Sophie*: I needed a bit of money (when I was at UCL). I was very skint so I came here (Portobello Market) and sold a few of my clothes.
> *Louise*: A few of the vintage things you'd bought for yourself?
> *Sophie*: Yeah, the things I felt I could just about let go. And it worked really well. I enjoyed it. I loved it. It's an addictive thing to do . . . (Notting Hill).

For others, as the following vendor intimates, selling at a boot sale is frequently a follow-on from participation as a buyer. Indeed, for some the motivation for buying at boot sales is primarily to stock up to sell later: 'You never know what you'll come back with, golf clubs, aroma-therapy oils, ballet shoes. We've got a house stuffed full of junk. When there's enough, we'll go out and sell all over again' (Mrs Coates).

And yet for others – and primarily here we are referring to men – there is a particular logic to disposal-for-sale strategies which has its roots, we would argue, in discourses of masculinity and which, particularly in the case of car-boot-sale-disposal, serve to reproduce conventional gendered consumption practices. Involving an array of commodities encompassing primarily electrical goods, DIY tools and materials, gardening equipment, car sundries and audio goods, the critical feature of men's disposal strategies at car-boot sales is that they are governed seemingly primarily by utilitarian and instrumentalist considerations and by technical discourses. Many of these acts of disposal as money-making are riven through with constructions of Man as builder/repairer of the domestic form – here money-making often comes from the left overs and cast-offs of DIY projects (see Chapter 3). Others, though, are about attempting to sell on items/goods that have been 'upgraded': redundant and/or obsolete PCs and printers, personal stereos, audio systems, vinyl that has been replaced by CDs and so on.

This form of disposal continues to intrigue us. Rather than turning to philanthropic motivations, then – and give away – there is a desire to sell, to elevate exchange over use values, even when things are faulty and admitted to be (witness the discussions surrounding the solder in Chapter 3). Why this is we can only speculate about, but we would note that rarely – if ever – did women talk about selling such faulty items, tending instead to dispose of them at 'rubbish' venues: in skips, at land-fill sites and in household dustbins.

To conclude this discussion of disposal dispositions, and in order to emphasize that dispositions, in practice, are ruptured and not mutually exclusive, we draw at length on one case-study individual, Lily, the London fashion student and part-time model. Lily is interesting in that she adopts different disposal practices at different times and for different kinds of commodities. So she invokes reasoned yet subjective judge-ments about the value, quality, brand and appropriateness of particular commodities. In making such judgements she draws on a number of discourses, including philanthropy, respectability, political critique and money-making. Her disposal strategies are thus complex, highly variable in space and time and, as such, are particularly insightful in trying to illustrate the ways in which disposal strategies are mediated by a number of considerations that in turn depend upon commodity, market and geographical knowledge. Not simply about making space, nor purely an ethical argument about recycling and philanthropy, Lily's disposal dispositions invoke reasoned reflexivity and reveal a complex series of judgements about commodities, their residual and potential exchange value and their appropriateness for particular destinations. She thus reveals the deeply layered processes governing her selection of commodities for disposal. Lily is a high investor in second-hand worlds who knows the range and variability between sites and displays the full range of disposal techniques – from dumping at the nearest charity shop to selling (to make money to buy new things) at up-market London designer dress agencies. Scrutiny of an extended passage from Lily's transcript reveals both the range of disposal strategies she employs and her motivations for them:

Lily: I've bought lots of junk from charity shops. I think that's great – wear it once and then give it away to another charity shops . . . I quite like that folly as well, of only wearing it once or twice, it doesn't really matter as you can give it away again, this constant cycle . . . I have completely regular clear-outs. I get so bored of my clothes so quickly, so quickly, I just have to have a regular clear-out. More or less enforced as I've moved addresses that often in London. I always have to clear out my clothes. But that's once a year

Kate: And would you take them to the nearest charity shop?

Lily: Just the nearest charity shop. I just drop them there. I don't think about the charity I just think about getting rid of them, and I can't bear to throw them away because they've still got some wear in them.

Kate: Well, somebody's going to find them and they'll be their treasure.

Lily: You can make an awful lot of money from agency shops as well, and that creates a whole new cycle. I had a lot of clothes to get rid of [. . .] urm, my boyfriend's ex-girlfriend . . . these clothes were just sitting there and they were getting all fusty, and there was that many of them that I [. . .] sorted through them and took them to an agency shop and they sold them for me [. . .] I nearly made £400 which is a lot of money which then I can spend on different things . . .

This excerpt reveals how Lily has regular clear-outs in order to literally make space, and how this is in part the result of the rapid turnover time of her fashion tastes, as she gets 'so bored', so quickly. In these instances, Lily's disposal is about efficiency and control rather than charity or philanthropy: Lily wants to keep her personal 'taste cycle' going as her fashion tastes move on quickly. Second-hand purchasing in turn makes such space-saving strategies comparatively risk-free and easy – because clothes are relatively cheap (for her), she can almost borrow them from the charity shop, and she enjoys the 'folly as well, of only wearing it once or twice'. Lily is also aware of the latent and residual value in her clothing, in part presumably as a result of the rapid movement of her taste preferences, and doesn't want to imagine her clothes 'dying', telling how she can't 'bear to throw them away'. Here, then, Lily is drawing both on philanthropic notions of donating to deserving others and also on a desire to extend the life of her cast-off commodities. Finally, she is happy to dispense with any sense of philanthropy when discarding others' clothes (in this case her partner's ex-girlfriend). Seemingly unfettered by worries about exposing her taste and body size and shape – of literally revealing her wardrobe to others – with no emotional or aesthetic attachment to this woman or her clothes, and possibly with a desire to 'erase' this woman from her (and her partner's) life – to make emotional space – she is more than happy to dispose of these items in ways that will make her money and fuel further consumption.

Sourcing

While disposal is one mechanism through which goods end up in second-hand spaces of exchange, another is sourcing. Our exploration of car-boot sales, charity shops and retro shops revealed sourcing to be an activity few traders were prepared to discuss at length, at least in terms of its specifics. Indicative primarily of the intense competition between traders for goods – in itself a consequence of the growth in the second-hand market – this, nonetheless, does not foreclose comment on its generalities. Broadly, then, our research identified two forms of sourcing: one where individual traders source-to-sell themselves and the other in which sourcing (and its associated work) is devolved to an intermediary or trusted third party (TTP). As we show, these variants span the three sites we researched, but the second is associated with, and indicative of, commercial levels of investment in trading. It works therefore to separate those for whom trading is business from those for whom trading is primarily 'fun', 'a hobby' or an occasional thing to do, and only secondarily about money-making. Correspondingly, a feature of sourcing is the way in which individual traders switch from the first form of sourcing to the second – a tendency particularly prevalent among retro traders and certain car-boot-sale vendors.

Individual Sourcing (from Multiple Sites)

Associated exclusively with retro and car-boot-sale traders, individual sourcing is a search strategy that frequently weaves together multiple second-hand sites. Concomitantly it is an activity that is invariably time-consuming and, at least for those sourcing through discernment (retro traders) often fruitless and frustrating. For example, Tina (Manchester) tells how she goes to a number of sites and spaces in her search for stock 'You can just go round anywhere really . . . car boots'. Celia (Nottingham), meanwhile, scours the obit columns, searches through adverts in the local press, visits local antique fairs and trails off on (often unproductive) sourcing journeys to people's homes. Simon (Nottingham) talks about how 'one of the hunting grounds was car boot sales' while Paul (Bristol) explores a range of sourcing spaces: 'You used to get a lot from charity shops but can't now 'cos they're too expensive . . . we get stuff from small ads in newspapers, Trade It magazine'. Paul is an interesting example here as his shop-sourcing strategies have evolved out of his own love of rubbish and junk. His sourcing strategy is one which has developed fortuitously rather than as part of a grander plan, and spans a full range of sites, from local newspapers through to house-clearances in properties he was squatting in, through to other people's rubbish collected from skips. It is a highly time-intensive strategy, both in terms of scouring multiple sites and in terms of the repair work such cast-offs often require. Yet Paul's is a strategy that yields considerable mark-up as he deals primarily with other people's discarded 'rubbish' (washing machines, hi-fis, fireplaces) He discusses how:

> I've been interested in junk for a long time . . . I don't throw anything away [. . .] I spent 10 years on the dole so you don't throw anything away. I used to collect stuff anywhere, like going to derelict houses and getting all the fireplaces out [. . .] there was always loads of junk in squats. We used to go skip hunting [. . .] and we used to get washing machines. And with a washing machine there's usually only like a couple of things can go wrong [. . .] but people just throw them away [. . .] so we used to get washing machines, take 'em home unblock the pipes and then sell 'em for £50 to students [. . .] and one day we came across this skip that had

computers, hi-fi equipment, old tailor's dummies, weaving looms, rolls and rolls of material and apparently the girl who lived there [. . .] was a fashion student [. . .] so we emptied the skip once and when we came back it was full again, so we emptied it again [. . .] we spent a week emptying the house into the van and filled a shop with it . . .

Similarly, Mary, now retired from full-time employment, is a good example of how individuals source from multiple sites in ways that map onto our disposal strategies above. Mary spends much of her time 'doing' car-boot sales for charity fund-raising, and is driven largely by philanthropic motivations. She employs a number of strategies, notably door-knocking and generally making it known in the area that she is a fund-raiser. As a result, some of her stock simply appears in plastic bags on the doorstep – often from neighbours who know that Mary sells. However, a large amount of it is sourced from the most affluent areas of Newcastle, where Mary goes knocking each week. On her door-knocking rounds, though, Mary also employs a second strategy – she makes careful note of which houses are up for sale and makes it her business to knock on the door once the sold sign appears. She asks if there's any stuff that they want to get rid of before they move and which could be donated to a good cause.

In pursuing these activities, many traders draw on knowledges gained from participation in other second-hand spaces such as markets and jumble sales, as well as car-boot sales, particularly here in relation to the types of goods that sell well and whom to buy from:

> My mum works in a charity shop and gets a lot of things from there. And she also works in a library so she knows what books are popular. They [his parents] get stuff from lots of places. Junk shops, charity shops in town, jumble sales. So they spend part of their week sourcing the goods to sell at the week-end . . . they get up early on a Saturday morning and do jumble sales to find things. The they might do an auction, then a boot fair on Saturday afternoon and Sunday morning. (Tom)

The result is the creation of complex, but highly localized and seemingly infinite chains of second-hand commodity circulation and re-use. Second-hand spaces then are a way of life for a number of vendors, but their chains of commodity sourcing extend far beyond individual traders' selling spaces. Instead, much like dedicated second-hand shoppers, traders weave together in sourcing practice multiple sites, seeking to buy (from the 'unknowing') to sell (to the knowing) in ways that are clearly about capturing competitive advantage and profit.

And yet there are differences in practice here that are important to note. As Bill (a car-boot-sale vendor) remarked: 'What you've got to realise is that most dustmen do boot sales. When I was a bulker driver they used to spend all their time racking through the rubbish . . . it'll be "I'll sell that". "I'll have that"'. Bill tells how he acquired his stock for nothing from the tip and, since he had a regular income, the proceeds from his car-boot sales went to top up household income. As a result of this illegal 'totting' Bill and his wife used to make between £100 and £500 each week. Here Bill goes through the types of things he picked up from the tip to sell on:

> Initially we sold reasonably good stuff because we thought we couldn't sell anything worse . . . But we got to the stage where we were picking up *rubbish* (his emphasis) from the tip. I went to pick up a broom handle and I thought 'well, that's 20 pence!' There was a saucepan which I was about to crush [describes it] when I thought 'no, no, I'll sell it'. It was ridiculous!

The significance to us of this testimony is Bill's revelation of is own gradual realization that anything he sourced might sell; that he could source to sell (at car-boot sales) without discernment. In short, he came to learn that 'rubbish' had value. And this is something that other car-boot-sale traders also revealed. Mal and Fran for example – who when we met them had bought up sack loads of 'old tatt' to sell on (at a considerable mark-up) at another car-boot sale. Far from being difficult, frustrating and time-consuming, then, this form of sourcing was relatively easy work. For retro traders, though, sourcing through discernment remains a heavy time investment, frequently overlain by necessary alteration, cleaning and repairing. Indeed, our field observations revealed the large amounts of work which go on behind the scenes: Carole (Portobello) spends her days at the back of the shop sewing/embellishing/ironing stock unless she has a customer in; Richard, Eve, Celia and Elaine (Nottingham) all sew, alter, clean and iron commodities prior to their sale; while Fiona (Portobello) spends her week washing and cleaning stock, ironing and pricing everything up.

Such direct, personal involvement in sourcing means that these traders actively shape the second-hand market by what they source and reject. Traders here, then, act as intermediaries or knowledge brokers who can manipulate the perceived value of a commodity. Like others who work with household cast-offs (such as refuse collectors, scrap dealers and, formerly, rag-and-bone men[54]), traders are intermediaries who can bring about shifts in the permeable cultural boundaries of commodity value. But in order to sustain this position, traders require detailed geographical, commodity and market knowledge; brokering also demands considerable commitment in terms of time and dedication. For many it is hard work and, with greater competition, becoming harder. Consequently, and as we show now, many have moved to a commercial-merchanting form of sourcing.

Commercial-Merchanting Model

The second sourcing strategy we identity relies less on individual search processes and more on (employed) intermediaries. Many of the traders we talked with, often as part of a career trajectory, have moved on from sourcing themselves and have come to rely on suppliers or buyers as trusted third parties (TTPs), who know their particular requirements and will take the hard work out of sourcing, leaving traders free to undertake post-sourcing rituals (cleaning, repairing, altering, ironing, pricing) and to staff the store. Sophie (Notting Hill) for example uses a group of 'expert buyers' who source vintage and retro clothing for her nationally. By contrast, Eve, who has been a retro trader in Nottingham for more than 15 years, explains how she now only sources from large centralized warehouses in the Midlands. Often with their own shipping companies for export, these sort and grade goods and often restrict the number of traders they deal with in any one city. Eve, then, is one of the few Nottingham traders with access to these goods. Relations here are about trader-trust: the warehouse sorters put goods into separate bags for which she pays by the bagful. Eve has to take it on trust that the prices will be fair and that they won't rip her off. And – later on – she has to sift through the bags herself.

Such shifting sourcing strategies towards the use of trusted third parties are paralleled in the charity shop sector where large centralized warehouses sort, grade and allocate to shops. Sorters in these warehouses perform the role of merchanting intermediaries, shaping which commodities go to which shops, when and where. And getting this selection process right is a key component in ensuring charity-shop success. But unlike the case with retro trading, in charity retailing this mediation is complicated still further by shop volunteers. Indeed, it is volunteers who sift and sort through both individual donations and deliveries – be these from centralized warehouses or from same-chain shops within the region. It is here that the passage of goods towards recommodification becomes open to question: for volunteers evaluate, subject goods to their own criteria, mediate what ends up on the shop floor, for sale. And – as we have argued elsewhere (Gregson, Brooks and Crewe, 2000) – this passage is refracted with questions not simply of economistic exchange and use values, but with negotiations about bodily presences within donated goods, specifically here clothes. It requires negotiating the associations which surround other people's discarded clothing, notably the tacit knowledge that frequently the clothes donated to charity shops are not just 'throw-outs' but are the discarded effects of the dead. Furthermore, other narratives of the body are used to assess, reject and accept donations and deliveries; to repackage and sell them on. Too much bodily presence, be this conveyed through signs of leaky, messy bodies, just too much general wear or smell, spells rejection. By contrast, that which displays little trace of ownership, which looks as new or which can be rejuvenated through cleansing, purifying, freshening rituals, is to be valued: a garment which can realize further value precisely because of what it lacks. And it is the volunteer who makes these critical decisions, who decides just which of these effects are still usable, wearable, re-enchantable, and which are not. The volunteer is in this instance, then, the cultural intermediary who has the potential to determine a commodity's future passage through time and space.

Such formalized sourcing methods are also echoed in our work on car-boot sales, where the more experienced traders, particularly those who do regular car-boot sales as an occupation, may subcontract out sourcing work to friends, relatives or those in the appropriate social network who are aware of geographical variation in pricing arrangements and the variations across different second-hand sites. Mal, for example, is a full-time car-boot-trader who goes with his wife Fran to one site each week in order to stock up for more lucrative events in Nottinghamshire at the weekend. On the day we talked to them Mal had spent £15 on what he classified as 'tatt', which he'd bought as a job lot to sell on at treble the price elsewhere, while Fran had purchased a small number of 'select' ornamental objects, again to sell on but at a different venue. We also found several other examples like this, where household/family members implemented a division of labour around purchasing for future sale, or where one went out sourcing while the other 'did' a car boot sale.

Such shifts toward more formalized brokerage-sourcing strategies have emerged partly as a result of structural shifts within the second-hand market, specifically the increasing difficulties in sourcing original items. Sophie articulates these difficulties in sourcing scarcity quite clearly, arguing that genuine articles are becoming more and more scarce, and more and more expensive,

> *Louise*: Has sourcing become more difficult recently?
>
> *Sophie*: Much more so. Things are becoming incredibly scarce. It's getting harder all the time because of a sheer lack of things. We just don't see much vintage around these days. As the years go on the condition gets worse and the challenge gets harder . . .

Celia (Nottingham) also talks about the problem of sourcing – in the case of 1970s clothing and shoes she says that the two key constraints are quality and availability. Many of the items were of such shoddy quality that they simply fell apart. Others were simply never available in spite of being iconized (she says that people come in wanting original 1970s Gary Glitter boots and don't realize that nobody ever owned such items apart from the man himself). In terms of older vintage garments Celia argues that it is incredibly difficult to get the sizes required by today's (larger) customers, as most of the dresses are a size 8 with tiny waists. And Tina (Manchester) also explains how:

> Clothing-wise its very difficult to get really old clothing. I mean I get asked for Victorian clothing and you just can't get it, it's so difficult. And 20s things [. . .] Shoes from the 50s is quite easy, 20s to 40s a bit more difficult.

And Richard too (Nottingham) underscores the shortage of particular commodity groups:

> If I had a lorry load of good quality 70s leathers I could sell them by the tonne.

But such changing orientations in sourcing strategy are also in part the result of traders' evolving career trajectories as they shift from an early and informal mode of sourcing through to increasingly formalized and distant supply chains which are more heavily dependent on trusted third parties (buyers, centralized warehouses). Kevin (Bristol) for example talks in some detail about how he started going to jumble sales and found that within the space of a year he had amassed a roomful of stuff, so decided to open a stall. It went so well that he decided to open a bigger shop and 'sculpture' the stock more, concentrating predominantly on 20s, 30s, 40s and 50s clothing. He has now moved on from sourcing from jumble sales in favour of using warehouses which pre-sort their stock.

Paul too (Manchester) like Simon (Nottingham) and Sophie (Notting Hill) reveals how his sourcing strategies have evolved and developed through time, beginning in an ad hoc way and becoming more discerning and organized as time has gone on: 'When I first started I would get stuff from jumble sales and boot sales . . . pricing every day . . . Those days have gone! . . . People I've been buying off have done it for about 7 years . . . buyers with experience'. And while such arm's-length sourcing arrangements free up traders' time, they do introduce a new tier of competition into the buyer-supplier relation which compounds the ongoing supply scarcity problem. Richard (Nottingham) tells how:

> It's very difficult now. Those kinds of things (beaded 20s or 30s dresses) are sent out to Bonham's and Christie's to be auctioned. And the places where we source stuff from, they'll take it out at source too because they can send it down to London vintage clothes auction which might be in a few months time . . . and they get a nice hefty cheque.

Shifting sourcing strategies are, then, in part the result of evolving career biographies. But they also reflect the commercial imperative. With this being most clearly visible in the case of retro trading, we end this section as previously, by discussing one individual who to us encapsulates these tendencies. Simon's biography reveals this shift through time and space as experiential learning and, increasingly, business acumen takes over from early enthusiasm and idealism. Simon began trading at Short Farm Market in London in the late 1980s, sourcing from car-boot sales and amassing large amounts of stock in his house. Talking about this period in the late 1990s, he reflects on the underdevelopment of the market, seeing this as critical to his initial trading success. He then moved on to the provinces, setting up shops in creative quarters in Manchester and Nottingham in the early 1990s. His first shop was in the edge-of-town student quarter of Forest Road in Nottingham, a 'relatively cheap location' and still home today to a small agglomeration of retro traders such as Daphne's Handbag and Helter Skelter. He then opened a shop in Nottingham's Lace Market, and underscored here the importance of cheap economic rent in defining alternative quarters. Currently, though, he owns and manages three shops in Nottingham's Lace Market, the most recent of which is a large, conspicuous and highly stylized interiors shop on a major thoroughfare adjacent to the newly constructed and high-profile Nottingham Arena (see too Chapter 2). It would be difficult to imagine a less alternative location and store space, and Simon is well aware of how market changes have forced such spatial and organizational shifts towards more conventional trading patterns. The market 'has changed; become a more 'diluted experience', 'it gradually just got bigger and bigger', 'it's difficult to do and actually make it worth doing, especially nowadays', he argues. To do 'it' well, though, and to make 'it worth doing' (i.e. pay) – as Simon does – depends not just on commercial skill but crucially on the ability to work with (and to one's advantage) distinct sets of knowledge. 'Successful' second-hand traders, then – be these retro traders, car-boot-sale traders or in the charity retail sector – are those who have a highly developed appreciation and understanding of the spatialities of supply and demand in second-hand worlds. In the following and final section here we interrogate more closely the ways in which commodity and geographical knowledges shape sourcing strategies, identifying three distinct forms of knowledge.

Knowledge

Geographical Knowledge

First, and quite straightforwardly, sourcing depends on detailed localized knowledges and an awareness of the place specificity of value. This is local knowledge, a geographical knowledge of the networks of different places and sites and of the difference that place makes. It is this knowledge that enables sellers to buy cheaply and sell on more expensively according to site and situation. As Trish acknowledges, there are 'people going into charity shops and buying up stuff and then taking it to a second-hand market – probably Brick Lane or somewhere.' Similarly, Simon explains how 'a cooker can be £10 on a tip but £300 in a trendy shop in London. It's where it's being sold that makes it worth what it is. That's why I take these guide price books to task as people read about New York shop prices and try to get the same in the middle of a field in Yorkshire'. And Simon talks too about the geographical variation in second-hand prices during the 1980s, arguing that:

> At the time there was a real differential between what was going on in London and what was going on outside London [. . .] I could go round (the provinces) and buy stuff for next to nothing and sell it. Most of the time it was going abroad – going to Italy, France, Germany – cos again they were ahead of the game [. . .] things like Bakelite, collectables, that kind of thing. I suppose when I started it was deco, art deco, chrome, that kind of stuff [. . .] dealers were travelling over from continental Europe to buy, because at that time the UK was a real hunting ground.

Paul (Bristol) is an interesting example of how geographical variations in value and individual knowledge (or lack of it) can spell competitive advantage, and points too to the existence of geographical regimes of value: 'In cities it's difficult to find, but (if) you go to boot sales in the countryside round here . . . I had a bit of Whitefriar's glass about 3 months ago, cost me £3.50. They didn't know, even I didn't realize it was worth that much . . . I sold it for £500 to a collector . . . and I bought a 1988 wooden sculpture for 50p. That went in a Christie's auction about a year and a half ago for £120'. Simon (Nottingham) echoes Paul's sentiments about Whitefriar's glass, saying how he used to sell bits of it really cheaply: '10 quid, 8 quid, 20 quid for a really good bit . . . and now a good bit of Whitefriar's glass is 200 quid . . . somebody had an exhibition, I think in Manchester, it all comes out and off it goes. You can't touch it any more'. The invasion of aesthetic value by economic value is, then, a recurrent theme in the second-hand world, and what mediates aesthetic and commercial value is the commodity, its histories and its geographies.

The case of car-boot sales is a particularly clear example of the ways in which knowledge about spatial variation can signal competitive success. While casual vendors' knowledges are usually confined to a small circuit of specific boot sales, full-time vendors are acutely aware of geographical differences and use these to effect in both their sourcing and selling strategies. As one commented, 'it matters what the area's like – if it's an area where there are more classy people who'll be looking for particular kinds of things, we'll bring out our ornament collection'. In a sense there is evidence here of market segmentation across different boot sales which is apparent through differential pricing strategies and through the range, condition, brand and quality of products available. Such market segmentation in turn has implications for the sourcing strategies of these full-time vendors and for the chains of commodity circulation which are evident, whereby experienced vendors source stock from cheap, down-market boot sales in order to sell on, with a considerable mark-up, at a higher quality sale in a more prosperous neighbourhood.

Clearly, then, these insights into the importance of geographical variation in sourcing strategies and localized knowledges begin to shatter the suggestion that contemporary exchange is a trivial, straightforward, unembedded process. Rather, the car-boot sale is revealed as a site of locally embedded exchange, a site which is enmeshed within the possibilities and potential for commodity reuse within proximate geographical neighbourhoods and thoroughly interwoven with the specificities of

individuals' particular knowledges of these neighbourhoods, their possibilities and product-specific local supply–demand relations.

Commodity Knowledge; Knowledge as Investment

Secondly, knowledge about particular commodity values is often
product-specific and is often seen as something to be invested in and
worked at. Although evident across the spectrum of traders we encountered, this was invariably a characteristic of retro trading. In the following
extract Elaine provides us with a classic illustration of this:

> Louise: How have you acquired this range of knowledge?
>
> Elaine: It's being so into the clothes themselves. You'll go into second-
> hand shops and not only will they have absolutely gorgeous
> clothes but they'll have the albums too. I've bought like Happy
> Hammond plays the hits with Burt Bacharach [. . .] And you'll
> see the clothes people wear on the albums, and they'll also have
> like original 60s knitting patterns, and I think once you start
> looking around [. . .] you can find all sorts of like household
> items and books that show you what the clothes were like. So
> you're building up your ideas from the histories of the times.

In a similar way Eve, a retro trader in Nottingham, gets her inspiration
from the biannual fashion shows, the trade press and specialist fashion
magazines. This second form of commodity knowledge relies on the
ability to build up ideas from a range of sources and to make (creative)
connections between, for example, images, music, streetstyles, architect-
ural design and so on. Elaine too illustrates the importance of these
connections:

> Elaine: It really is having the shop, reading the trade magazines, going
> to shows and exhibitions and trade shops, the media, *Vogue*. It's
> a whole range of things.

Simon (Nottingham) is also interesting in terms of commodity knowledges, which he argues are one means of ensuring competitive success.
He cites the example of a telephone he saw on a market stall that he
bought for less than £5. He asked the price but wasn't sure if the seller
had said £4 or £40. He said to the vendor that he'd like the 'phone and
a clock, and was told 'a fiver for the two'. He then saw the guy who
dealt in classic telephones and sold him it for £70 within 'two minutes'.

Contextual Knowledge

The third form of knowledge evident in our transcripts is knowledge as contextual. Often described as 'having the knack', a range of car-boot and retro traders talk about 'just knowing' what to buy and where to buy from. Richard, for example, argues that his partner Eve just has an innate skill: 'don't ask me how she knows, she just does . . . She's got an eye for it. It's just a knack. You've either got it or you haven't. You can't teach somebody'. Such knowledge is tacit, innate, not easily passed on, but in part it comes out of a personal history in the second-hand world, the arts or the cultural economy more broadly. A number of our interviewees, then, have a long history in fashion and many have moved across into retro trading from other creative sectors such as music or art. Sophie (Notting Hill) trained as an art historian and was 'always interested in the visual, aesthetic, creative side of things'. Simon (Nottingham) began in a band and supported himself by doing markets. He was always, he argues, 'interested in design and clothes and things, that kind of thing'. Paul (Manchester) had been to Art College and began a stall in Afflecks Palace; Elaine (Nottingham) trained as a designer and worked in the clothing business for some years before setting up her retro business. Others have developed knowledges not through any formal training in the cultural industries but, rather, through long-standing family or personal histories of buying and collecting second-hand commodities. Celia has a long family history in antiques and remembers how she used to go to auctions and fairs with her mother, looking for Victorian lace and linen. Others such as Eve have worn second hand clothes for 20 years and have developed 'an eye' for sourcing commodities which will sell. Similarly, Paul (Manchester) reveals how the knowledge to spot the next trend is an unteachable skill: 'once something becomes valuable, you don't see it . . . that's the fascinating thing, seeing what's going to be the next big seller . . . it's not predict-able. Something can be laughed at and then two years later everyone wants it'. And Tim (Bristol) argues that 'it was interesting to see how some people understood it [retro] straight away and other people, how-ever hard you tried, never actually grasped the concept'. This, then, is an instinctual form of knowledge yet one that is deeply contextual and contingent too. And while such knowledge is inherent it can also critically be knowledge which can be shared and appreciated between different retro retailers and which depends on being immersed in a creative scene where emergent trends can be both identified and shaped. As Sophie (Notting Hill) explains,

'I get a lot of inspiration from the clothes coming through the shop [. . .]
You kind of feed off each other, that kind of thing.'

In part, then, such knowledge is deeply geographical, in that it
emerges through the activities of groups of people who become identified as pioneering, innovative, in touch with fast-paced shifts of fashion
and style. It is grounded in particular places at particular times. And such
knowledges are one of the means by which people carve out a niche
for themselves in an industry in which making one's name so often
relies on marking oneself out as different from the mainstream or
dominant form of organization. But the difficulty with relying on tacit
knowledge as a competitive strength is that aesthetic and stylistic shifts
mean that knowledge is constantly under review, is constantly in flux
and is thus elusive and difficult to stabilize. To stay ahead of the game
in an ever more competitive style arena requires very specific forms of
knowledge and skill that depend on the definition of difference.

Conclusions

Conceptually in this chapter we have endeavoured to make a set of arguments about the instabilities of meaning in goods and have argued that
meaning and value are constantly in a process of production/re-creation.
We have two particular sets of comments that we want to draw out by
way of a conclusion. The first relates to commodity and geographical
knowledges about disposal and sourcing, and specifically their gendered
dimensions. The second connects to debates around value creation and
the commodity chain. To take each in turn.

First, running throughout the discussion in this chapter has been the
question of gender divisions. Despite being on the whole more fluid
and unpredictable than formal retail spaces, second-hand spaces are
nonetheless reproductive of traditional constructs of femininity and
masculinity: men and women dispose of different things, sell different
things, buy and look at different things; in short, their dispositions
toward and knowledges of second-hand exchange and consumption are
deeply gendered. For women, as we discussed above, participation in
second-hand worlds is mediated by constructions of body image and
is fettered by questions of respectability, public image, the embodied
self, nurturing, household provisioning and a moral economy of value.
For men, in contrast, gendered knowledges, specifically in relation to
the car-boot sale, hinge rather more around functionality and durability.
Second-hand disposal and sourcing, we argue, are activities that place

considerable emphasis on the skills and knowledges of consumers in terms of the ability to assess the sellability of items in terms of quality, durability, price, style, brand and fit. And what this suggests is that, while second-hand arenas of exchange and consumption have the potential to enable the development of critique and resistance – specifically here in terms of the moral economy of household provisioning – at the same time such spaces may serve to intensify dominant gendered discourses of consumption. That they do is, in our view, a reflection of the premium that such spaces inevitably place on expert gendered knowledges about particular gendered commodities.

Secondly, much existing work on circuits of meaning and value has drawn on the commodity chain or filière tradition and has attempted to define or capture the key point of meaning and value creation – typically by unveiling regimes of commodity production and fixing attention on the place of production. This conceptualization is, we would argue, problematic, in that it focuses attention exclusively on global power relations, is (backwardly) linear and tends towards reductionism and spatial fixity. In contrast, we have argued for an approach which is circuitous, focuses on journeys and movements (rather than fixed points or nodes within a chain), acknowledges the creativity of social actors in shaping the conditions of value creation (and destruction) and suggests, critically, that *time* may be as important a determinant of meaning (re)creation as space. Shifts in commodity value can take place in multiple directions, and de- and re-valorization processes are contextual, subjective and unpredictable. We are thus moving towards an understanding of commodity journeys through time and space that is non-linear, unpredictable, fortuitous and subjective. Commodities circulate in different regimes of value in space and time and value is defined not simply in relation to the rarity or collectability of a particular object (although evidently these are important qualities), but is intrinsically connected with the links between people and is clearly embedded in the specific possibilities provided by the fleeting place-specific conjuncture of individual consumers with particular objects. All of this, of course, is worlds away from more conventional determinations of value expressed through the production, distribution and marketing costs of particular commodities as codified in fixed, non-negotiable retail prices. And what this alerts us to is the existence of variable, embedded, frequently socially constructed circuits of value which, we maintain, have the potential at least to question, if not undermine, those conceptualizations of commodity value to be found in conventional retail environments.

Transformations: Commodity Recovery, Redefinition, Divestment and Re-enchantment

Introduction

In this chapter we continue our exploration of commodity de- and re-valorization cycles, looking more broadly at the role objects play in identity formation and maintenance. Having explored the ways in which people dispose of their commodities and looked at commodity journeys in Chapter 5, focusing on the various ways in which items come to be in particular second-hand spaces at particular times, we turn our attention now to post-purchase rituals; to those activities which are undertaken in order to make a commodity one's own and to give it special meaning and value. Here, then, our focus shifts from commodity journeys to transformative practices in time and space; from movements to moments in a commodity's life story; looking at the practices which follow crucial passage points into and through second-hand worlds. In short, then, we are looking here at commodity transformations in situ via rituals of possession. For most of the time objects are in ownership and are thus effectively out of the commodity sphere. Their value is ambiguous and mutable and they are open to cultural reinterpretation through shifts in taste and desire and through transformations in form or function through possession rituals. Such rituals are particularly significant in the case of second-hand commodities as people are often not buying the commodity we see but a particular attribute of it which will only be realized when they return home and either renovate, reminisce, clean, repair or transform it. More broadly here we explore the difference that the commodity form makes, looking at how, and

143

why, some things undergo divestment and possession rituals (while others do not).

We focus on three key possession rituals here. First we explore recovery rituals whereby former meanings and traces of ownership are retrieved, recaptured and reimagined. Most notable in respect of the memorabilia of iconic figures and celebrities – for example Diana, Maria Callas, Christina Onassis and Elton John – and clearly linking back to our discussion of disposal strategies,[55] it is the former life and times of commodities, and particularly their association with specific 'stars', which are valued here. Recovery rituals, however, go beyond the former possessions of the rich and famous, and extend to include goods from particular periods, 'the authentic'. Here it is the imagined memories trapped within the commodity that create value, and the consumer's work here involves recapturing these former traces of ownership in order to, quite literally, produce meaning. Secondly we look at a very different set of practices, namely divestment rituals where the commodity problem is, in contrast to recovering meaning, that there is too much trace of previous ownership, traces that need to be expunged, removed. In different ways, then, recovery and divestment rituals rely on the consumer's historical and geographical imagination, about who has owned, used and worn the commodity before, when, where and under which conditions. Thirdly we look at transformative rituals, including processes of alteration or repair, which quite literally make a commodity one's own, in terms either of fit, function or style. Through such rituals it becomes possible to transfer, obscure, lose or restore the meaning of goods when they change hands. And as commodities leave one consumption cycle and enter another, possession rituals enable the transferrence and/or destruction and re-creation of meaning from one commodity-world to another, thereby transforming an anonymous commodity into a meaningful possession, making a decommodified object singular.

This focus on possession rituals is important for a number of reasons. First and in conceptual terms, it enables us to further track products through various cycles of use and re-use, and also provides an important corrective to the many existing accounts of consumption which prioritize single acts of purchase at first-cycle sites of consumption. The narrowness of these representations which conceptualize consumption in terms of a momentary act of purchase have recently been recognized by those who prefer to see consumption as an ongoing, socially and culturally encoded process (see for example Crang, 1996; Crang and Malbon, 1996; Glennie and Thrift, 1992; Jackson, 1993; Jackson and Holbrook, 1995; Miller, 1987, 1995; Willis, 1990). However, important though this work is, it still focuses attention on the first cycle of consumption and ignores the ways in which commodity value is constantly in motion and is actively (re)created by consumers through possession and divestment rituals.

Secondly, this approach enables us to explore the ways in which consumer agency acts as a key determinant in shaping value, and reveals that people rarely (if ever) buy passively or uncritically but, rather, actively transform the meaning of goods – particularly, we argue, second-hand goods. Given that the meaning of goods is constantly in transit, this approach enables us to focus on the ways in which meanings are 'unhooked' and transferred, and at how consumers fetch the meanings out of goods or change the value of commodities through rituals (Belk, 1995a, Koptyoff, 1986).

Thirdly, this focus on rituals gives us some purchase on the role which property and possessions play in self-definition. This remains a neglected area of enquiry, and the importance of object attachment is still little understood (although see Belk, 1992; Pavia, 1993; Rudmin, 1991; Rudmin and Richens, 1992; Schouten, 1991). In particular, very little has been written on what individuals actually do with their purchases and on how they imbue them with value. And so in spite of ongoing, perhaps indeed renewed, interest in commodities, commodification and material culture, there remains a persistent and curious lack of work on the connections between the material culture of commodities – their temporality, circulation, exchange and possession – and the construction of identity. Perhaps the most useful corrective to this neglect is the work of McCracken who has drawn attention to the time consumers spend cleaning, discussing, comparing, reflecting and showing off their new possessions (1985). Other notable literature on how people relate to their material possessions includes work by Csikszentmihalyi and Rochberg-Halton (1981), Rudmin (1991), Dittmar (1992) and Moorehouse (1991) who looks at the customization of hot-rod automobiles by enthusiasts. In the following discussion we argue that the point about purchasing second-hand items is that the rituals involved in transforming the commodity into one's own result in high levels of attachment and the creation of new forms of meaning. It is to this that we now turn.

Of Mods and Men: on Potentiality, Singularization and Imagined Histories

For many consumers both the attraction and the value of a second-hand good lies in the imaginative potential of its former life. Second-hand goods are imbued with a history and a geography and, theoretically, all the things of material culture have the potential to become meaningful, even when they have been effectively withdrawn and deactivated as commodities through, for example, disposal, damage or decay. And as we saw in Chapter 5, this deactivation leaves commodities open not only to singularization but also to individual (and collective or institutional) redefinition. Commodity journeys are thus conceptually open and endless. And for us what is significant here is that the study of second-hand stresses that the commodification of goods bought for consumption need not be terminal – the cultural and economic longevity of a commodity's life can be infinite, value can lie dormant, meaning can be hidden from view, awaiting rediscovery. Shifts of category – from undervalued to priceless, or from worthless to valuable for example – are achieved most notably through the passage of time. Significantly too, objects can simultaneously be part of different value systems – an heirloom ring can have a clear market price and exchange value to a jeweller while at the same time being part of a closed personal sphere wherein it is deemed priceless, sacred, uniquely valuable and inexchangeable by virtue of memories and history (and see too Koptyoff, 1986). This paradox of value is particularly keenly developed in relation to the art market, wherein singularity is confirmed not only by a commodity's structural position in an exchange system but by 'intermittent forays into the commodity sphere, quickly followed by re-entries into the closed sphere of singular "art"' (Koptyoff, 1986: 83). And second-hand commodities, we maintain, are particularly meaningful, and take on an almost sacred character through, for example, contagious contact with famous and/or imaginary others (rock stars, film stars, designers); through rituals such as bequeathing, inheriting, alteration and personalization; or through singularity (gifts from loved ones, original one-offs). Such goods are valued, cherished and treasured because of their unique and special status. Their sacredness may be preserved or enhanced through investment rituals and disposal, under such circumstances, becomes particularly fraught.[56]

In what follows we draw on two particular modes of meaning creation that we identified during our interview work. Both modes revolve around the recovery of meaning and centre on the imaginative potential of commodities, although they differ in their gender dimensions and in the ways in which they mobilize issues of authenticity. The first mode of meaning creation revolves around profound association with, and attachment to, particular historical eras; this we call *meaning creation through historical reconstruction*. It relies on detailed and researched knowledges about particular historical styles and on the celebration of famous celebrities such as designers, rock stars and actors. This form of object attachment hinges on questions of authenticity and cultural capital, and has close links to music and club scenes. Throughout the course of our work we found that the most extreme examples of meaning creation through historical reconstruction were evident among individuals whose homes, clothes and artefacts all originate in the 1960s, and it is these people on whom we draw to illustrate our argument below.[57]

Quite why the 1960s looms so large in the memories of many second-hand shoppers remains a point for speculation. Undoubtedly in part, we would argue, this veneration and celebration is being mobilized by those who are the children of the 1960s generation, and who have their parents' memories replayed back to them through the course of their child- and early adulthood. But more than this we would argue that the sixties represented (or are being represented as) a time of progressiveness in fashion and design, of quality, innovation and excitement. This was a time when London in particular was pioneering new design processes and practices, when retailing and consumption practices and spaces were being transformed and when youth and pop culture inspired and energized emergent consumer youth cultures (Armstrong (2000b), Brooke (2000), Hulaniki (1983), Jackson (1998), Lobental (1990), Powell and Peel (1988), Quant (1967), Radner (2001), Time (1966), Woodall (1999).

The second mode of meaning creation we term *imagined history making*. Connected to both familial history and nostalgia, this form of object attachment is largely based around romantic and fantasized visions of the lives and times of imagined others, rather than the authenticated excavations associated with the reconstructionists. Significantly too, as we go on to argue, this latter disposition is most keenly evident among a group of middle-class professional men, for reasons which we go on to discuss below.[58]

Historical Reconstruction Through Knowingness

First, then, we look at the ways in which certain of our interviewees inhabit and recreate earlier eras through the clothes and commodities that they buy, wear, use and display. As we go on to argue, the absence of unified and universal definitions of value or prestige make it necessary to attribute high cultural but non-monetary value to aesthetic, stylistic or geneological esoterica.[59] This we see particularly acutely in discussions with a group of interviewees who dress and design their homes in 1960s style. Josephine and Ian are a young professional couple living in Nottingham. Their interior design, artefacts, furniture, records and clothes are, as far as is possible, all original sixties. Their house they bought in part because of the things that were left behind, there for them to rediscover and re-enchant:

> This suite was here when we moved in and one of the reasons I bought the house was because I loved the suite [. . .] the lady left us everything in the house [. . .] we have a late sixties oven that was here, and pieces of furniture in the dining room . . . (Josephine).

Josephine and Ian revere and reify the historical artefacts of this particular era, and are frustrated by the encroachment of the mass market onto their style turf. Throughout our discussions Josephine in particular talks about the importance of wearing the authentic item rather than the mass-produced copy or fake, as the following extract reveals

> *Josephine*: . . . I've noticed myself getting more critical. You see things in the shops which have been done in sixties style; immediately I hate it.
>
> *Louise*: You wouldn't want any repro-sixties stuff? You know an original piece when you see it?
>
> *Josephine*: It frustrates me [. . .] I find I'm going back even further in terms of my clothes because the sixties style is so reproduced in the shops nowadays that you feel as if you're wearing something from Top Shop . . .

In order to seek out original 1960s clothing and memorabilia, the couple find themselves having to go further and further afield and are planning a trip to Amsterdam to search out original items as London – their primary source – has, they argue, become prohibitively expensive.[60] Josephine looks for original crafted clothes, arguing that 'quality (is) the main thing. I like hand-embroidered stuff, hand-made and tailor-made'. Here we see that Josephine emphasizes the stylistic and aesthetic qualities of garments and talks with obvious pleasure about the cut of original garments that she sees as serious cultural artefacts, to be appreciated for the way they adorn her body. Her clothes are invested with meaning in this instance through the knowledges and discourses of fashion and aesthetics; specifically knowledge about 1960s clothing – its construction and shape. Such historical fashion knowledge is mobilized to construct a personalized way of dressing which emphasizes difference, individuality and knowingness.

Ian, meanwhile, collects 1960s vinyl records, 'all vinyl, yeah. Basically what I class as excellent musicians and bands . . . so they are rare . . . some of the singles go for about four or five hundred pounds, sometimes more'. He began listening to his parents' Buddy Holly records when he was about seven, and his taste has developed from then, through 'digging deeper and deeper all the time. You hear a band and you want to know who they were influenced by or what came before them, or the band that may have supported them'. When you listen to the music you can, argues Josephine, 'just close your eyes and you, like you might well have been there'. Ian dreams about living in the 1960s, saying 'I'd love it to be 1966 especially, there's just something about the year . . . 1966 was amazing. All the best records came out then'.

Throughout the transcript there is much talk of quality – how contemporary music is poor in comparison to original 60s classics, and how clothing isn't made to appropriate quality standards any more, how there are 'no French seams anymore, or proper tailored lining'. This seems to be a way of setting themselves up as the arbiters of good (elite) taste, in the classic Bourdieu sense. And so we see here that they work with a notion that cultural quality is more significant than economic value, and that value is inscribed to that which is authentic, real and thus meaningful, as is the case with Josephine's things that 'might have cost 50p but I'd be devastated if they got stolen'.

Martin and Emma, a couple of '60s afficionados in Manchester, tell a similar story of producing identity through recreating the looks and sounds of the 1960s with original commodities. Again we see here the importance of music (vinyl records in particular), the club scene, and the elitist tribalism of the contemporary Mod subcultural scene. Like Josephine, Emma's clothes are all 1960s originals, 'everything 100 per cent without a doubt. This is me', and again we see the cultural distinction made between individuals who are 'authentic', knowledgeable about the scene and high in cultural capital, and those who are just playing at 1960s revivalism and who buy and wear new mass-market copies of original garments. Emma and Martin talk disdainfully about such fakes, the

> girl wearing a half, a quartered black and white dress from Top Shop and some pair of clumpy boots [. . .] Spice Girl boots [. . .] they come along in their stupid little semi-platform boots and some wanky shift dress from

Top Shop and think they're Queen Bee [. . .] Or the trendy girl [. . .] with a sewn on target on the back [of a parka] which is so *immaculately clean!!* It's never been anywhere *near* a scooter or fallen off the back of anything in its life. It's a fucking state. (Martin)

Martin and Emma model themselves on the lifestyle of the original 1960s Mods: they 'want the original look . . . Like the original mods you see. . .looking at our roots and our roots are the original mods'. They feel that the 1960s were a profoundly important time in terms of popular culture and feel attached to, bonded to people who were teenagers at the time and who shared their passion:

you pick up a book and you know it's a second hand book, you know it's cool, it's got a history to it this book, somebody bought this book, they wanted it, they wanted this James Bond first edition cos they were into James Bond and I'm into James Bond so you've got a common bond with some person you'll never meet or ever see. (Martin).

Such passion for the decade extends though not just to clothes and records but to all the material culture of the home. Emma, for example, reveals the pleasure she gets from discovering such items: 'I've got 60s sellotape, 60s plasticine . . . and every little thing gives us so much pleasure, to find that 60s stamp, that's just the highlight of the day . . . and then you know, another day it'll be a tie or a book, anything' (Emma). Every item has a story attached to it, she argues.

The relation of both couples to the 1960s relies on accumulated specialist knowledge they have built up over many years, such that it has become a lifestyle project. Both couples reveal a strong emphasis on celebration and display, and were keen to show us their decor, clothes and record collections in enormous detail. They talk about the 1960s as a time of authentic youth and pop culture and feel that quality was superior then, and that material commodities of the time were both innovative and exciting. Their lifestyle, defined through the material culture of commodities, is about differential display and rarefied elite knowledges, encapsulated in the discussion of vinyl (rare, obscure, researched knowledge) and 1960s fashion (tailored, crafted, beautifully constructed). Both couples define themselves as part of a small, tight-knit, self-constructed elite based around authenticated, researched and intellectualized historical re-creation.

Others too talk in reverential terms about the 1960s as a time of fashion, design and retailing revolution. Diane, for example, refers in the following extract to famous 1960s film and fashion design as key influences:

> I've got a little brown cloth cap. Urm, yeah, all that kind of stuff like British new-wave films and *Room at the Top* and *Saturday Night Sunday Morning*. I just felt comfortable. It's my niche [. . .] I bought a Mary Quant mirror in there (Attica) for eight pounds which was lovely. It's got a little green plastic base with a stem and the mirror is a red plastic flower [. . .] My favourite coat in the whole world, which is like a brown swing coat, its like a little sixties thing and its got two zip pockets and little round white things on them [. . .] my favourite thing that I got was a little Sixties black and white mod dress that I got a couple of weeks ago and I was really excited about it. It's one of those split into four and it's black and white and I went wooow, that's so cool, I have to have that. (Diane)

Another (Charlie) talks about her 'lovely Jackie O suit, that was £5, perfect condition' while Rachel talks about the impact which the aesthetic and style trends of the 1960s inspire on her current wardrobe. She argues that 'The sixties were brilliant . . . That's when it all started to happen . . . I just don't like the 90s really, 90s fashion . . . My gran, we sit down and watch a 1960s film, a musical, and you see all the costumes, and it's just amazing. Everyone used to go out in suits and look smart and I like that, sometimes I like to look smart with my big coat, my big fur, to look glamorous, like a film star'. This was a time when cut, colour and line were the defining principles of a garment, 'kind of cool chic beatnik look, '67 when it was still fairly sharp . . . I like it hip and sharp . . . sharp suits, there's a nice balance between classic lines and colour, a bit of extravegence, a bit of dressing up, a bit of dandyism without being too over the top' (Tim).

And for this group of people such practices are about displaying knowingness and knowledges to and for appropriate audiences. Consequently, buying the 1960s for these people becomes a serious process, involving searching out the authentic in unlikely unknowing places, and looking disdainfully at those who are seen to have neither the knowledge nor the skill to understand the difference that authenticity makes.

Imagined Histories and the Archaeology of Memory

The second way in which meaning and value can be created through second-hand goods relies rather less on specific, researched and intellectualized reconstruction and rather more on romantic imaginings about the discards of either family members or unknown, 'ordinary' others. While this mode bears some relation to the historical reconstructionists (specifically in relation to questions of commodity production, quality, design and craftsmanship for example), it differs markedly in the sense that this second strategy is altogether more romantic and is based around musing and/or fantasy. Far less specific in its historical detail, this mode of meaning creation is about flights of fancy, about abstract imaginings. Significantly too, it is most keenly expressed by a group of middle-class men whom we interviewed.[61] Two particular strategies of meaning creation are evident within this sub-group: one relies on familial history and storytelling while the other is based around unknown imaginative histories. The following extract from the interview with Steven, the 30-something graduate and artist from Bristol we met previously, is illustrative of the first strategy:

> I remember having this thing about wanting to dress like my Granddad, wanting to have the same cut of suit in the same era [. . .] just kind of, really, Everyman clothes, really ordinary, loose fitting [. . .] I always had this thing about my Granddad. I think probably the first second hand clothes I ever wore were things I'd got off my grandfather when he stopped going outside. I always used to like the way he dressed [. . .] I've got a shirt that my Granddad, I've got a photo of him wearing it in the 60s, and like that, yeah, all the nostalgia of these, the photos of mum and dad when they were young, even before they were married, when they were sort of young and maybe a bit beatnicky and stuff, it's very attractive to me, the way they both dress. (Steven)

This extract reveals the strong sense of revisiting familial histories as a means of both shaping fashion taste and of imbuing old clothes with meaning, value and memory. Steven constructs his Granddad as some kind of Everyman – ordinary, unpretentious, hard-working; his very own working-class hero (and see too Laurence, 1997). Others too talk in wistful terms about their parents' and grandparents' style sensibility: Ian (Manchester), for example, discusses how his love of old clothes has a long tradition and is rooted in early family experiences and memories. He wears many of his father's original clothes, 'Urm, that brown cord jacket, that was my dad's'. Steven too has such evocative memories of the house he grew up in that he has recreated his own house in replica style, '(this room) is a hell of a lot like our old room in Shipham where my parents lived in the 70s, the colour scheme and the curtains which have fallen down now, but they were the same as those (swirly brown/white/orange patterned) cushions. I found that fabric, the cushions and my bedspread are 1970s.'

But as significant as the narratives of family history are those who create meaning through imaginative journeys. For Rupert, a 20-something graphic design graduate from Nottingham, charity shops are a fantasy space moulded around nostalgia – the commodities here seem to have the potential to open up and make accessible earlier constructions of working-class masculinity that he finds seductive and stylish. Rupert's discussion below of the Johnson's Control shirt is a classic illustration of this:

> *Rupert*:   . . . My favourite find is my Johnson Control shirt. That was £2.50 [. . .] I think it's a firm in Canada that's something to do with paper and printing [. . .]
>
> *Louise*:   And why is that a prize find?
>
> *Rupert*:   Because it's got big collars, big starched collars. It's very, very light. And the cut is very tight to the body. It's just the – you'd imagine someone wearing it in the States as a bowling shirt [. . .] It's a kind of workman's shirt turned cool . . .

For Rupert, this shirt is imbued with an imaginative history that makes it both special and meaningful, to the point that he has even tried to find out the history of the company to authenticate the garment. For him to cite the heterosexist working-class male hero through everyday clothing is a knowing practice that accords kudos and stylistic respect. Rupert enjoys thinking about and romanticizing the person who wore the clothes before him, and the attractions of second-hand clothing here, then, lie in reconstructing their imagined (authentic) histories. He talks about his authentic find, the garment he had the knowledge to spot, the history of toil that is ingrained in the fabric. Other interviewees echo such sentiments almost exactly. Tom, for example, tells how

> One of the things I've found myself doing more and more is trying to guess where things come from. Reconstructing what other people have donated [. . .] I feel like I'm getting a piece of clothing which has got a whole load of stories attached to it. Not just stories about who made it and under what kinds of conditions and where it was sold and how it was arranged in the shop, but also about who wore it, where did they go, what sort of adult was the person who bought it, urm, whether it was a Christmas present, whether it was a favourite pair of trousers . . .

Martin too tells how part of the thrill of buying and owning second-hand records lies in the imaginative potential of their former lives:

> That's what my passion is about, records. I buy a record, I know it's not brand new. I know it's old, it's been about, know what I mean, who's had it, I'll never know, but it's nice that aspect [. . .] who had it originally? What was their passion? Were they like me or were they just like a radio DJ at the time in the 1960s or were they an intense soul DJ? You'll never know . . . (Martin)

Here we see not just the fascination and allure of imagined others but the importance of the unknown and the unknowable.

Many of these transcripts are steeped in melancholy and musings for the variously imagined (and unauthenticated) sad, tragic or gifted lives of others: the collector of books, the buyer of shrouds, the writer who collects personal papers. And this in turn leads certain second-hand consumers to reflect on both the history and the geography of a commodity's journey, and to think about its many possible ownership cycles and consumption journeys. Ian (Nottingham) is particularly instructive in this regard in that he actively thinks through not simply cycles of use and reuse but also about biographical origins and production processes, as in the following extract where he talks about his passion for second hand books:

> It could be a really old book which is really valuable because of the kind of binding or because of who printed it. Or it could be a second hand book which isn't valuable but which is special to me because of the subject. Old things like books are works of art. They would have been printed by hand. Some would have been made of paper that was made by hand, the whole book would then be hand-bound. Each piece of type was hand-carved [. . .] I once bought the complete works of Goethe's *Faust* at an auction in the German language, and poking through the nine volumes at the back of one was an article taken out of a London newspaper from the nineteenth century written by Lord Byron who'd been to see *Faust* in London. That's the type of thing you dream of finding . . .

Ian is thus acutely aware of commodity chains – he enjoyed getting his early clothes tailor-made as he knew then about the quality and fit; he imagines who made his second hand clothes/books/furniture under what conditions, how and when. He actively seeks out books with inscriptions, annotated notes, fragments of paper, relics and signs of life from the previous owner and dreams about finding a music score or book from Beethoven. And what strikes us as interesting about such narratives of the imaginary potential of commodities is that they are almost exclusively from men. And the commodities which Ian and Rupert refer to are all wildly imaginary: silk waistcoats, silk smoking gowns, old white shirts, preferably Edwardian. Old, individual, handmade, with important and interesting issues to do with production and consumption, these clothes are the equivalent to the way Ian (Nottingham) talks about desirability in second hand books (about the importance of paper, binding, of understanding and treasuring hand-crafting), and to the way Ian (Manchester) talks about the histories locked into his vinyl records. Perhaps, we suggest, this has something to do with men's (generally) more limited purchasing activity within second-hand spaces. Ian, for example, rarely buys in charity shops, but imagines what he could possibly find there. For him, the charity-shop is a relatively unknown world of dreams and possibilities, rather than limitations. Women, in comparison, many of whom are involved in ongoing household provisioning, are acutely aware of the possibilities – and limitations – of charity-shop purchases, and reveal less by way of romantic musings about exceptional items, and more by way of practical knowledges about the acceptability, or not, of donated clothes. It is to one facet of this acceptability that we now turn.

Divestment Rituals: Leaky Bodies, Inhabited Clothes

While both excavating 'the authentic' and reconstructing imagined histories of commodities such as books, accessories, furniture and clothing offer scope for the revalorization of second-hand goods, other sets of consumption practices suggest that revalorization is connected intimately with divestment rituals. Most clearly visible with respect to clothing purchases, these divestment rituals allow the new owner both the erase and to personalize, and through this to 'free up' the meaningful properties of possession (McCracken, 1988: 87). Indicative of a significant oversight within the current consumption literature – a tendency to avoid thinking about embodied consumption (although see: Corbett, 2000; Crewe, 2001; Gamman, 2000; Grogan, 1999; Malson and Swann, 1999) – second hand clothing obliges individuals to negotiate with that which a known/unknown other has already worn; with clothes that have been inhabited and that frequently bear the trace/s of this habitation – in evidence of leakiness, in the shape of the wearer, in practices of wearing. Perspiration marks, stains, the pounding and fading associated with washing cycles, grease, mud, tears. Consuming items of second hand clothing through both charity shops and retro shops, then, requires the negotiation of this unknown other, his or her body and practices of wearing. But it requires individuals to confront too both the constructions and taboos of personal bodily dirt and death, and their own thresholds in relation to these. Particularly acute with respect to charity-shop clothing, where clothing is neither cloaked within the safety net of temporal distance and authentication accorded by retro shops, nor juxtaposed – as in car-boot sales – with previous owners, it is this instance and the consumption practices associated with charity shop clothes purchasing that we focus on here.

Negotiating the Other: Wear and Tear and Bodily Traces

In the following extract Val, the 50-something secretary we met earlier in Chapter 4, reveals:

> *Val:* [. . .] a lot of the stuff that you get in charity shops has hardly been worn, although one thing that I do do is to look at the label because if things have been washed a lot of times then the label usually washes out, and it gives a good idea of how old things are.
> *Nicky:* Would that influence you in whether to buy something, how many times it seems to have been washed?
> *Val:* In a way yes
> *Nicky:* So what are you actually looking for?
> *Val:* I'm looking for something that's not very old, which hasn't been worn very much . . .

An important point here in her assessment of charity shop clothing, then, is about the absence of signs of wear: her evaluation of the traces of washing is one that is about the amount of wearing that a garment has had and – as she goes on to make explicit – about its relative new-ness. This, however, is not an understanding of newness that is bound up within fashion cycles. Rather, newness is about practices of wearing, and for Val it is the presence/absence of the bodily that is being evaluated. In a telling phrase, it is something 'that hasn't been worn very much', that lacks traces of the bodily, that she is looking for; an item characterized by absence. Washing labels, then, provide her with the vital clues: they are her key to unlocking previous wearing practices and her means for detecting absence.

As the testimony of others reveals, at the same time as looking for signs of bodily absence, signs of bodily presence – and particularly of over-presence – is as significant in shaping charity-shop-clothing purchasing. Here, for example, Janet (a 40-something 'housewife' from Bristol) recounts how pairs of jeans were rejected:

> *Janet*:   A couple of pairs of jeans I've looked at, I've thought ooh, I'll try them on. I've taken them in and there's been blood in the gusset. I'm like 'Eurghh!' And I've taken them up to the counter and said you either want to throw them out or clean them . . .
>
> *Kate*:   Say they were really good jeans, though. You wouldn't think about taking them home and washing them?
>
> *Janet*:   No I wouldn't. I mean if somebody that dirty has worn them I don't want to know . . .

Similarly Barbara – a 50-something woman living on benefits – reveals:

> I had an unfortunate experience the other day. I don't want to put you off your tea! There was this rather nice little T-shirt, you know, it was a kind of rusty colour which I wanted. New Look. And I tried it on and it fitted very well, and I though – 'oh the smell'. It was like somebody had thrown up on it. But there was no mark on it or anything, and I did say to the person, well it fits OK but it smells a bit. And she said, 'well would you like it for 50p?' And I said, 'no thanks, I don't want it for anything' . . .

Now, what we find insightful about these two extracts is that they show how too much bodily presence, particularly a presence associated with visual and/or olfactory leakiness, works to render garments valueless; potentially even impossible to revalorize. Indeed, in both cases it is important to note that it is not sufficient for shoppers simply to reject these items at a personal level. Instead, both Janet and Barbara make a point of articulating their disapproval to shop volunteers, who are seemingly contaminated by association. When we think back to our discussion of washing and/or steaming in Chapter 3, then, this is shown to be not just a set of practices about establishing appropriate standards of retail display, but one that works to contain risk by working to erase and/or mask bodily traces.

Constituting Self: Body Boundaries/Body Layers

Beyond this though, charity shoppers appear to have distinct limits, boundaries, which they constitute through the purchase of second hand clothing. So, in answer to the question 'is there anything which you'd never look at in a charity shop?', we were consistently and without hesitation told 'underwear' by everyone we interviewed. Moreover, the majority went on to add nightwear, shoes and bedding to their list. As the following extract from an interview with Lydia – a 30-something University technician – reveals, this is about making demarcations between those garments worn closest-in and is inscribed too with strongly normative narratives of personal hygiene:

Kate: Would you buy things like shoes in charity shops?

Lydia: I'd be less happy about shoes to be honest cos of that whole foot infection number. I've had um some bizarre slipper things which came from a retro shop, but they, I think they were actually brand new. I think if it was hiking boots, sort of Doc Marten ones, I'd probably buy them, but then if they were wear next-to-your-skin ones, or sort of court shoes I would think twice about that. But having said that I'd have a pair of shoes off somebody I knew

Kate: Cos you know their infections!

Lydia: Well exactly. But also if you wear other people's shoes they're worn different aren't they, cos it's very personal, how you wear your shoes down

Kate: So it would be the fact that they were worn and also

Lydia: Hygiene

Kate: Hygiene. What about underwear?

Lydia: Well as a rule, most charity shops, well you can't buy sort of, tight-fitting knickers, as a rule. I mean, I'd buy a second hand bra, cos a bra is only [. . .] I think it's all to do with what bits you're exposing. I mean I'd buy cami-knickers, probably, but they're not so tight. But they'd have to be clean. I'd have to wash them before I wore them . . . I wouldn't buy tight knickers [. . .] it's the gusset, it all comes down to gussets!!

But, what this extract also suggests is that charity-shop purchasing appears to be riven through with notions of layering, layers which themselves are constructed in terms of risk and closeness to the body. For some of our more casual charity shoppers, then, the extent of charity-shop purchasing begins and ends at outerwear – coats and jackets. For others, though, it extends to encompass items worn increasingly closer to the skin – jumpers, tops, trousers – and this, we would argue, is a pattern of purchasing that has strong connections with practice. Judy, for example, whom we met earlier in Chapters 3 and 4, began her charity-shopping 'career' buying what we would label as relatively safe items of outerwear, such as a Windsmoor winter coat for £1.50. Later, however, and as her skills and knowledges have developed, she has expanded her purchasing to include more tops, trousers, and the occasional pair of barely worn/unworn shoes/boots. We would interpret this pattern as indicative of a progressive negotiation of the pollution taboos inscribed in various forms of second hand clothing. So, the safest, least risky second-hand garments, we maintain, are those worn furthest away from bodily surfaces – coats, jackets, jumpers. Although worn by others, their inscription with the body of the unknown other is less than that with other clothing categories. Small wonder, then, that these are the purchases which beginning charity shoppers frequently start off by making. By contrast, tops, dresses and trousers are riskier – clothes worn closer-in. Some of them come into close contact with intimate body zones; others have the potential to have absorbed various body fluids, notably perspiration, and – notwithstanding washing – often continue to display traces of these fluids. Purchasing such items, then, requires one to negotiate these pollution threats head-on, to place on one's own bodily surfaces clothing which has been similarly placed on and permeated by an unknown someone else.

There are, however, rather more subtle distinctions at work here too which point to the complex ways in which class and the age of garments might mediate decisions about which commodities are taboo, as the following extract taken from a discussion with Charlie (a 20-something fashion student studying in London) reveals:

> *Charlie*:   If they were unusual I'd buy second hand knickers, but not just cotton briefs.
>
> *Kate:*   Right. What would have to be unusual about them, without being too nosey!
>
> *Charlie:*   They'd have to be a very glamorous-looking French knicker for me to think I'll have them and wash them [. . .] I couldn't buy anything from a second-hand shop that was '90s. It's got to look old . . .

Here we see how temporal distance serves to metaphorically cleanse an under garment, as if time might somehow work to nullify the problematic associations of closeness and intimacy. In a similar way, the following extract from conversation with Rupert – the 20-something graphic design graduate – reveals class distinctions in consuming rituals:

Louise: Is there anything you wouldn't buy at a charity shop?

Rupert: Underwear. Shoes . . .

Louise: What, even if you saw a fantastic pair of Paul Smith pants?

Rupert: Well then I might have to reconsider because, by definition, if they're Paul Smith boxers it's more likely that a young trendy person has worn them as opposed to an 80-year-old granddad that hasn't washed

Louise: So you don't mind the bodily odours of a young person?

Rupert: Well I do mind. It would have to be an exceptional pair. I'd be more likely to buy a designer pair of pants because a young person's worn them. I'd imagine they had better body hygiene and the fact that they're buying designer suggests that they're trying to pull and so they'd be especially careful about washing. They'd be washing hard

Louise: So you don't mind old men's sweat under the armpits on a shirt but you do mind old men's willies and bums?

Rupert: Yes, and I'd always wash it before I put it on. Just in case . . .

Louise: In case of what?

Rupert: In case it's got BO odours and sweatrings and all that clinging to it . . .

Here Rupert reveals the potential for the disruption of the taboos surrounding certain categories of clothing. While in general he makes it clear that he wouldn't consider purchasing underwear in a charity shop, he might make an exception in particular circumstances. And these circumstances depend on his construction of the type of body which he associated with Paul Smith underwear: a youthful, potentially sexual, scrupulously clean body, with which he can identify and which holds less fear for him than certain imagined others – old(er), and by his definition therefore unclean.

Negotiating the Death Taboo: Illness, Disease and Dead People's Clothing

While the pollution/contamination threats of bodily dirt constitute one set of bodily narratives to be negotiated in relation to second hand clothing, the other is that of the association between charity-shop clothing and the material effects of the recently deceased. In the following extract, Tom – the 30-something graduate student/single parent we met in Chapter 4 – wrestles with some of these associations:

Tom: I have quite a lot of clothes for [child's name] from people that I know; things that their children have grown out of, which is really nice.

Nicky: Does that make a difference?

Tom: Yes, definitely

Nicky: In what ways?

Tom: Because I guess that I know the stories behind the clothes, and how they were worn and who wore them, and whatever, and in some way, urm, getting stuff from charity shops has an added excitement to it, what if you know this is from a dead child? What if this is from a dead child and they were wearing it when they died?

That Tom can come up with nothing by way of coherent reasons for why it might matter that these are the clothes someone might have died in is instructive. Probably he is right – there are no logical reasons why it should matter, but in articulating these ideas Tom suggests that somehow, in some imprecise, unspecified way that is impossible to pin down, it does. In part what we think is going on here is a negotiation of suspicion, chance, even luck, and a need to air this discursively, to confront taboos around the wearing of dead people's clothing. Taken to its extremes with Anna – who previously scoured charity shops for shrouds, which were then transformed into dresses – the significance of associations with death is revealed again in the following discussion, this time involving others of an older generation:

Phil: Oh I usually like things I can wash, and if I don't wash them I put them in a plastic bag in the freezer and leave it for a few days.

Kate: Oh right!

Phil: Yes I read in a *Good Housekeeping* or something, because they're good as, then they're germ-free you see

Kate: So what would you put in the freezer then, coats and things?

Phil: I shall put that dress actually, the one I paid out, although it's new I fancy it's got the smell of a charity shop

Judy: Actually knitwear would be quite good

Kate: You don't dry-clean things, then; you'd rather put them in the freezer?

Phil: If I can't put them in the washing machine. They're so expensive, cleaners!

Judy: Like that bear (fur) coat that I bought, it cost me £7 and to clean it would have cost £16! So I just hung it outside! It still smells like someone died in it though. I can't help it, I'm not paying that!

Phil: No I don't blame you, hang it outside in the fresh air on a frosty night, preferably . . .

What we think is going on here is the subconscious re-enactment, the rearticulation, of historical narratives that entwine the clothes of the recently dead with narratives of illness and disease. Certain possession rituals, then – here enacted around coats – would seem to have more than a little to do with oral and/or popular traditions concerning disease-eradication procedures. So, notwithstanding various advances in understanding the processes of disease and virus transmission, and the power of discourses of scientific rationalism, these associations and connections remain, persisting within the popular imagination, particularly among older respondents who remember diseases such as TB and scarlet fever. Second-hand, particularly adults' clothing, then, continues to be inscribed with death and disease, however 'irrational' this might be. And consuming these clothes, consequently, remains construed as a risky practice.

In the previous sections, discussion has focused largely on pre-purchase practices of scrutiny; on the presence/absence of the bodily and the acceptability (or not) of its presence. As important, though, are post-purchasing rituals. And, as we show now, these concern divestment and personalization through cleansing rituals.

Cleansing Rituals: Divestment and Personalization

As almost everyone we spoke with about charity shopping made clear, purchases of charity-shop clothing were taken home and subjected to a range of cleansing rituals.[62] Involving both washing – with one's own particular brand of liquid/softener – and less frequently, dry-cleaning,[63] this is illustrated both in the extract immediately above, and by our conversation with Lily – the fashion student we met earlier:

Lily: I mean I don't buy underwear or anything like that, but I think that once something has been washed and pressed or dry-cleaned and repaired, it's like nobody ever wore it before, and – there have been occasions where I've dry-cleaned something twice!

Kate: What was that?

Lily: The suit I was talking about before, the pink and yellow suit. It
was so lovely but it wasn't quite clean and I just really wanted it
to go through again, I really, really did . . .

Cleansing is the means by which the bodily presence of the unknown
previous owner/s is erased; the means through which the taboos of
wearing other people's clothes are countered; and – simultaneously and
critically – a means of personalizing, of using one's own washing rituals
to make a garment smell as if it belongs. The rituals of cleansing purchases, then, are practices of erasure and reincorporation. They work
to counter the polluting, contaminating threat of this previous unknown
body and to reconstitute clothing through the bodily associations of
the self. Cleansing rituals thus secure a safe, imaginary distance from
previous owner/s. Akin to a process of cooling off, they allow a garment
to shed previous associations; to become a metaphorical clean sheet for
the re-enchantment of meaning. Moreover, cleansing, purifying and
personalizing seemingly work to protect the body's own protective
surface, the skin; to reconstitute it, reconstruct it as a critical boundary,
the imagined container of the self.

Alteration and Repair: On Customization, Making Good and Making Do

The third and final set of possession rituals we consider involve making
an item one's own through either alteration/customization or repair.
The transformative practices we encountered throughout the course of
our research are grounded in sets of practical and/or expert knowledges
that are often, though not exclusively, gender-specific. Such transformations are a means of investing meaning into a commodity, a means
of making it one's own, and possession rituals are thus vital processes
in the personalization of commodities. Many talked, for example, in
some detail about the important and memorable purchases which they
had made, and which in many cases had been carefully repaired or ren-
ovated and now formed part of a collection or display, as the following
reveals:

My more memorable purchases are the bits of bric-a-brac that needed a
bit of care and attention – a bit of repairing and a good scrub and polish
up – my art deco knife set and an unusual deco lamp which needed a bit
of work doing. But I got it for a few pounds and they're fetching 100s
now. It's those kinds of things that are memorable. (Katie)

In terms of specific categories of goods, clothing alterations and transformations are predominantly (though not exclusively) done by women. For some shoppers, the alterations were in order to make a garment fit, or to make it one's own. Lily, for example, tells us about numerous articles of clothing which are altered so that they fit; darts are inserted into men's waistcoats, shoulder seams changed. Here Lily is using her skills as a trainee fashion designer to alter the construction of garments from scratch. In other instances she adds things to garments to personalize them, including fringes on scarves and linings in jackets for example. Such possession and ownership rituals are about saying 'this is mine, this is part of me', which is quite unlike the divestment rituals discussed previously which are about acknowledging that an item belonged to someone else, and has a history of which they weren't part.

For others, transformative work centres less on personalization through stitching-to-fit or on customization as on changing the commodity form. One woman, for example, was clearly tempted by a skirt for £1 that she saw at a car-boot sale: she liked it but was not sure about the size and kept holding it up against herself. Eventually she rationalized her decision to purchase by saying she could always make it up into something else. What is important here is that the consumer has the vision to recognize the potential of a commodity that might not be apparent in its current form and the skill to effect this transformation. And in some instances the resulting transformations can be dramatic: Tina for example bought a skirt that was reworked into a pair of trousers, while Christina reveals that

> I used to pick up the odd quality item, some old lady's sort of tweed jacket which, if you altered it slightly, took the collars off – actually looked quite interesting [. . .] I used to buy quite a lot of, what's the word, gaudy old dresses with bizarre material and then sort of do things with them later on . . . I did buy old ladies' flowery dresses and alter them, use the material actually. And I used to get curtains from charity shops, to sort of decorate rented accommodation, drape them over ugly furniture. (Christina).

And another, Anna (London) told us how in the 1960s she used to buy

> nightdresses, long nightdresses, all types of different nightdresses and dye those all different colours (to wear as) day dresses, yes, and I used to buy laying out gowns [. . .] When they bury people, they lay them out and put them in the gown [. . .] they were beautiful. Cotton. I was thinking

the other day that they'll be nothing like that now, probably paper. But these were cotton with hand embroidery on, hang neck [. . .] with a yoke there and with embroidery here, and puffed sleeves [. . .] they had like cloth buttons, like little flat cloth buttons. I used to dye those and wear those as well.

Anna opted to buy these shapeless gowns in part because she loved the quality and construction of the garments, in part because they were cheap and plentiful ('all like a penny, and tuppence'), and in part because they suited her body at that time, 'you could guarantee that they were going to fit me, they were shapeless and I was dreadfully fat'. In addition Anna also undertook quite dramatic steps to alter garments that were intended for another person, another body, another style:

> we used to buy things from charity shops, me and me mates, and chop them up and put them together in a different way[64] [. . .] You used to get a dress . . . an old fashioned dress with a waist and a belt, and you used to discard the belt, cut it up, cut a chunk up here and move that up there so that it came under the bust so it looked better, so it didn't look so frumpish.

What is important here is that the consumer has both the cultural capital and the skill and ingenuity to recognize the potential of an item that might not be apparent in its current form.

Others, however, are more realistic in their assessments of a garment's transformative potential – and their ability to undertake such work. Judy, for example, tends to buy things that she imagines she will be able to repair and/or transform. In practice though, she rarely gets round to this so things have a habit of remaining in the repair box. And Emma too is interesting in that, while she can see the potential for transformation locked within a second hand garment, she doesn't possess the requisite skills to undertake this work herself, and pays a third party (in this case a male tailor) to undertake the alterations for her:

> This suit [. . .] it was like rent-a-tent, it had lapels over here. But it was the material, it was in such good nick. I saw the material and thought interesting. It cost me a fiver, and he took it in, the trousers were wide, late 60s, but it was such good material so I had covered buttons put on it and the jacket tailored slightly, lapels shortened. It's amazing the different look. I mean there'll be some sort of Crimplene dress or something and it'll be a complete granny dress, like down to your shins,

and I know immediately that once that's taken up it'll look like a little
60s dress. A world of difference. It's just knowing what you're looking
for (Emma, Manchester).

The significant point here, it seems to us, is that such tailoring skills
seem to be decline at present, in part because people have less time on
their hands (as Anna says, 'I can't even bear to stitch buttons on nowadays, I don't have time'), in part because the clothing industry is in
decline nationally and therefore there are fewer demands for sewing
skills in the workplace, and also because stitching, sewing and making-
up skills are practised less familially in the home and formally through
education. Speculating further, it would seem likely that as such skills
decline, so alteration work will increasingly be undertaken via the paid
labour power of skilled third parties, which both increases the relative
cost of a second hand garment and, potentially at least, erases one
process of commodity meaning-creation, that of possession rituals
through alteration and transformation. In terms of personalization and
possession, the demise of such skills might reduce the meaningfulness
of second-hand commodities that are transformed by the anonymous
hand of a commercial third party.

For other commodity groups, including here homeware and decor-
ative items, similar transformations in commodity form are evident.
Rehmana and Clare, for example, both bought domestic table lamps
at car-boot sales. In both cases the lamps were bought for their bases,
and were subsequently altered and customized in line with their taste
and aesthetic preferences. For other commodities, though, restoration
and repair are undertaken not for display or aesthetics but for use.
Electrical items, hi-fi systems, televisions, lawn mowers and bicycles are
all examples of goods we witnessed being bought extremely cheaply
at car-boot sales,[65] in many instances by those whose comments made
it transparent that they had the practical skills and/or the equipment
to (attempt to) get them working again: Mr Brown, for example, from
Nottingham is an ex-electrician and buys bits of plugs and wire at car-
boot sales to repair or restore other commodities; and the previously
discussed instances of the solder and the battery-operated bicycle also
reveal repair/transformation for use. But, while these rituals are
governed primarily by utilitarian and instrumentalist considerations,
and – unlike our clothing examples above – are seemingly unfettered
by questions of aesthetics, fit or embodiment, there are nonetheless
parallels between the two commodity groups, in that both rely on
specialist knowledge, on investments of time in undertaking repair

work, and on risk, in that there is a chance that the items will never work (in the case of tools or equipment), will never fit (in the case of clothes), will never be aesthetically right (in the case of transformed clothes, ornaments, homeware) or will never justify the time involved in making them right, their fate consigned to the sewing box, the shed, the garage or the attic.

Spaces of Juxtaposition and Display

While the possession rituals discussed above are key moments in revalorization and, as such, are critical in shaping the biographies of things, it is important to note that they frequently connect too with post-transformation practices that themselves foreground the significance of revalorization and recovery. And so while alteration, transformation and repair revalorize a commodity at a particular moment in time and space, the ongoing practices of wearing, displaying and using transformed commodities further adds value. In particular, here, we see how recovered goods tend to be incorporated within consumption practices that juxtapose 'the new' with second-hand, in ways that enable both to comment relationally (and spatially) about each other, and in turn about the subject. In general terms, and in the particular case of clothing, there was evidence throughout our work that few people desired to dress entirely in second-hand clothes. This, it was commonly argued, would be read as signalling poverty and exclusion from first-cycle consumption spaces. Indeed, Tom, the fine art student from Nottingham, and Christine (Chapter 4) are the only examples we came across of people who buy and wear exclusively second-hand. Others, though, such as Christina and Jane, talk poignantly about the difficulties of achieving respectability through exclusively second hand clothing. So, when second-hand consumption is induced through poverty, as in Christina's case, there is little evidence of playful juxtaposition. Instead, respectability is sought by matching cheap 'new' goods (underwear and T-shirts) with second hand staples (trousers, coats). A far more widespread tendency within our respondent group, though, is for people to juxtapose new with second-hand in ways that are about fashion and style. Lily is a good example of this, in that she argues that she would never dress entirely in second-hand for fear of looking 'like a tramp'. So Lily teams the jacket from her Chanel look-alike Oxfam suit with jeans, and the skirt with 'black tights and a black jumper which looks really cute, really really cute'. She similarly juxtaposed new with old in putting together an outfit for Ascot:

I wore an outfit that everybody loved, absolutely loved. It was a themed outfit. The dress was a Nicole Farhi flapper dress that I bought at a warehouse six months beforehand, knowing I'd wear it on an occasion at some point, it was too beautiful to pass up. And I bought a hat from Liberty, which was my only real extravagance, which looked fabulous. I had a white scarf, which I attached a fringe to, to give it a fringed look for the '20s, and a little white bag that I bought from the high street, and little shoes. . .and a long string of pearls which my dad lent me, which were costume jewellery which reached my knees [. . .] I was photographed in the *Telegraph* which was rather nice.

Here then we see how Lily mixes designer second-hand (the dress), with designer new (the hat), with high street new (the shoes and bag), with customized old (the scarf) and with borrowed old (the pearls) to create a look which reveals her unique style and fashion knowledge. Rupert too, formerly a creative student like Lily, also juxtaposes new clothes with old, as shown in Plate 6.1. Here we see Rupert in his prized charity-shop Johnson Control shirt, which he teamed up with French Connection jeans and Nike Shox trainers. Our interpretation of these practices would be to argue that to dress entirely in Johnson Control-type second-hand workmen's wear would run the risk of being seen to be a manual worker, rather than the professional creative worker that he is. So what we feel appears to be going on here is a practice of wearing which signals that new clothes lack the temporal archaeologies associated with the second-hand Johnson Control shirt – and all of the style and taste associations which go with this – but that 'the new' offers something else in this display strategy, namely the stylistic safety net the brand confers, which cannot easily be achieved through dressing entirely in second-hand. The Johnson Control shirt seems to us to refract knowingly against the brands and is being used to frame a particular reading of personal style that also demonstrates a sophisticated awareness of, and commentary on, fashion and style.

And a similar story is evident too in the spaces of the home, whereby juxtaposition of new with old provides both stylistic safety and also a level of utility not possible through the second-hand world alone. So that while many interviewees adorn their home with second hand artefacts, and display these appropriately and knowingly, few (with the exception perhaps of Josephine and Ian who lived in a shrine to the '60s, with period kitchen equipment and no central heating) can or do live without contemporary domestic commodities such as up-to-date sound systems, televisions, microwaves and so on, and many juxtapose

Plate 6.1 Rupert

key second-hand pieces with new and/or repro goods from mass-market stores such as Ikea and Habitat. Here again we see how the brand and aesthetic of the new provides a safe commentary on the taste and design credentials of the old.

Conclusions

There are three sets of conclusions we want to draw from the above analysis. One relates to theoretical reflections on commodity biographies, the second concerns the embodied geographies of second-hand, and the third and final is about agency, consumer:object relations, meaning and value creation.

First, then, in this chapter we have tried to move toward a more theoretically aware 'biographical' model by presenting the full range of
biographical transformations which commodities undertake, exploring
the ways in which particular moments in a commodity's life story are
realized: what has a commodity's career been to date, and how significant is this in informing decisions about how to make it one's own?
What are the recognized significant moments in a commodity's life and
what are the cultural markers for them? How do commodities change
through time and space and in relation to different episodes of ownership? And for us the key thing here in shaping value is the various ways
in which commodities are adopted, changed, put to use, culturally redefined. And we would argue that, for the majority of the material
commodities in which we are interested here, biographies can only ever
be partial. From last chapter's discussion of rubbish and junk, through
to this chapter's discussion of rituals of possession, and on into next
chapter's discussion of collecting and gifting, there still remains a sense
in which these moments and movements are a partial view – who knows
what will happen to the clothes and artefacts made one's own and transformed when their owner dies, moves or no longer sees any use or value?
And what will happen to the everyday clothes and commodities of
today? These are invisible and undeterminable future biographies,
unpredictable chapters in a journey still yet to be written. All commodities have social, technical, cultural and economic biographies; they mean
different things to different people at different times and in different
places, classified and reclassified into endlessly reconstituted cultural
categories (Koptyoff, 1986: 68).

Secondly, we want to reflect on the complex ways in which value is
inscribed in second-hand adult clothing and its intimate connections
with the body. As we have seen, in the space of the charity shop both
second-hand exchange value and use values rest on the presence/
absence and/or erasure of previous traces of ownership and consumption. Clothes which look 'as new', which have been barely worn, and/
or which don't betray traces of wearing, command a higher price in
charity shops than those which do. Moreover, in order to wear these
clothes, to open them up to re-enchantment through consumption and
to access their second-hand use value, it is frequently deemed necessary
to undertake cleansing and purifying rituals. Although, as we have
noted, even these practices fail to re-enchant certain categories of clothing, notably underwear and night attire. So, the value of second-hand
adult clothing can be seen to vary: some categories are valueless, others
have greater value, but seemingly this value is in all cases mediated

through bodily presences/absences, rather than, as with first-cycle clothing, simply production costs or the brand.

And yet, as our research suggests, this isn't quite all there is to second-hand adult clothing. Indeed, garments such as Victorian underwear, night shirts and so on, the very categories of closest-in clothing which cause problems, become prized and sought-after in a retro or vintage setting even though the practices of washing, laundering and dry-cleaning might be considered to be potentially damaging to such items. And this is important. It is as if distance, history and the authenticity encoded in such purchases override the potential contamination of the bodily here; as if the bodily loses its potential to contaminate with temporal distance; as if time enables commodities to cool off, to be decontaminated, deactivated. Whereas, with charity-shop purchases no such mediations exist. Instead, by comparison, the majority of goods sold therein are of a relatively recent vintage, mass-produced, closely entwined with the presence of their previous owner/s – and therefore requiring acts of symbolic release. So we would suggest that space here matters to the ways in which the bodily gets entwined within second-hand clothing. And – unlike retro/vintage shops – charity shops, we maintain, are constructed negatively in relation to the body. Bodily dirt, contamination, pollution, these are ever constant threats within charity shops – associations which they continually have to negotiate and counter, which permeate and threaten to contaminate the goods they sell and which consequently loom large in the purchasing and consumption practices of charity shoppers themselves. This is, then, a combination which places an emphasis on practices of containment and metaphorical layering; which reconstitutes the body as a surface capable of infiltration, porous, and consequently requiring protection, protection from the lingering traces of the bodily presences of the unknown Other caught between the weft and the weave.

Clothing, then, is not just about fashion and adornment, body shape, disguise and aesthetics, or even functionality, but is an extension of our own corporeality. It becomes us; we personalize it and possess it through our own leakiness. And this corporeal presence matters. It is what makes the recent discards of the unknown Other so troublesome. Corporeal presence then, the personalization and possession which remains trapped in the cloth, is critical to the exchange and consumption of second-hand clothing. Indeed, it is what makes second-hand adult clothing a unique category of second-hand good.

Thirdly, and finally, we want to reflect on questions of value, agency and meaning-creation. In spite of the enormous momentum of the value-homogenizing attempts of big retail capital, individual agency retains some power in the interstices, in second-hand spaces where multiple means of value-creation are possible. Individuals hold the power to singularize commodified goods, to recommodify notionally terminal goods and to decommodify notionally worthless objects. Through both culture and cognition, the biography of things evolves in quite unpredictable and inconsistent ways. Commodity value shifts contextually and biographically as individuals undergo rituals resulting in singularization and sacredization, and as objects are pulled into (and out of) their usual commodity sphere. Further, we would argue that quite unlike Marxian accounts of value, where fetishism masks the social relations of production and makes the production process (wherein value is created) remote and misperceived; our work offers a useful corrective and suggests that power and value can be imbued in commodities long after the original production has ceased, through cycles of use, transformation and reuse. And thus individuals act as counter-forces to retail commodification and massification – by their actions to discriminate, classify, reify and singularize commodities, in short to mark themselves out, through their purchase, use and display of commodities, as different.

Gifting and Collecting

Introduction

The previous two chapters have examined movements into and out of second-hand worlds, both journeys of disposal and transformative practices. In both cases, though, we have been interested in circumstances where the relationship to second-hand goods is largely personal and individual, where objects come into (and out of) individual's ownership and possession rituals, and where it is primarily 'the consumer' who decides on purchase and its links to recovery, divestment and disposal.[66] In the final chapter in this section we turn to consider two distinctive variations to these practices, where this nexus is disrupted. Our focus here is on 'gifting' – where the object is constituted through and comes to encode the relationship to (significant) others – and 'collecting' – where ownership conventionally is divorced from 'use' through the special status accorded 'the collection'.

In addressing gifting and collecting together, however, we are developing an argument that goes beyond ownership and questions of inalienability, and beyond traditional long-established arguments about the 'sacredness' of 'the gift' and 'the collection'. So, whilst we acknowledge that 'the gift' and the object in 'the collection' constitute examples of bounded-objects, where transformation, alteration and cannibalization are regarded as inappropriate practices, we want to argue too that they share a highly particular time-space frame that makes their joint consideration appropriate here. Both 'the gift' and 'the collection', then, are locked into a time-space 'freeze', where objects are locked out of the commodity sphere through relations that both make their return frequently problematic and that work to hold their time-space trajectories in suspended animation. Think, for example, of classic instances of individual's collections – stamps in albums, coins in display boxes, books on shelves and so on. Locked into particular spatialized arrangements, these are corralled by their keepers in ways that frame their significance and control their biographies, often long after the death of their keeper. Similarly with 'the gift', where the significance of the relationship to exchange works in many cases to hold objects within particular domestic spaces – even in storage spaces such as lofts, garages and the backs of wardrobes and drawers – long past when they might otherwise have been discarded.

There is, then, a theoretical rationale for our juxtapositon of gifting and collecting, but there are also empirical ones. One, of course, is the frequent elision between 'the gift' and 'the collection', the practice through which 'the collection' becomes the basis for 'the gift'. Already well rehearsed in the literature (see Belk, 1995), we do not discuss this further here, beyond noting its existence. A second, however, and our focus here, is the difference that the second-hand arenas that we are interested in make to the practices of gifting and collecting. As we show in this chapter, gifting is not a common practice associated with these arenas, and when it does occur it is located primarily outside of the conventional gift economy of Christmas and birthdays. This is important: not only does it indicate the immense difficulty that second-hand worlds like these pose to providing acceptable gifts in a gift economy that is striated by mass consumption – notably the impossibility of acquiring the latest children's toys through such arenas – but it signals too that 'the gift' here is about a gift of the giver's skills and pleasures in shopping, as much as the object itself. Gifting here thus is often about small items, classically of the 'I saw this and thought of you' variety, or of 'unexpected' and/or amusing 'finds' that work to materialize particular social relationships and networks. More rarely, though, it can work as a disguised form of 'disposal', where inappropriate purchases – mistakes – are offered to others, at least before being returned to the (nearest) charity shop. Generally, though, gifting through these arenas is argued to be connected intrinsically with particular sorts of commodities – books, bric-a-brac and baby clothes – and not others, adults' clothing being the most significant omission. In the object of 'the gift', then, we see once more how certain second-hand goods – particularly certain categories of clothing – are frequently deemed too risky to purchase for (significant) others, and how the rituals of unlocking meaning, recovery and divestment that are key consumption practices in these arenas are themselves intensely personal acts of consumption.

In comparison, at least for those with the money to spare, collecting is a common practice within these particular second-hand worlds. Again though, these sites are argued to exert a critical set of influences on practice. We argue here, then, that collecting through charity shops, car-boot sales and some retro shops is a creative way of regulating exchange (Miller, 1987), a way of constricting and controlling purchasing possibilities, both through the object and the time discipline of its purchase. Moreover, we go on to suggest that there are differences too in the consumption practices of collecting. So, whilst some of the collections amassed through these spaces are subjected, as per convention, to sacralisation and display, others are shown to be collections-in-use. Furthermore, we argue that these forms of collecting work not simply as individual acts of collection but as socially regulated consumption practices (Koptyoff, 1986); that they are embedded within particular 'taste and display' communities that themselves are about specific combinations of risk and certitude. Finally, we show how at least some of these collections are rather more vulnerable to the loss of 'aura' and disposal than their more rarefied counterparts collected through the more elite spaces of art houses, antique and collectors' fairs and certain auction houses, but that – while collections may be cast out – what remains is the practice of collecting. We conclude the chapter therefore by arguing that, like gifting, these forms of collecting display traces in practice of the second-hand worlds that constitute them. In the context of these worlds, gifting and collecting respectively suggest both the limits and the possibilities of practice: where one is foreclosed by these worlds, the other seemingly is enabled to the point that 'the collection' itself maybe subverted, destroyed and disposed – re-assigned to 'rubbish'.

Hard Gift-work and the Limits of the Possible

Gifting is one specific consumption practice that has been afforded considerable attention in the literature. Traditional anthropological studies in particular have explored the ways in which gift-giving comprises both altruism and egoism, and how it is simultaneously a form of exchange, of social communication and of socialization (Gregory, 1982; Malinowski, 1922; Mauss, 1966; Strathern, 1988). Much of the literature on the gift attempts to break out of the duality between gifting (with its associations of reciprocity, sociability and spontaneity) and commodity exchange (with its emphasis on profit, egotism and instrumentalism) and stresses certain parallels between gift exchange and more ostensibly economic practices (Appadurai, 1986; Bourdieu, 1977; Mauss, 1976). This it does by developing an exchange model of gifting. Under this conceptualization ritual consumption festivals such as Birthdays, Valentine's Day and Christmas are interpreted as festivals celebrating hedonism and materialism, where the gifts given are intended as much to reveal the social standing of the giver as to demonstrate unselfish love to the recipient (Thrift and Olds, Miller, 1993; Belk, 1987; Sherry and McGrath, 1989). One discernible thread running through the literature on gift-giving, particularly that relating to ritual celebrations, is the way in which gifting is seen as a frustrating, resented or hostile act. Certainly, in relation to events such as Christmas, the substantial consumption work involved in finding appropriate presents – not to mention the enormous financial outlay involved – arguably represents a bind and a chore. Akin to domestic provisioning through household food shopping, and with all of the associated gender connotations, gift-buying here is seen as indicative of the hard work that characterizes much consumption, and specifically second-hand consumption (Sherry, McGrath and Levy, 1992, 1993). Such studies have assumed an exchange model of gifting, which sees the practice as instrumental (designed and purposive), rational, dispassionate, pragmatic, reciprocal, egotistic and giver-dominant (Belk and Coon, 1993). Far from shopping for love, or unselfishly buying for others, gift-buying under this model involves the hard labour and financial excesses of economic one-upmanship, where the commodity is reflective of the social standing of the giver and demands appropriate recompense via equivalent reciprocal gifts. Taken one step further, and when extended to self gifts too, such approaches go as far as to pathologize gifting: shrouded in a rhetoric of deservingness and bound up as part of broader processes of motivational bargaining, gifting under this conceptualization becomes part of a process of consumptional mental accounting or just rewards: the father who buys a child a car for passing exams, the rewards for children's good behaviour that Santa Claus bestows, the therapeutic mood-enhancing gifts we buy for ourselves when we have done badly, are low, lonely. Founded on notions of treat and reward, gifting here is argued by some to lead to compulsive consumption behaviour, to self-indugence, to greed, yet ultimately, always, to disatisfaction: the reward is never enough, the satisfaction remains elusive (Baker, 2000). The conflation of the gift with the exchanged commodity is, under such models, complete.

And yet as was alluded to in the introduction, we are offering a somewhat different take on gifting to that which is presented in much of the literature. Specifically here, we want to disrupt the conjoining of gift and commodity exchange which is apparent in such constructs. And while we would not wish to advocate a return to duality, we would argue that gifting within the second-hand arena is markedly distinctive in its practices, motivations and dispositions; it cannot be simply and straightforwardly reduced to an instrumentalist, rational and economically symbolic act. And so when one shifts the focus from first-cycle consumption spaces to second-hand sites, a rather different picture emerges. For sure, many of the financial and time difficulties associated with provisioning for ritual festivals that are encountered in the first-cycle retail world are every bit as evident in second-hand spaces: to try to 'do' Christmas through the purchase of second-hand gifts would be almost impossible; it would certainly be exceedingly time-consuming. This is undoubtedly why we encountered very few people throughout the course of our research who routinely engage in wholesale second-hand gift-buying for festivals such as Christmas.[67] But if we broaden our focus to take in presents bought for others outside of the commercialized giving-festivals a rather different take on second-hand gifting begins to emerge. Here we are not talking about envy provocation and giver-dominant modes of gifting where the donor seeks control and command. Rather, gifting within second-hand spaces is more akin to the agapic love paradigm which is expressive, spontaneous, emotional and altruistic (Belk and Coon, 1993). And what we find here is a process of looking, buying and giving to others which creates or strengthens a symbolic link between the donor and recipient (Miller, 1998). Less about reciprocity and dispassionate instrumentality, the gifting here encountered is a process where money and the economic value of the commodity becomes irrelevant but where the symbolic commodity value takes on great significance. This is about taking delight in serendipitously finding the perfect gift for a loved one, the gift which is unique, spontaneous, a treat, just right. And here too we have a search process which is devoid of the notions of drudge and labour which typify accounts of gift-buying in first-cycle spaces, but which is, rather, characterized by fun, delight and pleasure.

Katie, for example, an academic from Nottingham who regularly purchases at car-boot sales, reveals the pleasure she derives from seeking out second-hand gifts. Katie particularly enjoys gifting carefully chosen second-hand commodities including antique silver spoons and glassware to close friends and relatives. The time involved in the selection, alteration, renovation and often personalization of such gifts represents a significant, non-monetary investment which, for her, enhances the meaningfulness of the act. The pleasure derived from the selection and giving of affordable yet highly personalized gifts was reiterated in the following extract too from Maureen, a grandmother from Nottingham:

I've got four grandchildren . . . I get pleasure from buying them presents. I love giving them things [. . .] I remember I bought an absolutely beautiful pink and white organza girls dress. It was fit for a princess. New and so cheap. The woman had bought it when she was pregnant. She wanted a little girl but had a boy!

Others talk about how buying for others at second-hand sites both makes people more generous and alters the nature of the gift. Lucy, a student from Nottingham, buys anything she likes: 'We just used to go and distribute it around because it was so cheap. Whatever we saw and we liked we'd just stuff in a bag and if it didn't fit us we'd give it to our friends'. Another interviewee, this time an elderly man, talked about the pleasure he derives from buying for others. He had, for example, found 'a set of Mills and Boon books to give to Lily downstairs, a lovely lady who can't get out now'. The set were wrapped up in a Nettos bag and they were to be a gift to Lily. He often did this and would never accept payment 'after all, they've cost me nowt and I've had the pleasure of getting out and talking to people for most of the morning'.

Others talk more in terms of treats: as Simon, the student from Sheffield reveals, the gifts he buys are not necessary purchases which come with the gloom of obligation but are random surprise presents:

I bought a lot of ski-wear. I bought a pair of salopettes – I treated my girlfriend. They were £6, and a ski suit that was £10 [. . .] I bought my brother a Ralph Lauren shirt for like £1.50 and like there was nothing wrong with it other than the person had probably grown out of it or lobbed it away or whatever [. . .] If I was to go into a charity shop with a girl then I would then flick through some of the girl's stuff to see if I saw anything that I thought she might like.

And we see too how fun infuses the gifting process in second-hand spaces, where prices are negligible and small finds become amusing mementoes, a source of shared jokes and amusing memories, as Simon explains:

I bought a couple of these (CDs) as a joke: cos like for 25p they're quite amusing [. . .] There's a girl in Christian Union who we decided to call Lulu because they said she looked like Lulu, and it just became a standard sort of joke for a while, not for very long. And when I was in a charity shop I saw these two Lulu singles – two for 25p – and so I bought them, wrapped them up for her, put a big bow on them – special gift sort of thing. So that was 25p well spent.

In all of these extracts, we see how the language of second-hand gifting practices reveals its pleasures and its fun: it is framed in terms of thoughtful practice, a treat, stumbling across something that a specific someone might just like. For these individuals it is the pleasures in the practice of consumption that explains their gift-giving behaviour; the ritual and delight of seeking out presents becomes almost more important than the object itself. The real gift here, then, is the process of selecting and giving, not the commodity itself. The gift itself is merely the tangible symbol of the social relation. And so even for those who talk about the considerable labour involved in the pre-purchase (selection) and post-purchase (transformation) phase of second-hand gifting, there is evidence too in their talk that this is an activity that gives them pleasure and endorses the ways in which second-hand gifts can be highly personalized, meaningful commodities – none binding tokens through which social relations are enacted. The following extract from Pat, a retired Yorkshire GP's wife who often buys gifts at car-boot sales, reveals the pleasure she derives from investing time and effort in second-hand gift giving:

> We buy things to renovate, to re-cover or repair and then give them away as gifts. Its more work for us but it keeps us happy and we feel our presents are really personal and thoughtful.

And yet we stand by the proviso that we raised at the outset that gifting in second-hand worlds can be a fraught, time-consuming and frustrating exercise – in short, hard consumption work – and qualify our discussion of pleasure and fun with the clear proviso that this form of participation can only extend to those with the requisite financial wherewithal and often the appropriate class position too. For certain of our interviewees, who buy second-hand for largely financial reasons – i.e. through necessity as much as through desire – it would be impossible to enjoy the pleasures and treats associated with 'fun' gifting since spare cash for such purchases is simply not available. Shopping for need, we maintain, largely excludes one from participating in unnecessary and frivolous second-hand treating for others. A second proviso, and linked to the above, is that this type of gifting practice depends upon a certain middle-class subject position which deems such consumption behaviour appropriate. It depends, in short, on a particular aesthetic connection between giver and recipient, both of whom must 'see' the practice as appropriate. This is in many ways an extension of 'clever shopping' in which gifting gets constituted as a game that tests participants' skills through careful selection. By contrast, such practices would be deemed highly inappropriate by certain taste communities, and specifically by those poorer shoppers who see second-hand gifting as evidence of financial poverty and exclusion from first-cycle consumption spaces. In short, they could be read from this subject position as a cheap shot, as miserly, as evidence of poverty and as a sign that the giver undervalues the recipient. Under the shopping-for-need model, we maintain that appropriate gifting practices are directly and positively related to spend.

Such comments endorse the ways in which second-hand worlds place both possibilities and also, however, real limits on what is possible for certain subject positions in terms of gifting. Certain forms of gifting, we would argue, are almost impossible in the second-hand arena, and certain commodity categories are deemed almost un-giftable. Here we would identify three particular limits of the possible in terms of second-hand gift practices. The first relates to taste communities and social networks, the second concerns the temporalities of key gifting rituals and the third involves class position and questions of respectability. We shall take each in turn.

The first notable example of these limits in practice relates to adult clothing which, on the whole, is rarely gifted. There are three sets of reasons for this. First, there is the obvious difficulty in finding garments that fit. Secondly, and perhaps of greater significance, are the ways in which second hand clothes are deemed risky and dangerous because of their previous bodily associations with unknown others. To gift old clothes to another is altogether too difficult, too dangerous, potentially too insulting, for who knows where these clothes have been, whose bodies they have adorned, whose bodily traces may linger on in the weft and weave of the fabric?[68] Thirdly, and most significant of all, are the difficulties that second hand clothes pose in terms of matching distinctive and personal fashion tastes. Such difficulties make the gifting of second hand clothes an anxious and testing process which few part-icipate in. And those who do engage in these practices reveal just how important shared taste communities are to this kind of gifting. Indeed, the only examples we encountered of individuals gifting second hand clothes were those who were buying for significant others, usually their partners or close friends. Margi, for example, bought a Jean Paul Gaultier shirt for her partner and she has bought a few items over the years for her good friend Trish. Simon too talks about buying ski-wear for his girlfriend, Tom discusses buying jumpers for his girlfriend and Anna tells how she always looks for things with her partner in mind and recently bought him some Chinos. Anna Barratt is also instructive in her discussions about gifting clothes arguing that 'I might buy something for Claire (daughter) but no, on the whole I don't . . . because I don't really know anyone else who likes these weird things that much. But Claire and I have got very similar taste so I'd be quite happy buying things for her, but not anyone else'. What these examples suggest is that few people take the risk of buying second hand clothing as gifts for others, and those that do participate in such practices in ways which endorse and mark out key social relations of love for significant others. The gifting of second hand clothing involves overcoming one's anxieties about appropriate selection and taste. It relies, then, on certitude in relation to shared-taste communities among friendship and kin groups and on aesthetic knowledges about identity and taste. In this way we see how the gifting of second-hand adult clothes marks out key distinctions within social networks.

The second limit of the possible in terms of gifting practices relates to key consumption rituals and the problems that these pose for second-hand gift economies. The difficulties here can be most vividly illustrated with reference to Christmas, but the arguments apply equally well to other key moments in the gift economy such as birthdays, Valentine's Day, Mothering Sunday, Christenings or the birth of a new baby. These key points in the gift economy are fixed in time and space, they are non-negotiable and require the consumer to gift at precise moments. This in turn poses severe limitations on what is possible in terms of gifting through second-hand. The first and most obvious point is that to gift appropriately for Christmas through second-hand would probably involve searching for most of the year in a way which would be onerous, time-consuming and frustrating, in which case it becomes barely distinguishable from ongoing household provisioning modes of consumption. Secondly, and perhaps more significantly, Christmas involves, for a great many people, buying not only for significant others but primarily for children, many of whom ask specifically for things that they (really really) want, which may involve reference to particular consumer catalogues such as Argos, to television advertising campaigns and to peer-group pressure. Children's Christmas lists are often specified in precise and detailed ways. They are often written down and posted to Santa Claus, and expectations run high. All of this of course is in turn bound up with the rhythms of product life cycles and is reinforced by powerful and pervasive advertising drives on the part of toy, game and clothing manufacturers and retailers. As a result it becomes impossible to satisfy the latest craze through second-hand, as such statement products are simply not available in the second-hand arena. And not engaging with such ratcheting-up of demand at key moments in the calendar runs the risk of one's being deemed an inappropriate parent. Here, then, we see with some clarity the limits of what is possible in terms of second-hand gifting for key exchange rituals. Such constraints operate too in the case of Christmas shopping for adults, although perhaps less vividly. While it is theoretically possible to step outside such commercialized rituals and to cancel Christmas, to postpone buying until the January sales or to place and agree prescribed limits on spend per person, this rarely occurs in practice and still relies on careful choice even within prescribed price points, choices which may simply not be forthcoming in second-hand spaces.

Thirdly, and finally, we maintain that the limits of gifting through second-hand are deeply connected to class identity and subject position. And so while second-hand gifting might be possible, defining even, of certain middle-class aesthetic sensibilities, gifting through second-hand is a practice that rarely occurs among working-class families and friend-ship groups. To do so would be read as a sign of meanness and would signal a lack of respectability. It would just be too risky, not simply in the taste sense discussed above, but in terms of appropriate outlays. Within such taste communities it is important to engage in spending that is appropriate, excessive even, precisely because this is taken to be a signal that certain people matter, even if such excessive consumption is at the cost of debt and deprivation.

In these various ways then, we have shown how the selling space, the time cycle, the commodity-type and the rituals of temporality influence what is possible – and what not – in terms of second-hand gifting. And what this approach has enabled us to do is to look less at the commodity itself and more at the ritual of giving. It has also exposed quite clearly the limitations to gifting in second-hand worlds, and the flaws and failings in conventional narratives of the gift: all too commonly reduced to economic transactions within conventional models, we have endeav-oured to decouple the gift from the commodity, to restore the cultural dimension to gifting practices. More generally, what the above discus-sion has revealed is that consumers at second-hand sites become agents for the transfer of meaning, in that they selectively distribute certain goods with certain properties to recipients who may or may not have otherwise chosen them – and who may or may not want them (Belk, 1995a, 1995b). And quite what the recipient does with such gifts pro-vides the basis for the next episode in a commodity's journey – perhaps it will be stored or stashed, hidden from view, the unwanted discards of a chance purchase; perhaps it will be discarded, back into the charity shop, car-boot sale, bin or skip; perhaps it will, in turn, be given as a present to another; or perhaps it will be displayed, treasured, sacralized, to form part of a collection. It is to this that we now turn.

Collecting through Second-hand Worlds: the Practice of the Possible

Collecting, like gifting, is a specific consumption practice to which much attention has been given. Identified as a metaphor for 'our times' (Belk, 1995; Pearce, 1995), this is a practice that is widely represented in the literature as about the selection of areas of collecting and the production of 'the collection' by an 'empowered (priestly) collector' (Belk, 1995: 62), who works in a socially sanctioned manner both to salvage and to sacralize objects, to produce 'aura' (Kopytoff, 1986). Collecting then is seen to be intrinsically about the constitution of boundaries and borders, both around objects and to differentiate between them; through 'the collection' it simultaneously defines-in and separates out, and is considered to remove objects from the sphere of 'ordinary use' (Belk, 1995; Pearce, 1995). At the same time as forwarding a particular representation of collecting practices, however, this same literature has popularized a specific reading of the types of second-hand sites that we have been concerned with here, as sites where goods are defined as 'rubbish'. Pearce, for example, characterizes charity shops and car-boot sales, as well as house-clearance auctions and junk shops, as 'the characteristic locations of rubbish' (p 386). Collectors, then, are seen within this literature to be in possession of knowledge/s that enable them to see and select, to rescue goods from certain second-hand worlds which represent the unknowing repositories of the detritus of 'the consumer society' – and which certainly are constituted as worlds away from the elite auction rooms, art houses and trade fairs, and as the very antithesis to the temple to collecting, the museum. As well as inaccurate and possibly nostalgic (for a time when car-boot sales and charity shops were happier 'hunting grounds' for this form of collecting), this literature pedals a particular binary between those who collect and those who do not, and locates collecting's significance primarily in the object and the collection.

By comparison, we want to argue here that those who describe their relationship to second-hand goods – if not themselves – in terms of 'collecting' are using this consumption practice not simply to produce and service 'the collection'. Rather, we maintain that collecting is intrinsically both about controlling exchange and embedded it in consumption rituals that go beyond building 'the collection'. So, we demonstrate here that collecting works in these arenas as a way of selecting and controlling what to buy in charity shops, car-boot sales and the like, and as a ritual of participation; that it is embedded in practices that blur the conventional association of collecting with non-use; and that it is an intensely personal activity that sets clear regulatory limits around other peoples' collecting practices. Finally, we show that 'collecting' here is not the one-way 'traffic' to 'aura' that so much of the literature tends to assume, but that 'aura' can indeed be lost and collections disposed of, but that what remains is the ritual of collecting, the consumption practice.

Creative Control and Rituals of Purchasing: Constituting Limits to Purchase through Collecting

In the course of this research we encountered an enormous variety of 'collections', encompassing the highly predictable – for example, books, vinyl and 'collectables' – through to the idiosyncratic. The list, then, is as diverse as it is possible to imagine, from domestic irons, telephones and knitting patterns, through to 'fuzzy felts', postcards and photo cubes. And in a sense this is important; collected only from charity shops, car-boot sales and retro shops – as well as the occasional jumble sale – it means that virtually anything 'for sale' at such sites is open to revalorization through collecting. But what is common to all these collections is the spontaneity of their instigation. Indeed, rather than according with conventions of rarity and prescribed value regimes, most of those we spoke with articulated how their 'collections' had suggested themselves to them. Steven for example – the artist we met initially in Chapter 4 – talks about 'the random collection of the charity shop' as providing the impetus for his subsequent collecting, and of how his collection of photo cubes started because 'I hadn't seen them anywhere else but my grandmother's mantelpiece, she had two'. From nostalgia has come five years of collecting and 25 to 30 pieces. Similarly with Sue – from the group of Bristol-based friends. Here 'snowdomes' and 1970s annuals and books are a nostalgic invocation of childhood, again suggested by an initial find. Diane – whose increasing immersion in the 1960s we referred to in the previous chapter – collects album covers. Suggestion for her is all about visual appeal; as it is in a very different

way for Val, whose interest in cats provided the trigger to a collection
of a wide range of domestic goods (mugs, teapots, toasters, etc.) either
'with a cat on them, or shaped like a cat'. In these, and many other
cases like them, the initial purchase provided the means to suggesting
and then defining the content of 'the collection'; but what it provides
too, as we show now, is a means of defining out other goods – of controlling purchasing in these arenas – and the basis for a particular ritual
of participation.

Lydia is in her early 30s and a media technician working in a university setting in Derby. Unlike the vast majority of our respondents,
her interest in second-hand clothing is marginal, and instead she scours
charity shops looking for books and particular sorts of bric-a-brac – cups
and saucers and Pyrex dishes for instance. She is an avid collector of
books and it is this that provides the basis for her practices of looking
through second-hand sites. As we see in the following extract, particular
authors at particular times provide both the key to how she looks and
the control, yet they also work to constitute collecting practices as 'the
hunt':

> . . . cos I used to collect Agatha Christie books [. . .] and you'd go in and
> for you know, six months there may not be one there at all that you
> haven't got, and then all of a sudden the last one you want is THERE!

A core metaphor for many collectors – as others have noted – the
attractions of 'the hunt' were articulated by many others we spoke with.
Mark, for instance, who collects coloured irons and plastics from the
1950s, talks explicitly of 'collecting as hunting', and as an obsessive
practice, focused around capturing elusive items – 'like collecting
football stickers, the more you get the less likely you are to get the ones
that you haven't got'. Likewise Tom, from London, who collects
carpentry manuals, and Karen – again London-based, but who currently
collects Thermos flasks – talk of 'the thrill of the chase'. At the same
time, however, the purposeful 'hunt' is overlain for some through the
added attractions of 'the unexpected'. Lydia again:

> . . . one of my Best Finds Ever was going to a charity shop and finding
> the whole of the Forsyte Saga, all nine books, and I already had the first
> three, and this was just, at the time this was really the most exciting thing
> in the world to me [. . .] I quite like the fact it's so totally unpredictable,
> because if I wanted to buy say an Ian Fleming book, I could walk into

Smiths or Waterstones and more or less guarantee that any book I wanted, I could walk in, and if it's not on the shelf I could order it. Whereas if you go into a charity shop, you just don't know what's going to be there at all [. . .] We went away for the weekend to Buxton [. . .] and we went into the town on one of the evenings when all the shops were shut, and I got all excited cos in the window of Oxfam was a copy of *Romola* by George Eliot, which my aunt's actually named after. And I knew this book existed but I have never seen it. And I was like 'Oh we have to come back! We have to come back when it's open!' And I was lying in bed thinking, 'Tomorrow, if it's not open tomorrow, I'll I'll go and put £2 in an envelope and I'll write them them a note saying "PLEASE can you post this book to me?!"' And I wasn't sure whether I was being a bit obsessive about this book which I know is still in print, and it's not exactly difficult to get a copy of! But we went back and it was open, so I managed to get that book, and I managed to get another book which I didn't expect to get . . .

Here we can see how 'the unexpected' – in this case both multiple 'finds' and the rare 'find' – adds value to Lydia's collecting. So much so that it is these – 'the unexpecteds' – that get remembered and celebrated in talk, as 'Best Finds Ever' and/or Memorable Moments.

Although the foregoing makes clear that it is 'the collection' itself that provides the rationale both for 'the hunt' and the scope for excavating 'the unexpected', the same material establishes unequivocally that collecting is a consumption practice based on a particular way of looking through certain second-hand sites. Specific, focused, often detached and dislocated, this is frequently about distancing 'the collector' from the mass of goods available, almost as above these. Indeed, rather than requiring intensive effort in looking, many of these 'collections' can be added to through the cursory glance of the practiced, knowledgeable, collecting 'eye' – literally, through a quick 'in and out'. Witness snowdomes, irons, photo cubes and cat memorabilia for example. Others, while they require more methodical practices of looking – books and vinyl being the obvious instances – are still dealt with relatively quickly, certainly when compared to the rituals of clothing acquisition. Collecting, then – at least as practised within these second-hand arenas – is for us both a way of regulating purchasing and a way of constricting such possibilities. The converse of 'bargain-centred' purchasing, it is about exercising creative control in the market both through 'the collection' itself and through the time discipline associated with its practices of looking (and see too Miller, 1987).

Taste and Display, Collections-in-use: Collecting and Consumption Practices

The literature on individual collecting practices makes clear connections between 'the hunt' and 'the chase' and the separation of 'the collection' from ordinary, everyday use. Indeed, the cycle of collecting – anticipation, desire, temporary pleasure, its dissipation and reformulation and narration through the metaphor of 'the hunt' – is hinged here both to sacralization and to the work of classifying and curating 'the collection' itself (Belk, 1995). In part a reflection of the importance of the museum and museum practice/s in shaping the field, and indicative too of the considerable emphasis placed in the literature on particular – merchant and investor – models of collecting and their traditional foci (stamps for example: see Gelber, 1992), our research suggests that the relation between individual collecting practices and consumption-as-use is rather messier and altogether more blurred than these narratives imply.

To be sure, we did encounter individuals whose practices accord with the standard representation of collecting. Some, then, like Ruth and Andrew – whose mantelpiece and living-room shelves are lined with a display of ornamental delftware collected exclusively from car-boot sales – are collecting through objects that were produced as giftware and for collection. And the same is the case with Sue's snowdomes, Mark's irons, Karen's Thermos flasks and Lydia's Pyrex dishes however, were once – presumably – in everyday use, as objects in domestic household consumption, even within social reproduction. Currently, though, they feature prominently in living-room displays and, as such, would appear to be the epitome of decommoditization and sacralization. And in a sense of course they are. But we would want to argue too that the display of collections like this has a 'use' also and that it continues to be embedded in everyday consumption practices. Indeed, we maintain that working with objects in this way is both a way of recovering and encoding meaning/s for individual collectors and a way of ordering domestic space through things; it is then a consumption practice that – whatever its constituent content – is about regulating the gaze (of others) and about constituting certain domestic interiors though appropriate spatialized performances. Located exclusively in 'front' and/or 'public' rooms, in the manner discussed classically by Goffman – typically in living rooms and/or dining areas – these 'collections' are noticed, if not explicitly talked about, by others and work to encode 'the collection' as both an appropriate individual consumption practice and a socially acceptable way of 'doing' particular interior spaces. Moreover, we would argue that these modes of doing become key practices within particular social networks; that they are constitutive of networks of 'taste and display' communities. Witness the affinities between Sue, Mark and Steven's collections, where aesthetic taste and design knowledge/s work both to shape collecting through a combination of knowingness and nostalgia, in ways not dissimilar to the retro retailers discussed in Chapter 3 or the parallels between Val's ornamental cat display and Ruth and Andrew's delft collection.

Yet others, however, take the connections between collecting and use much further, to the point where, as we see now, these seem to be collections-in-use. Lydia's books are one obvious example – bought to read, as well as to add to 'the collection'. But there are others. Her partner for example collects old DIY manuals (from the 1940s onwards), to use and display, in a manner similar to that of Tom's collection of carpentry manuals. Others, though, place their 'collections' in routine everyday use. Diane's album covers, for example, while they work as a display, are actually converted into a form of 'wallpaper"' 'I've got loads of cheesy record covers on my wall at home . . . the walls are painted purple and I've got loads of easy-listening record covers on the wall'. As well, Steven's photo cubes constitute an ongoing artistic project:

> I think the first one I just put images in, photographs of people I knew or photos cut out of magazines and things, and I just, it was a way, just seemed to be a brilliant visual device for showing flat images, but also having three dimensions. And I still haven't – after five years of collecting them I still haven't quite worked out what they're gonna be good for. I've just got this faith they'll be, there's something I could make out of them.

For Val it is important that at least part of her collection can be used:

> Mugs, small ornaments, you know, money boxes and that sort of thing . . . but preferably something which you can use, with ornaments – well you can just get too many ornaments . . .

Hence the significance to her of toasters, teapots and mugs. And, in one of our most extreme examples, we have Paul – a part-time University lecturer and writer based in London. Paul collects numerous things, including 'paper effects' from household clearances – love letters, accounts, unwanted diaries, etc. These he stores in boxes and suitcases and uses as resources for his writing projects:

... People's documents, I got a bit obsessive about collecting all the, all the kind of stuff that is basically left after people have died, like their, probably ranging from their school certificates, their swimming certificates through to their National Insurance thing, through old passports, things that you just have in a box, that you think you shouldn't throw out, like your health cards [. . .] so it was all their little documents [. . .] occasionally you'd get a collection of letters, like love letters, things like that, so for me as a writer it was a brilliant source. I've got like 1930s love letters, I've got letters from prison sent to people, boxes of postcards that people kept [. . .] filing card systems with examples of all the printing works from say a 1930s printer, things like that, so [I was] always thinking, 'this could make a project, this could be used in a book'. Of course what happens is you just end up collecting more and more junk and then you have 20 cases full of other people's things.

Collecting here, then, is a consumption practice where sacralization does not necessarily take 'the collection' out of use. A significant counter to the conventional wisdom, we regard this as in some cases an effect of collecting's location here within the domestic arena. Collecting for some, then, is a practice that is located within ordinary homes and ordinary spaces, in living environments that are often shared with significant others and that confine and constrict the possible. Some collections, then, may only be acceptable – tolerated even – precisely because they serve a dual purpose, as about display and use. In other senses, though, there is a sense in which in putting 'the collection' to use individuals are openly and deliberately contesting the norms of collecting practice. Rather than constituting themselves as curator/s-cum-caretakers, then, some of these 'collectors' are endeavouring to work with their 'collection' to produce something else again – literally to distinguish 'aura' through their own creativity. Most clearly articulated and demonstrated by two 'artistic' figures – Steven and Paul – this is a practice that we come back to later. For the moment, however, we want to examine further how collecting can work as a regulatory, and not just individual, consumption practice.

Risk and Certitude: Collecting as a Regulatory Practice

... It's a bit scary though, when you come into a community that's into that sort of thing, and all their houses are such a reflection of their taste – as somebody who's just done that here, it's terrifying actually. I think

'Oh my God!' 'What if I' – as someone who has never had a house you know, and now I have – 'What if I haven't got any taste?' 'How would I know?' – [*laughter*] (Maria, among group of friends)

We begin this section with a critical extract from the group interview with Sue, Mark and Maria – the Bristol-based friendship network first discussed in Chapter 4. Discussed there in terms of its importance in shaping practices of exchange, Maria's comments about anxieties around taste take on a new meaning when we see them in the light of collections of irons, snowdomes and the like. This, then, is a friendship group for whom collecting and its rituals and display practices matter profoundly. It is a group, though, for whom collecting works as an expression of self-declared aesthetic taste; and for whom the collection therefore has to be personally selected, not prescribed by external value regimes. Critically too, it is steeped either in design history or in nostalgia.

We see this again with Steven, who not only collects photo cubes but particular types of soft toys:

I rummage through the inevitable bin of soft toys, and there's only once in 25 visits that you'll find one, and when you find one it's just, it's a joy – I found one in Wareham, at the weekend – a knitted panda about 8 inches high, with no nose or mouth. It's to do with, actually that relates more strongly to my work, cos my paintings are a lot about stance and gesture of a figure and it's, you kind of judge soft toys in a similar way, like if they have a kind of like, benign posture and the kind of, an open face, and some that I've got, I just really like them [. . .] I wouldn't exhibit them [. . .] it's just a subtle, it's such a nuance thing, two very similar soft toys, and I suppose you wouldn't get that in toy shops cos you would get say three lions or something and they'd all look the same.

And again for Karen, it is design rather than nostalgia that provides the primary linking theme, and coloured 1950s plates, white plastic household containers and Thermos flasks have all figured as key collecting themes. To us this set of collecting practices is suggestive in the extreme. Associated exclusively with university- and/or art-school-educated individuals, who are frequently employed (or self-employed) within the creative industries, this suggests that collecting in this case works as a constitutive consumption practice: one that not just defines the self, but that enables connections to be made with others – one that matters to and in the constitution of friendship networks. When Maria talks about these practices as 'a bit scary' and as 'terrifying', then, we can see just what is at stake here: to be part of this group, to 'fit in' with its practices, it is critical to engage in this particular version of collecting and to display this prominently for the (silent) scrutiny of others. Small wonder, then, that Maria's talk betrays a degree of insecurity and anxiety.

Similarly, we find within Karen's transcript the same evidence for insecurity/ies around taste-based collecting. Talking about one of her collections, Karen recounts how she discovered that one of her 'friends' had replicated her 'collection':

> I have got one friend who used to be my flat-mate, and she and I have frighteningly similar tastes – and it actually got quite fraught, we actually had arguments about things, you know, like who spotted it first, and I would avoid going with her to Brighton – though I think I've got that in check now . . . She sort of followed me in my enthusiasm for white plastic – I was rather sharp about that, I went round the flat and she'd got – it was a bit pathetic – she'd got this Thermos flask and I'd got quite a few of them, and it was exactly the same as mine – I couldn't believe it . . . [*Kate*: Why didn't you like her doing that then?] Well I suppose because I have this thing that second-hand shopping is – when you go to new shops someone else has already vetted everything, and particularly in a lifestyle-y shop like, what's it called, Habitat, it's already been selected so you can buy into it. But if you don't do that then you go round being more eclectic, then if someone else just copies what you've done it's just rather irritating – I suppose one feels that how your home and the objects you surround yourself with and your clothes are an indication of your personality, therefore it's sort of, I don't know, buying into it.

Indicative as this is, almost certainly, of attempts to fit in within a particular collecting aesthetic and practice, and of personal insecurities about how to achieve this, just how transgressive such practices turn out to be is instructive to note. Interpreted by Karen both as 'the copy' and as encoding a lack of taste-certitudes, 'copying' is to her evidently an unacceptable and inappropriate practice within this friendship network. But more than that, it devalorizes the original collection too – precisely because what was constituted initially through self-declared taste has been reproduced. So, in a manner that resonates strongly with a process that we met first in connection with repro-retro, the duplication of the original collection leads to disaffection. Indeed, Karen took the radical step of disposing with this 'collection' entirely, making room to collect something else instead.

Taking the evidence against this backdrop, we can perhaps see why others engage in collecting practices that are less 'risky', at least in terms of the displays of cultural capital. Collections of delftware, of cat memorabilia, of books, even of album covers, work as 'collections' for others precisely because they construct clear limits and clear parameters to collecting knowledge/s and practice. Already categorized as 'collectable', often within clear value regimes, these are low-risk objects to engage with collecting. Pre-selected and pre-determined, as well as socially sanctioned, these are collections that work through certitude and where the investment of the collector is in the work of looking and hunting. By comparison, when certitude is rejected and when collecting becomes a personal, self-declared display of taste, collecting is a consumption practice striated by anxiety, as risky a display of cultural capital as it is perhaps possible to make. Which brings us to issues of disposal and the loss of 'aura'.

Creative Destruction, Disposal and the Loss of 'Aura'

'Aura' is one of the most significant constituents of collecting practice. Seen to define 'the collection' and to separate it out from ordinary objects in everyday use, it is that which makes things special. Symbolically, then, the loss or even destruction of 'aura' is of considerable significance: it is the point at which the collection is desacralized, where objects return to sites where they might be redefined as 'rubbish' or reclaimed for everyday use, and where they enter another consumption cycle. And certainly our research is revealing in this direction. So, while we encountered many 'collections' where 'aura' was indisputably still intact – the delftware, the books, the album covers and so on – there were others where 'aura' was either in the throes of being lost or where it had been. It is these that we focus on here.

Steven and Paul provide the two best examples of the former, and critically both work creatively with their 'collections'. What we see with Steven's discussion of his photo cubes is a desire to transcend 'the collection' through creative work, to add value to it, but in a way that goes beyond the original to destroy the collection. 'The collection', then, is an initial frame of reference, which provides both the creative inspiration and the seeds for its destruction as 'collection'. Moreover, 'the artist' figures here as the powerful, determining, creative agent, as omnipotent – as creator, curator and destroyer. Although the process is slightly different with Paul, there are some resonances. Here paper effects become constituted within the creative process as resources, to be used but in a non-renewable, non-sustainable sense. So this 'collection' has already lost its 'aura'. Used and incorporated it resides in boxes and in storage, awaiting disposal. But again it is 'the artist' figure whose work provides the basis for the collection's destruction.

Karen provides one of our best instances of another tendency. Indeed, in the previous section we saw how her collections can be disposed of, there through devalorization. Elsewhere in this interview, though, Karen reveals that this practice of disposal has occurred before. So, when she tires of particular collections, the objects get boxed up, eventually to be sold on at Greenwich Market:

> I think, I don't know, I just go through phases – for example, I think I had quite a lot of 50s stuff, well ceramics, they were lurid and I went off that, and I got heavily into green, this sort of green aspect, which is actually more 40s I guess, or not 40s, 50s, so it's dictated by colour . . . I kept it for a bit and once I'd had it in boxes a year or two, well you look at it and think 'Well I'm probably not going to put it out again, I shall go to Greenwich Market and sell it' . . . I don't like the thing of getting more and more and more, so I would probably always have roughly the same quantity, there'll be some new in and some old out.

There is, then, a distinct sense here that 'collections' are just as vulnerable to the process of 'casting out' that we discussed in Chapter 5; and that some collections consequently never quite manage to achieve the degree of 'aura' discussed in the literature.

Quite why this should be the case is, we think, both a reflection of the spaces through which these 'collections' have been assembled and an indication that collecting for some is perhaps not quite the distinctive consumption practice that it is frequently represented to be. So, in a situation where individual collectors are able to select and 'hunt' through personally declared value regimes, we would argue that it is collecting as practice that comes to matter rather more than the collection itself. Rather than 'the collection' singular satisfying the collecting imperative, then, we would argue that second-hand worlds like charity shops, car-boot sales and some retro shops make multiple collections possible – at least for those with the certitude and taste knowledge/s to make such selections. Consequently, for such individuals, 'the collection' could be one of many things. Moreover, it is constituted within distinctive consumption cycles, and can be devalorized just like other consumption goods, cast out. But what continues to matter is the consumption practice that is collecting – the cast out, then, is replaced with another collection. For us what this suggests is that collecting here is indicative of a very particular relationship to goods, that is a declaration of a personal, idiosyncratic, if socially sanctioned practice, but where 'the collector' is not just the agent of salvage and sacralization but the agent of destruction too.

Conclusions

Although very different and distinctive practices, when conducted through the second-hand worlds that we have considered here, both gifting and collecting reveal the significance of these worlds to practice. Indeed, we have seen in this chapter how these worlds place limits around gifting practices, literally making certain forms of gifting impossible and constituting certain objects as beyond 'the gift', and how they enable more expansive versions of collecting practice, that push to the limits (and sometimes beyond) normative collecting practices. We think, then, that such findings are of intrinsic importance for what they have to add to existing accounts of gifting and collecting. They establish, in short, that there are limits to gifting that are both highlighted by certain second-hand arenas and obscured in accounts that assume the first cycle. And they show too that collecting is not quite the uniformly distinctive and special-case consumption practice that it is frequently represented to be.

Reflections/Future Directions

Aswe established at the outset of this volume, the research discussed here has been something of a 'mission', one that has as its core that the first/second-hand distinction matters profoundly, both to developing existing understandings of exchange and to enhancing current accounts of consumption and consumption practices. And, if the previous chapters have done their work, then we will have gone at least some way to achieving these objectives. However, rather than ending with a reiteration of our core findings, we want to close on a more speculative set of notes: to reflect on what we see as three of the critical issues facing second-hand worlds in the early twenty-first century and to highlight the significance of these worlds to future research in the field. These concern respectively: questions of over-capacity and rationalization; the degree to which these worlds may be read as 'alternative' or indeed as progressive; and what we now regard as their primary significance – what they have to contribute to understandings of 'rubbish'.

Over-capacity, Rationalization and Closure

As we have been writing this volume the 'unthinkable' has started to happen, at least in terms of some of our preoccupations over the past few years. Rather than seeing various second-hand outlets opening up all around us – the picture that had dominated the 1990s – we have begun to see evidence of closure. Charity shops, then, have started to shut (see Chapter 3), and retro shops have closed down too – among them some of the entrants of the late 1990s. And we have witnessed closure too even amongst our research respondents. So, for instance, Elaine – one of the retro retailers we featured – ceased trading in the summer of 2001. For us this is no temporary blip. Instead, given the tendencies of the previous decade, we anticipate that rationalization is

195

inevitable; a reflection not just of prodigious expansion but of the way this expansion has developed, and its limits currently within the UK.

The charity-shop sector, as the most extensive and geographically widespread of these worlds, provides perhaps the clearest indication of some of the problems currently facing second-hand trading. Developed rapidly by a suite of charities for the most part aiming to achieve a national coverage, expansion has brought about intensive competition, for both stock and labour. Tales of 'bag wars' in certain local areas, then, are both frequent and legion, as too are those of 'volunteer poaching', as shops compete among themselves for the small, and possibly dwindling, pool of volunteer labour. Compounded by their location within relatively high-rental units and charged to deliver in terms of fund-raising expectations, this is clearly 'crunch time' for the sector and for the charity retail project more generally. Indeed, without the ability to control stock quality (or flow), rationalization strategies would appear to be one of the few remaining options for charity retailers to enhance profitability. The picture of trading difficulty is similar for retro shops, where stock flow and quality has become progressively harder to regulate through the 1990s. Connected by retro retailers to the rise and proliferation in charity shops and car-boot sales, this has led many of those who remain in business to spend large periods of time sourcing abroad, where supply chains allegedly are more reliable and predictable. In the UK, then, market saturation and its attendant stock-flow problems – which, in turn, relate to the buoyancy (or not) of the consumer spend situation – means that the foreseeable future for many second-hand worlds is likely to be 'harder', 'leaner' and 'meaner'.

But what this situation is also about is finding the appropriate spatial 'fix' for various forms of second-hand trading. For those second-hand outlets that make the connection to local causes, there is undeniably still a strong tradition of stock flow. Hospice shops within the charity-shop sector, school and/or hospital car-boot sales, even the Scout jumble sale, continue to be forms of second-hand exchange where 'donations' are readily made available, where 'quality' is talked about as 'high' and where profitability continues to be realized. And that these forms of second-hand trading continue to be so successful is, for us, because they make the connection between local and/or community-based services and local economies of redistribution. They work, then, precisely because they can be seen to be about both a geographically specific moral economy and a locally embedded public good. 'The local' then provides an appropriate spatial fix for certain forms of second-hand trading, and it is these connections to place that account for the continued buoyancy of these forms of trading. By comparison, and at the other extreme, although no less successful, are those retro retailers who have transformed their activities into second-hand versions of independent retailers in the first cycle. With guaranteed stock runs, sourced internationally, these retailers have established that the appropriate spatial fix for their operations is provided through the more organized and established supply chains of continental northern Europe and parts of the United States. Connected to both a more firmly entrenched and established tradition of reuse and recycling, at least in parts of continental northern Europe, and to a more developed notion of 'thrift shopping' in the United States (Hoff, 1997), these international fixes highlight the difficulties for those second-hand traders caught in the middle – charity retailers. Trying to implement national-scale retail operations through disorganized, unpredictable and at best regional supply chains that are undermined by and in direct competition with the local/moral nexus, charity-retail chains would be the most likely beneficiaries of any moves to rationalize and centralize practices of reuse in the UK. In the meantime, though, their supply difficulties mean that they are likely to bear the brunt of over-capacity in the second-hand market. The most visible face of the expansion in second-hand worlds through the 1990s, they are likely to be the focus of widespread rationalization in the decade following; an indication of the limits to the possible in a context where central and local government commitments to reuse and recycling remain at best half-hearted and patchy, and where second-hand markets are polarized as 'local' and 'global'.

In What Sense 'Alternative'?

Initially, when we first formulated this research, we saw these second-hand worlds as illuminating 'the alternative'. Like a few of those we talked with, then, we saw these sites as potentially another critical moment in consumption, one that went beyond consumer boycotts and campaigns and that was located in a 'red'-'green' nexus, in which the act of purchase could be simultaneously anti-consumerist and anti-corporate and pro-reuse – both a critique of manufacturer's product cycles and an acknowledgement of the temporal durability of things. Conducting this research, though, has forced us to think hard about some of these arguments, and to revise them radically. Rather than constituting an 'alternative' economy based on the exchange and consumption of used goods, we would argue that the expansion of the second-hand market and its proliferation in various sites in the UK through the 1990s has meant that second-hand has become more closely entwined with exchange and consumption in the first cycle. The clearest indication of this tendency is provided by the significance of 'the brand' and 'the label' to purchasing practices: highly significant to exchange and consumption in the first cycle, in the second-hand market these are possibly of even greater significance since they are constituted here through value regimes that conjoin them powerfully with 'the bargain'. Here, then, 'the brand' is to be had for less: an imperative that replicates the success stories of UK retailing in the late 1990s, the 'discounters' (Keynote, 1997, 1999). Moreover, here 'more' can be had for less, a practice that proved seductive for many of those we talked with. Far from being anti-consumerist then, for some these second-hand worlds are attractive precisely because they enable, even legitimize, 'excessive' consumption of that that confers respectability and status, the brand and the label.

Similarly, we have had to revise many of our initial assumptions about reuse and its significance to practice. At the outset of this research we anticipated that reuse would figure prominently in talk, as a primary motivation for purchasing through second-hand worlds. But, as we showed in Chapter 4, it rarely featured. Moreover, when it did it was talked about exclusively in terms of the temporal durability of things (consumer goods), and not – as we had envisaged – in relation to issues of environmental degradation and the politics of commodity production. So, for example, no one made connections between second-hand clothing purchase and, for instance, arguments about cotton or silk production, or about the potential implications of widespread purchasing in the second-hand market for first-cycle production workers. Reuse, then, was not – as we had imagined it to be – a politicized practice. Rather it was construed more as a conservation practice, where preserving and/or extending the lives of things/consumer goods has come to matter rather more than thinking about the connections of such practices to the conditions of commodity production.

Another of our initial assumptions about reuse was that connections would be made between this practice and other practices of reuse located outside the conventional money economy. Practices such as the gifting of children's clothing within extended families and the circulation of maternity wear among women's friendship networks are indicative of other contemporary forms of reuse, as too is some of the work of consumption, particularly repairing and/or mending articles of clothing (replacing broken zips and buttons, 'turning' collars and cuffs, darning socks, 'patching' elbows, etc.) and 'converting' clothing (from dress to pillow case/s; unravelling and reworking jumpers, etc.). Indicative of practices that are 'alternative' in the sense that they are positioned out-side the conventions of monetary exchange and invoke both notions of a moral economy and the importance of 'thrifty work' to consump-tion as practiced, the absence of such connections highlights how reuse through the second-hand market is reworked primarily through de-and revalorization – through the commodity form. If we are to draw any conclusions from this research about the political potential of reuse as a critical consumption moment, then, it would be to say that the conditions of exchange work to exert profound effects on this practice. Reuse, then, can be a critical practice – when it occurs without money. But when it occurs through the market its potential is lost.

Overall, then, and after much deliberation, our general conclusions about the political possibilities of the second-hand worlds we have examined are that it is more appropriate to see these sites as an intens-ification and deepening of the economy 'proper', as its parallel rather than its critique. Moreover, we think these sites raise difficult questions for reflexive consumer practices, in that while some – notably charity shops – are anti-corporate, others – particularly certain forms of retro retailing – are firmly located in conventional capitalist strategies of entrepreneurship and expansion. Furthermore, purchasing exclusively through the second-hand market – as just a few of our respondents did – seems to us a highly debatable political strategy, one that invites the same degree of scepticism raised in relation to earlier 'green' takes on anti-consumerism, and that leaves unanswered the effects that such forms of provisioning might have on manufacturer-retail supply chains and the commodity chain. As a political strategy, then, these second-hand worlds provide no answers or solutions for critical consumption practices, and work to spotlight critical questions for the reuse/recycle lobby.

And yet, unexpectedly, unpredictably, these worlds have displayed a degree of progressive potential. Undeniably, then, there are, hints here – however tentative, partial and circumscribed – of (some of) these second-hand worlds as located within a moral economy. Most clearly visible in discussions of provisioning within poverty, and in the traffic in children's and baby clothes, there is a strong sense in which these worlds are (still) seen to be about needs and normativity, and about redistribution. They are located, then, in an understanding of an econ-omy where people's material needs continue to prevail over arguments about the sustainability of objects and the desirability of their reuse. At the same time though, and much more pervasively, we have seen here how participation in these second-hand worlds requires people to establish the principles and premises of exchange, to work out how to buy, when, what to buy, and even to think about objects for their potential – for what they might become, to think beyond the boundaries of the object. These worlds, then, problematize exchange and consumption. They compel those who participate within them to think hard about these practices and to question what, elsewhere, can be at least in part a taken-for-granted, routine, mundane and repetitive act. So, for us some of the progressive potential of these worlds is located in their relationality and their appeal to consumer agency: in the way in which they have enabled people to think harder about the prevailing, dominant figures shaping the first-cycle retail landscape – both about what they offer and, more importantly, how they offer it. Prescribed certitude, 'easy' shopping, a 'selected-for-you', singular, marked-out and safe, compliant package that eliminates many of the anxieties and risks of consumption: this figures as the ever present Other for many within second-hand worlds, but particularly for those with the certitude and cultural capital to do differently. Undeniably attractive for many, as it is abhorrent to others, one of the key questions for those seeking to further critical consumption practices remains the power of first-cycle retailers to sell (with) certitude. Maybe, then, just maybe, the increasing visibility of second-hand worlds may work to at least question whether this type of certitude continues to matter. They might, but we remain sceptical on this. Indeed, as we show now, for us the progressive potential of these worlds lies less in their connections to purchase than in their links to disposal.

Biographies, Geographies and 'Rubbish'

If one thing is clear from our excavations of certain second-hand worlds it is that the biographies of things are increasingly being constituted through potentially limitless cycles of de-and revalorization. The proliferation and expansion in second-hand sites, then, has meant that the processes of reappropriation through divestment and re enchantment have become both increasingly commonplace and socially diverse. No longer confined to 'the poor' and to specific subcultures, these worlds have become an acceptable, even desirable way to 'do' style in the first decade of the twenty-first century and an appropriate way of spending leisure time. And they are – through the medium of the charity-shop bag drop – a routine part of everyday life. Casting out, then, has become a commonplace consumption practice for many households. Without doubt too, though, these worlds have meant that the biographies of things are far more extensive than they once might have been. Once 'captured' within these spaces, then, objects can both remain within them and return to them. So, for example, as we witnessed repeatedly in charity shops, objects can either stay ad infinitum or – in the well-managed charity shop – circulate between branches within areas, literally for months on end. And similarly in car-boot sales, where 'unsold' goods simply get boxed up, for the next time. And then there is the case where charity-shop purchases return to the charity shop . . . In all these instances there is the tacit assumption that somewhere, sometime, someone will always be there, eventually, to re valorize these objects. But, in the interim, these worlds freeze these objects in time-space – holding them in storage, out of 'use', much as in the collection – stretching their biographies, potentially to infinity.

While they do this, though, there is a parallel sense in which these same worlds limit and/or foreclose the geographies of these objects. The process of casting out, then, is by definition about displacement, from the household to the sorts of sites that we have been concerned with here (and others). But this displacement is highly restricted geograph-ically, shaped by decisions which – if our research is anything to go by – are almost exclusively pragmatic, determined by the nearest or by which bag comes through the door when. Yet where objects end up matters profoundly to their future biographies. Objects, then, can and do frequently end up in totally inappropriate places – 'retro' clothing in 'bargain' and/or discount charity shops, bric-a-brac in charity shops in middle-class neighbourhoods, and so on. Consequently, objects circ-ulating in second-hand worlds can become locked into spaces where they are literally matter out of place, at least in terms of prevailing value regimes. Yet, because of the 'someone-sometime' ethos they remain trapped within these, caught in a time-space web. The source of endless fascination and anticipation for some, and utter frustration for those trying to make their business through these worlds, the geographical limits of displacement represent the difference that space makes to even the content of many second-hand sites. And clearly they constitute some of the limits that many of those working in the second-hand market have to attempt to find a spatial fix for.

Subjected to potentially endless cycles of de/revalorization, or even locked in the store of the charity shop, in car-boot-sale boxes or on the hanger in a retro shop open for a few days a week, the question these worlds raise, perhaps above all others, in terms of objects' biographies is 'at what point does anything, ever, become "rubbish"?' Indeed, what is 'rubbish'? That which is discarded for sure, but if – as we have seen here – that which is discarded is increasingly being placed and held in suspended animation, oscillating between devalorization and revalorization, and then returned to this state, then is there any longer any basis for terminal states such as 'rubbish'? Our inclination here is to think not, and to suggest that one of the most progressive, if unintentional, consequences of the proliferation in second-hand worlds has been the critical gap which they have inserted between disposal, the act, and its location. No longer automatically the dustbin, the skip or the household-waste-disposal site, the proliferation of these worlds inserts meaning into disposal in a way that insists on the potential for objects' revaluation as they are in the throes of devaluation, and simultaneously questions the essentialist, linear descent to 'rubbish' that is one of the core planks of representations of the consumer society.

We end this exploration and excavation, then, by suggesting that the most important issues for future studies of consumption perhaps are less to do with connections between the act of purchase and consumption practices – with why some things matter – and rather more to do instead with how certain things that mattered once come not to matter. Devaluation is a critical fulcrum point for processes of consumption, and not simply in terms of the histories of objects – the classic mass use/descent to rubbish/recovery as 'collectable' narrative of the cultures of collecting literature. Rather, devaluation is a critical consumption practice; routine, mundane even, but central to facilitating further acts of purchase and to enabling the space for new things to come to matter. In comparison to purchase-consumption connections, though, we know very little about this, and often assume a lot. But is devaluation within individual households simply a mirror of product cycles, and a citation of 'fashion' and its attendant anxieties? Is it instead a core facet of identity 'work' – as significant to constituting particular identities as the much more intensely interrogated act of purchase? And how does devaluation connect to use? Is it about a loss of use, too much use, overuse – or all these things and more, indicative of a ceaseless, yet only temporally satiable relation of desire? At present we can only hazard guesses here. And indeed only speculate as to how second-hand worlds might themselves work to encourage devaluation and intensify consumerism. But what seems clear is that these worlds mark out both a paradox and a cusp: simultaneously about revaluation (and reuse) and devaluation, they define our relationship to things in the early years of the twenty-first century as increasingly uncertain, provisional and temporary, and as caught between the reuse of matter and its designation as 'rubbish'. Rather than being inconsequential sites of 'rubbish', these worlds are ones where the very meaning/s of 'rubbish' are being redefined and worked out, in and through consumption practices.

Appendix

Research as Practice: Research Design, Methodological Approach and Analysis

The research on which this volume is based is the outcome of two separate, though linked, ESRC projects, both of 12 months' duration. The first looked at car-boot sales (research award number: R000221288) and the second at charity and retro shops (R000222182). In view of this background we detail the methodological approach undertaken for each project separately below. As is clear from what follows, key differences are evident between the two projects. The car-boot-sale study is, for example, more extensive, involving a greater proportion of large-scale survey work. The second project, looking at charity and retro shops, is in contrast more intensive in scale, its analysis more discursive and more textual. Significantly too, and as a result of these differences in research design, the results reveal different approaches to analysis, with the car-boot study producing more by way of descriptive and quantitative indicators (about goods in circulation, for example), while the charity and retro studies reveal more by way of consumption investments, practices and premises.

But it is important to acknowledge too at the outset that a series of common aims and approaches to both research design and analysis are evident across the two projects. Empirically, for example, both projects demonstrate the need to think spatially, temporally and organizationally about the range of sites and the practices that they involve. Common conceptual threads run through the two projects too, specifically a focus on knowledge, performative consumption, possession rituals and their intersection with determinations of value. And, finally, we hope to demonstrate that the volume produced here could only have been written with hindsight, for a key concern is that of relationality, both between first-and second-cycle sites and, perhaps more significantly, between and across our three case-study sites. To study each space in isolation would mask the complexities and connections the three sites reveal; they are very much more than the sum of the parts.

Although undeniably rich, it is fair to say that one of the limitations of our study of car-boot sales was its confinement to one second-hand space: it became apparent very quickly that one of the key features of the second-hand market is the connections, and the differences, between various spaces of second-hand exchange. In order to develop a full picture of second-hand consumption, then, we had to extend our lens to a range of other sites and spaces. So we hope that this work provides an interesting study of both additionality and progression: yes, the first study was conceived in isolation, but it is made altogether richer and more instructive when looked at alongside that of the subsequent two sites. We hope, then, that this volume is not simply the product of bolting two projects together but, rather, that it is an exercise in development, and that it demonstrates the way in which methodological approaches and means of analysis can be complementary while simultaneously evolving through time to become more sophisticated and insightful.

The Car-Boot-Sale Study

The methodological strategy adopted in our first project on car-boot sales comprised a staged phase of research that we outline below.

Media and Trade Search

First we examined press reports on the growth and characteristics of car-boot sales as well as media representations of the car-boot-sale phenomenon. This entailed on-line searches of *The Independent, The Daily Telegraph, The Financial Times, The Times* and *The Guardian* and manual searches of the tabloids. Relevant articles from local newspapers were also collected. This material provided considerable input to our analysis of the debate over car-boot-sale regulation as well as an initial input into our work on theorizing consumption through the case of car-boot sales.

National Local Authority Survey and Key Informant Interviews

The second stage of our car-boot-sale survey comprised a postal questionnaire survey of all local authorities in England and Wales in order to determine the extent of variation in car-boot-sale occurrence and particularly to glean information on the complex and highly varied regulatory context within which car-boot sales operate. A total of 350 returns were received from this survey. The survey was then supplemented by

key informant interviews with a range of public and private sector organizations involved in the public debate over car-boot-sale regulation,
including the Federation of Small Businesses (FSB), the British Chambers
of Commerce, the National Association of British Market Authorities
(NABMA), the Local Authority Co-ordinating Body on Food and Trading
Standards (LACOTS), with car-boot-sale-promoters, and with local authority representatives. In the latter case we chose two closely proximate
local authorities from within our study area, both offering contrasting
approaches to the regulation of car-boot sales, and interviewed them
about the historical development of their approach to car-boot sales and
their explanation of this. With key organizations involved in the public
debate over car-boot-sale regulation we were concerned with identifying
their role in the debate, their reasons for involvement and their varying
accounts of both the objectives behind the debate and its chronology.
With commercially oriented car-boot-sale promoters we were particularly
interested in their development and the scale of their operations and
in the extent to which they contest and/or circumvent the regulatory
operating environments provided by local authorities.

Observation Work

Our third strand of research comprised detailed participant observation
surveys of a range of car-boot sales in the North East, South Yorkshire,
Nottinghamshire and Derbyshire. This phase of the research process
comprised two stages, an initial pilot phase (August–September 1994)
and a longer period of sustained ethnography conducted between April
and August 1995. In the pilot phase the intention was to visit as many
and as varied car-boot sales as possible. The second phase of field work
involved attending car-boot sales intensively every weekend from Easter
onwards (typically two/three boot sales were visited each weekend), and
a sustained six-week period of booting (including various midweek events
as well as weekend sales) from July through to mid-August (a schedule
involving as many as six or seven sites per week in both the study areas).
Each of the detailed case-study sites were visited on at least five separate
occasions and detailed field notes were produced on each occasion,
detailing the site, its organization, layout, items for sale, nature of buyers
and vendors and so on.

Goods-in-Circulation Survey

The fourth strand of the research methodology comprised a goods-in-
circulation survey which aimed to determine which goods are bought

at car-boot sales, by whom and for what purposes. This phase of the research was undertaken in May 1995 via on-site survey work at a range of car-boot sales in Nottinghamshire and South Yorkshire (n=4). As well as offering various practical advantages for the research team, these localities were selected as they demonstrate the full range of licensed and unlicensed, large and small sales; they illustrate the varying regulatory environments in which car-boot sales operate and their socio-economic composition is sufficiently heterogenous for us to examine the ways in which class variations in consumption practices mediate car-boot-sale activity. A total of 263 consumers were questioned as they left these car-boot sales and completed cards detailing their socio-economic characteristics, types of goods bought, expenditure totals, intended use of goods bought, their frequency of attendance at car-boot sales and mode of participation (i.e. buying, selling, looking, or some combination of all three activities). In spite of the logistic practicalities which these case-study locations of Nottinghamshire and South Yorkshire offered us, it must be pointed out that our endeavours to question people at the entrances and exits to car-boot sales, armed with the familiar market-research equipment of warm clothing and clipboards, was a difficult, awkward and often embarrassing encounter. In parallel with the difficulties we subsequently encountered when trying to stop and question consumers outside charity and retro shops, we experienced similar feelings of discomfort and awkwardness when questioning car-boot-sale goers. In this case difficulties were compounded by the standard rhetoric surrounding car-boot sales at the time: wielding clipboards as adult women constituted us as 'outsiders' with respect to boot-sale participation and – more problematically – as potential DSS or Trading Standards 'snoops'. After several troublesome weekends during which our attempts to collect questionnaire data persistently and consistently came up against the label 'suspicious', we adapted our research strategy and employed student labour to complete the task. Students reported few of the suspicious and challenging encounters which we had experienced, perhaps because a combination of comportment and age rendered them less open to being read as DSS/LA employees.

In-depth Consumer and Seller Interviews

In-depth interviews were conducted with 30 vendors and buyers in order to explore their particular experiences of boot-sale consumption. In the vendor survey we were interested in the ways in which goods were sourced, how they were prepared and displayed and how pricing arrangements were determined. The interviews with buyers were semi-structured and probed buyers about their reasons for attending boot sales, their purchasing behaviour and rationale, their intended uses of goods purchased, and the ways in which their consumption behaviour at a boot sale might differ from that of conventional first-hand shopping.

The Charity- and Retro-Shop Study

In the case of our charity-and retro-shops project, we endeavoured to mirror the research strategy adopted above, with some necessary adaptations in order to take into account the spatial, temporal and organizational differences between the study sites.

Media and Trade-Press Searches

This comprised the collection of reports, features and articles on charity shops and retro shops, as well as second-hand shops/shopping more broadly, and encompassed on-line searches of broadsheet newspapers (*Guardian, Financial Times, The Times, The Telegraph*) and manual searches of the tabloids, fashion and consumption magazines (*New Consumer, Elle, Marie Claire, Vogue, Id, Arena, GQ* for example), the trade press (*NGO Finance, Mintel, Euromonitor, Fashion Weekly*) and internet sites such as *Just-Style.com*. It included material on second-hand shopping, retro revivals, vintage fashion on the catwalk and charity shops' presence on the high street ('unfair competition', 'professionalization', and more recently the difficulties in finding and retaining volunteer labour and over-capacity in the sector); web pages on alternative/ethical consumption; the retro scene and thrifting generally, information on retro shops and the retro scene from listings, magazines, newspapers and student magazines; and a monitoring of the fashion pages of the men's and women's magazines for guides to second-hand shopping and style and features on the retro look.

Observational Fieldwork

This stage of the research comprised an extensive phase of observation-based field work in both charity and retro shops. In the case of charity shops we visited all the charity shops which we could find in numerous, contrasting retail locations. These included the South-west (Bristol, Bath, Taunton and Weston super Mare), South Yorkshire (Sheffield, Doncaster, Barnsley and Rotherham), the North East (Durham, Newcastle,

York and Hexham), the Midlands (Nottingham, Leicester, Derby and Birmingham) and London and the South-east (Chelsea, Covent Garden, Bayswater, Notting Hill and Portobello, Brighton and Orpington). All told this observation work encompassed some 300 charity shops spread across a range of neighbourhoods. In each place we noted our impressions of each area, the other shops in the vicinity and the location of each charity shop. We also photographed the window display, noted its content, layout, posters, etc. – materials which formed the basis for subsequent deconstruction (did this appear to be a 'professional' shop or a traditional 'rummage-style' charity shop; what levels of irony/knowingness were involved apparently in the display, or did it appear literal; how did colour (co-ordination) figure; how did this window relate to first-cycle displays around it; where did new goods figure, if at all, and so on). This analysis formed an initial way in to establishing the shop's position, its connection to the charitable cause, assumptions about its customer base and shop culture. We would then look around the shop as shoppers, gleaning our impressions of the internal imaging and branding of the shop, price ranges, the layout of the goods, type of stock, the percentage of new and second-hand, the proportion of men's, women's and children's clothing, the degree of information about the charity itself and its visibility, volunteers (social characteristics, dress codes, comportment, visibility), and other shoppers. At the same time we noted what was happening in the shop at the time by way of interactions, conversations, etc. The (subsequently written) field notes, together with the survey results from Mintel, provided not just the requisite research materials for examining the changing geographies of second-hand exchange, but the necessary basis for selecting our case-study charities for depth interviewing. It also confirmed the suitability of our chosen locations/charities for detailed participant observation work. It also highlighted that customer profiling through the market-research clipboard tactic would be difficult to accomplish: already this seemed an overly intrusive method with respect to our observations of charity shopping as practiced, and – if conducted at the entrance to the shop – a potential customer 'turn-off' (although see Parsons, 2001).

We then selected two charity shops for the more intensive period of observational ethnography. We opted to concentrate our participant observation charity-shop work in two very different charities located in strongly contrasting retail environments: one (Oxfam) was an established shop near Sheffield's Devonshire Green Cultural Quarter – the site for high-fashion shops and bars/night clubs and an annual alternative festival. This had recently become one of Oxfam's Originals stores, selling high-fashion retro clothing and bric-a-brac alongside the usual staples (fair-trade goods, Christmas cards and a selection of 'giftware').[69] The other was a small shop, the first to be opened by the charity (Action for Blind People) in Weston-super-Mare, a traditional seaside tourist town noted for its number of charity shops. In both shops we decided to go beyond our initial intention of eliciting information through informal interviews, and to work in both as volunteers. Both shop managers and other volunteers were informed of our research interests, and we worked in these for at least four months, working weekly shifts. At the end of each shift we would write up a research diary, noting particular anecdotes, conversations, observations of the day-to-day running of the shop and the interaction and possible tensions between management and volunteers. Where possible, we also attended shop meetings, training days and social events. Enabling us to examine in depth the production of charity-shop space through the interactions between charity retailers, managers, volunteers and consumers, this phase of the research had us working as window dressers, till persons, sorters, shop stockers and even temporary shop managers. For supportive secondary material for these case studies, we also did a number of shifts in other charity shops, in one case doing a three-week weekly shift, in another a day shadowing the manager and volunteers.

We conducted a parallel phase of extended field observation for retro shops in key centres (Nottingham, Manchester, Sheffield, Bristol, Bath, London). Again, as with the charity-shop example (and unlike the car-boot study), it soon became clear that questionnaire surveys of retro shops and shoppers were likely to be problematic. Field observation revealed that many of these shops are temporary – either occupying short-term leases or open for trading only for ad hoc hours; that they are frequently staffed by helpers rather than by those who own/manage them; that traders are often away sourcing stock; and that sourcing is a highly competitive process about which traders were less than willing to be forthcoming – at least in a specific sense. Again, then, we decided that more was to be gained from the depth interviews and participant observation phases of this case study.

For the retro side of the study the key participant observation sites were Sheffield's The Forum, a converted warehouse containing a number of shops/stalls selling designer clothing, CDs, ethnic goods and retro second-hand clothing; Manchester's Affleck's Palace, a converted former department store; and Nottingham's Celia's and Baklash, again a large converted warehouse selling retro fashion. Detailed observation work in retro shops, then, took place over a further four-month period and involved a couple of days per outlet, in which we would spend a few hours or two/three afternoons at a time 'hanging out' (in The Forum, Celia's, Baklash and Affleck's Palace) in the shops, wandering around, sitting in the cafés and so on, as well as casually chatting with stall/shop staff as appropriate. In this case we visited the sites both alone and together, an approach which meant that we could compare readings and cover these sites at different times of the day/week. Again, these experiences, anecdotes, conversations and observations were recorded in individual field diaries, and again these materials enable us to examine the production of these spaces through practice.

In-depth Case-Study Interviews

Our aim here was to undertake in-depth interviews with key personnel working in charity and retro shops. Given that charity shops are typically larger in organizational scale, often forming part of national (and sometimes international) chains, it was important here to interview shop managers, area, district and regional managers and heads of retail operations within a cross-section of charities, so that we had interviews along the chain. This we managed to achieve fully with four charities (Oxfam ICRF, British Red Cross and Action for Blind People). We also managed additional interviews at various levels with Scope, Sue Ryder and Weston Hospicecare. Comprising 14 interviews altogether, this cross-section of charities (spanning national/local, high street/side street, large/small distinctions) enabled us to consider the key tendencies within the charity-retail sector, notably professionalization, branding, imaging, where 'the charity' figures in this, contrasting sourcing and sales strategies and relation to first-cycle retailers/retailing.

The retro-case-study firms were rather different: rarely part of a larger organization, such shops tend to be independent units where the owner/manager is the key decision-maker, and may well also be the buyer, shop worker and stock controller. Here, then, we interviewed manager/owners and key shop personnel in a range of retro shops including Celia's, Wild, Baklash, Acrylic Afternoons and Atomic in Nottingham; Affleck's Palace in Manchester and a range of other retro traders in Manchester, Bristol, Sheffield and London's Notting Hill and Portobello. These interviews covered sourcing and sales strategies, the range and diversity of goods, customers and their characteristics, traders' personal histories with respect to the retail/fashion industries, and general thoughts about the retro scene. These were also supplemented by shorter interviews with a handful of key individuals involved in the retro scene in Nottingham

and Sheffield, including retro music DJs an 214
members.

In-depth Interviews with Consumers

This section of the research comprised depth interviews w.
hand shoppers and explored consumer motivations, practices
relation of second-hand consumption practices to identity. While
originally intended to interview 40–50 charity-shop consumers and 40–
50 retro shoppers, in practice there was considerable overlap between
these two groups. For the purposes of analysis we have classified these
interviewees in terms of their talk: those who primarily talk about retro
shopping we term retro shoppers (38 people in total) and those who
predominantly talk about charity we analyse as charity shoppers (47
in total). These respondents were recruited through various strategies
including leaflets and flyers which we left in charity shops and retro
shops, advertisements in local newspapers, listings magazines and on
a virtual web page, and through snowballing via social and friendship
networks. Advertisements in student newspapers and posters on university noticeboards gained a low response rate, but personal, work and
friendship networks provided a much more fruitful source of interviewees who in turn introduced us to other willing participants. Some
of these contacts came from personal friendship and family networks,
others from work contacts (colleagues as well as students), and snow-
balled on to encompass their friendship networks too. As with all such
strategies, there were gaps that reflected the nature of our social networks. We therefore contacted via letter and follow-up phone call a
number of over-60s social groups, parent and toddler groups, a charity-
shopping fanzine and 70s music clubs and societies, yielding between
them further interviews. While we feel confident that our respondents
cover a broad range of age and social-class categories, there are certain
gaps and/or shortfalls in our respondent group that it is important to
be explicit about. Specifically, the vast majority of our interviewees were
white – our only non-white respondents were one black woman (a retro
retailer) and one Asian retro shopper (a 70s-afficionado student). In part
we feel this reflects the ways in which second-hand consumption, and
particularly charity shopping, is a predominantly white activity – at least
if observations made throughout our fieldwork are anything to go by.
But we also acknowledge the impact of our own positionalities as white,
middle-class female researchers here, in that this – and recruiting at least
in part through our social, work and family networks – tended to produce

ather more of those shopping with fun, pleasure, for a laugh and so on. Secondly and a corollary: notwithstanding making considerable efforts to access both very poor and other socially excluded groups, we encountered extreme difficulty here. In part this seems to us indicative of the effects of our research foci: not only were we attempting here to recruit 'poor' and/or 'socially excluded' groups, but the interview situation required people to be willing to talk – often at length and expansively – about the effects of this on consumption patterns. To us, then, it is not surprising that only 8 of our 47 charity shoppers could be categorized thus. Thirdly and finally we note that our interviewees tended to be 'high-investor' consumers, people with a firm commitment to second-hand shopping or with strong opinions about this. And in spite of trying to interview those who shopped on a casual basis or not at all, this approach proved to be not terribly successful. This is indicative of the way in which people who don't do something are usually unwilling to engage in lengthy discussions about why they don't (see too Barker and Brooks, 1998). And with casual shoppers, we found that these proved unable (or reluctant) to go much beyond the 'I just pop in' level of discussion.

Interviews usually took place at the respondents' homes. This was particularly important for retro shoppers, since displaying and talking about purchases comprised a central part of the discussion. Others took place at workplaces (ours or theirs) or in neutral spaces, usually cafés.

Interview Analysis

We end this discussion of research design and methodological approach with some comments on analysis, particularly in relation to how this evolved throughout the course of the research process. Much of the analysis of survey material for the car-boot project focused on the regulatory environment and on the space as a landscape of extraordinary consumption. In the regulatory case our understanding came primarily from survey work with local authorities, from interviews with key agencies and actors and from textual analysis of media representations. In the case of our interpretation of the car-boot sale as a landscape of consumption we relied more heavily on our reading of the space obtained through observational work and field diaries, supported by some interview material. In contrast, our analytical approach in the second project on charity and retro shops emphasized far more patterns of talk and discursive markers, and involved a much closer reading of our transcribed interviews. Here our in-depth interviews become valuable not simply for what is told or for the text into which they are transcribed, or even for the conversation which takes place, but critically too for the *ways* in which such stories are told (Laurier, 1998, Smith, 2001). And as Laurier argues further, there are geographies in this talk; places are made, remade and unmade by the practice of conversing (Laurier, 1998; and see too O'Neill and Gibson-Graham, 1999). Throughout this analysis phase we came to see the discursive as a key way of understanding the practices and material culture of consumption, to see talk as a citation of discourse; to connect talk with practice; and to think about talk in relation to space and its production. This mode of analysis argues that talk must be taken seriously as a citation of discourse. Talk, then, is not just about what is said: for talk to work as communication it is required to draw on shared and/or negotiated sets of meanings (interpretive repertoires[70]) which themselves point to the power/knowledge assemblages which constitute key discourses. Consequently, talk needs to be analysed for key patterns and slippages, for the use of key discursive markers such as repetitive phrases and metaphors, and as a performance of position for an assumed audience.

In order for this focus on patterns of talk to work we had to think through our analysis of the transcripts quite carefully. For all of these interviews the interviewer wrote a short description of how the interview had been set up and where the interview took place. This enabled consideration of the implications for the interviewer/interviewee relationship in the interview. Analysis proceeded by all three researchers reading and re-reading each transcript, making notes of initial impressions, repetitions, connections, implications in talk, patterns of response/s and phrases which we found ambiguous or difficult to analyse, or which we thought surprising. We then circulated these notes, each making further notes on each other's analyses and noting areas for further discussion as well as clashes in interpretation. We then grouped the transcripts together, writing up all our notes according to transcript type (such as high investors, or retro traders) and discursive themes. To do this we used a number of conceptual tools and markers: for example, we adopted the term 'investment' from previous similar work on cinema-going and, later, on men's magazines (Barker and Brooks, 1998; Jackson et al., 2001), in which investment is defined as the range of ways in which people cared about, identified themselves according to and talked about participating in leisure pursuits. Thus we identified critical discursive markers that revealed to us the respondent's level of investment. Those who cared a lot about or who were heavily involved in the practices of second-hand exchange and/or consumption would have elaborate, often well-rehearsed ways of talking about either shopping or trading (buying and selling anecdotes, bargain boasting) and would have and could talk at length about established routines, referring to them as part of everyday life and of their identity. By contrast, low-investment talk would include less knowing talk on bargains, places and practices, and respondents would commonly assert that they didn't have much to say about the topic. This stage of the transcript analysis also revealed considerable differences in high-investment talk. High-investment talk was not always synonymous with pleasure: one high-investor consumer talked at length about the time-consuming drudgery of trying to clothe her child adequately; another about the hassle of trying things on. Neither was high investment always something to be celebrated: some of our high investors were self-deprecating, describing themselves as addicts and these consumption practices as addictive. So, alongside thinking about investments, the analysis has had to account both for the different practices involved in second-hand exchange and consumption and the range of ways in which people talk about these practices. Drawing again on previous research, and work by Hermes (1995), we looked for specific discursive markers which would indicate the various ways in which respondents engaged in exchange/consumption practices – indicating for example how consumers look, display, buy, sell, transform and wear particular purchases and their celebration/rejection/ satirization of this. More than one charity shopper for instance jokingly referred to an acknowledged 'ideal' investment comprising buying a good-quality garment and then transforming it with needle and thread, but then went on to say that they hardly ever did this, and that most things stayed in the carrier bag before going back to the charity shop! So such a shopper is aware of the 'good-shopper' investment of thrift-iness and the clever transformation of the bargain, but remains distinctly ambivalent about getting around to doing this.

Interviews with personnel in charity and retro shops were analysed similarly, focusing on the key markers and discursive themes in the transcripts and the ways in which these could be compared and contrasted. In the charity-shop case for example, we found that with the heads-of-charity-retail interviews the dominant discursive mode was profession-alization, while key marker terms were conventional business buzzwords – empowerment, progress, good and so on. We then compared and con-trasted these with the discursive themes present in the transcripts of shop managers (as well as with the talk we heard around us while work-ing as volunteers), some of which made explicit reference to notions of community, philanthropy and social networks. We also used our field-observation notes, charity literature and participant-observation research diaries to triangulate with these findings. The retro-trader-interview transcripts were analysed in a similar way, and here we were looking to capture the tensions, contradictions, juxtapositions, clashes and ruptures in their patterns of talk, and at key discursive markers about work, such as risk, freedom, fun and commercialization.

For all transcript groups, then – shoppers (retro and charity), shop personnel and management – we had a plethora of key terms, markers, patterns of investment and patterns of talk; an analysis akin to the 'mind maps' discussed by Bedford and Burgess (2001), but which in our case goes beyond individual transcripts to be about groups of transcripts. These 'maps' provided the basis for further analysis – through writing, in itself another tier to the interpretative process. Here we have taken particular, and manageable, 'slices' of our material to interrogate in depth: 1970s revivalism; narratives of the body in clothing; 'profession-alization' in talk and practice; second-hand shopping; retro retailers' and discourses of 'work'. And it is here that we have used, at least in part, some of the more schematic ways of working with qualitative data outlined by Jackson (2001), where connections between discursive rep-ertoires and discursive dispositions are emphasized. So, we have explored, for example, charity shopping as fun, pleasure, treat, time-out and as hard work, drudgery, time-consuming and *not* fun; and retro retailing as 'creative', part of the 'alternative scene', as *not* work. Yet, at the same time, we have been mindful to connect such talk with practice – with what people do – and not just leave things at what they say they do. Which is where ethnography comes in. And we have emphasized too that such schematic interpretative strategies are analytical devices that simultaneously reduce and obscure the complexities and ambivalences expressed in individuals' talk and practice. In writing, then, we have been keen to reincorporate such complexities by illustrating how individuals relate to these categories – messily. To show how they blur this talk and practice, run analytical codes together and elide repertoires. Our intent here, then, has been to acknowledge that interpretative strat-egies are but ordering devices – ways of making sense of talk and practice that run the risk of writing out the opacity of the everyday and the ways in which talk and practice are continually citational, mutable and open to slippage.

All of this of course begs the question of whether we could have analysed the material collected for the car-boot-sale study in a more sophisticated way that more closely parallels the charity and retro study. In part the answer to this is 'probably not', since a large proportion of the first project involved mapping out the geographical and regulatory context of car-boot-sale activity, and designing appropriate questionnaire and interview schedules. In part, however, the answer to the question might also be 'perhaps', in that the analysis of the car-boot-sale study interviews could certainly have been more sophisticated and could have interrogated the question of talk more closely and more critically. Beyond this, however, we would note that our approach to the study and analysis of car-boot sales was highly appropriate to both the time and the space of study: little had been written at that time on 'alternative' consumption spaces and practices. Taken in context, then, our focus on the spectacular and specular attractions of this space, on the centrality of practices of looking and watching in the constitution of this space, and on the centrality of performativity to participation in this temporary space was highly appropriate: observation and field diaries were then, and still are, seen by us as highly appropriate research tools in this particular context.

Notes

1. The literature on malls and department stores is considerable, although much of it still primarily textual. For examples grounded in consumer practices see: Domosh, 1996; Dowling, 1993; du Gay, 1996; Lehtonen, 1997; Morris, 1988. Key instances of other work would include: Blomley, 1996; Bowlby, 1985, 1987; Chaney, 1983, 1990; Crossik and Gaumain, 1998; Goss, 1993, 1999; Hopkins, 1990; Laermans, 1993; Lancaster, 1995; Leach, 1984; M. Miller, 1981; Porter Benson, 1986; Reekie, 1993; Shields, 1989; Williamson, 1992.

2. It is important to note here that these terms are not being used interchangeably. Rather, throughout this volume they are used in two precise senses. 'Principles' refers to the purpose of exchange, and to how exchange is conducted, its social relations. 'Premises' by comparison is used in connection with the sets of assumptions encoded in exchange; it refers to what exchange is considered to be about. This meaning is particularly important, in that we explicitly are not talking about 'premises' in the buildings sense of the term (see Chapters 3 and 4 in particular).

3. For accounts located within the commodity chain see Gereffi, 1994; Gereffi, Korzeniewicz and Korzeniewicz 1994. For more critical readings see Bedford, 2002; Crewe, 2002; Jackson, 1999; Hartwick, 1998; Hughes and Reimer, 2002; Leslie and Reimer, 1999; Raikes, 2000; Raikes et al. 2000. Classic accounts of consumption and identity include F. Davis (1992); Featherstone, 1991; Lunt and Livingstone, 1992; McCracken, 1988.

4. A related question, but one that we do not consider further here, is the international market in second-hand goods (see for example Transberg Hanson, 2000 on second-hand clothing), as well as flows constituted by international emergency aid relief appeals.

5. Although there are various arguments that can be mobilized to suggest that food is no different to other goods located in the second-hand market – for example, that waste matter is used for fertilization and subsequently works to produce further goods (food) for consumption – we would want to retain

this as a distinction that matters, for two reasons. First, because what we are talking about here is first-world consumption practices, and secondly, because we are referring to goods whose form – if not condition – remains the same between first hand consumption and entry to the second-hand market. For us, this does not happen in relation to food. Indeed, the only instances of food being consumed in this way that we can think of involve flows to the animal food chain, with pigswill being a prime example. For most households however, certainly currently within the UK, casting out food is mostly destined for the dustbin and the landfill site, possibly the compost heap, sometimes for donations (for school 'harvest festivals' for instance) but rarely, if ever, for the market.

6. Although others have recited to us how they unearthed 'collectables' such as Whitefriars glass ware and Clarice Cliff ceramics – usually at car-boot sales, and mostly in the early 1990s.

7. And see too: Benton, 1989; Commoner, 1990; de Shalit, 1995; Pearce et al. 1989; Pepper, 1993; Redclift, 1996, cf. Harvey, 1996.

8. The literature here is vast, but a useful cross section of material includes: Klein (2000) and Roddick (2000) on branding and anti-globalization politics; Fuentes and Ehrenrich (1983), Hale (2000), Johns and Vural (2000), Ong, 1987, and Ross (1987) on the politics of production; and Barrientos (2000), Blowfield (1999) and Renard (1999) on ethical trade.

9. The temporary, transient and marginal characteristics of car-boot sales are also hallmarks of both jumble sales and nearly new sales (Clarke, 2000) and precluded their selection. Notwithstanding their importance, and their distinctive social composition, they had too many similarities with car-boot sales to be robust comparative cases of the diversity within 'second-hand'. Furthermore, we would note that – given the proliferation of spaces of second-hand exchange through the 1980s and 1990s in the UK – jumble sales have declined in visibility. Indeed, many people we talked with during the course of this research argued that they had declined in quality too – as a direct consequence of the proliferation in and popularity of boot sales and charity shops.

10. This is not to deny that knowingness figures as a mode of participation with car-boot sales, but it is to say that this became increasingly hard to satisfy through car-boot sales through the 1990s – as many of our respondents pointed out. In part fuelled by the expansion in the second-hand market and the parallel growth in codified 'expert' knowledge (in the form of guides, magazines and web sites), the disjuncture between 'unknowing' sellers and 'knowing' buyers is rarely found. Indeed, the increase in 'expert knowledge' is widely regarded by dealers, traders and second-hand retailers to have led to widespread price inflation across the second-hand market.

11. The leading charity retailers of 2001 – 'the Big Ten' – are Oxfam, Imperial Cancer Research Fund (ICRF), British Heart Foundation (BHF), Cancer Research Campaign, Scope, British Red Cross, Barnados, Help the Aged, Sue Ryder and Marie Curie (Charity Finance Report, 2001). Much as in conventional retail, their rank is a measure of number of shops and total profit. All have a national presence in that their shops are located in most towns and cities across the UK.

12. Charities with the most net closures in 2001 were: ICRF (26), Sue Ryder (18), Oxfam (16), British Red Cross (13) and Scope (13). Overall, charities responding to the 2001 survey reported 243 closures – 'almost twice as many as the previous year (126) and three times as many as the year before that (80)' (Charity Finance Report, 2001, p 43: source Goodall, 2001). Indeed, in 2001 at least three charities, including NSPCC, had pulled out of shop operations altogether.

13. 2001 figures record 6256 shops generating an income of £388m and a total profit of £72m (Charity Finance Report 2001, Table 17a: souce Goodall, 2001).

14. A key issue here is the VAT situation. Should VAT be introduced on donated goods, it is widely acknowledged that this would bring about a significant decline in shop income that would be difficult to transfer onto the customer. Mintel's 1997 estimates were that the imposition of VAT on donated goods would cost charity retailers £33.5m (46 per cent of their then current income). In turn, it is likely that this would lead to the closure of significant numbers of charity shops. Additionally, problems of donation-decline (Cheary, 1997; McCann, 1997), the collapse of the rag market, staffing difficulties, the employment status of volunteers, the potential for charity mergers and proposals to heighten the regulation of house-to-house collection in Scotland provide on-going issues of debate (Charity Finance Report, 2001).

15. The main debate over car-boot sales occurred during 1993–5; however, more recently further calls for their regulation have been made. As we write, Bob Russell (MP, Lib Dem, Colchester) has lodged a motion to regulate car-boot sales, and the current Minister for Consumer Affairs (Melanie Johnson) is calling for police and trading standards to regulate events. Already this debate looks to be a rerun of that that occurred in the mid-1990s, in which boot sales are being represented as the site of illicit and illegal trading and populated by a cast of rogues, thieves and fraudsters.

16. There is a range of legislation that local authorities can draw on, in theory, to control the frequency and location of car-boot sales. One avenue is to deploy existing market law. This, however, is the subject of considerable uncertainty, if not confusion, when translated into the context of particular

local authorities. In legal terms, the definition of a market as a concourse of buyers and sellers is one which encompasses car-boot sales, and under common law those local authorities with market franchise rights have the right to object to any 'rival' market occurring within six and two-thirds miles of their own (Pease and Chitty, 1990). Alternatively, they can use this franchise if they so choose to license other markets including car-boot sales. The second area of legislation that local authorities can draw on is planning law (Larkham, 1995). Under the Town and Country Planning General Development Order 1988 (DoE, 1988), the use of land for holding a market is classified as a permitted development (and therefore does not require planning permission), provided that the land is used for not more than 14 days in any one year; that the land is open land; and that the use of the land is temporary (that is, used on one day a week, where the character of the land does not change, and where on the intervening 6 days the land is clear). The majority of car-boot sale operators circumvent planning law by shifting sites after 14 events. Beyond this, various other legislative powers may be invoked by local authorities, including: Section 37 of the Local Government (Miscellaneous Provisions) Act 1982, which requires a one-month period of notice of intention to hold a market and which permits fines of up to £2500; Enforcement and Stop notices; and Article 4 Directions which withdraw permitted development rights but which require Secretary of State approval (Reardon, 1994). However, the fear of possibly incurring considerable compensation payments deters many authorities from resorting to Article 4 Directions (Chapman and Larkham, 1995).

17. LACOTS was established in 1978. Its main role is to provide a consistent interpretation of trading standards and food hygiene legislation. However, as the then Chair of LACOTS Bill Mackay indicated in his introduction to the LACOTS discussion paper on car-boot sales, the organization also acts to identify new patterns and/or practices that may influence the balance between consumer protection and the operation of the free market. In the case of car-boot sales, both remits triggered LACOTS' involvement.

18. NABMA is the association of local authorities who operate, or are able to operate, markets by virtue of charter, statute or otherwise. Established in 1919 by 14 local authorities in the Midlands, and then joined by a Northern group of local authorities, the association is comprised of an optional membership. Still dominated by Midlands and Northern authorities, and therefore with a majority of Labour-controlled local authorities as members, the association acts to promote the interests of market authorities.

19. Clause 21 of the DCO Bill, debated in Parliament in 1994, proposed the abolition of market franchise rights. The rationale behind this was an attempt to deregulate market environments. Dating back to the medieval period, market franchise rights can be used by those possessing them (largely the metropolitan authorities) to protect a monopolistic operating environment: effectively such rights prevent the appearance of any 'rival' market within a radius of six and two-thirds miles of a market protected by market franchise rights. Predictably, these proposals had the effect of mobilizing the anti-car-boot-sale lobby, most of whom responded to the Department of Environment consultation paper on the abolition of market franchise rights. It was in the course of the passage of the DCO legislation through Parliament (1994) that the most forceful attacks on car-boot sales were made by this lobby. The clause pertaining to the abolition of market franchise rights was eventually removed from the DCO legislation.

20. *Only Fools and Horses* (BBC, 1981–94) is a popular television sitcom featuring two lead characters (Del Boy and Rodders), who run Trotters Independent Trading Corporation from the back of a Robin Reliant in Peckham, south-east London. The 'plot line' of each episode typically revolves around Del Boy endeavouring to sell various goods acquired in dubious circumstances, which transpire to be shoddy, faulty or in some way undesirable (for example, digital watches with no batteries, videos that are incompatible with UK recorders and so on). Del Boy and Rodders therefore can be seen to accord with the 'wheeler-dealer' activities that allegedly prevail within car-boot sales, as do the words of the theme tune to the series: 'No income tax, no VAT, no money back, no guarantee'.

21. Arthur Daley is the character immortalized by George Cole over several years of the classic British television programme *Minder* (Thames Television, 1979–94). Portrayed as a likeable if scurrilous rogue, Daley made a living ostensibly from second-hand car sales. However, this activity was supplemented by dealing in various stolen commodities that were usually moved on with the help of his 'minder' Tel (Dennis Waterman). Although the last series of *Minder* has long since been made, Arthur Daley has been encoded in popular culture as an instantly identifiable, and well-loved, petty criminal: witness his appearances in various advertising campaigns for the Leeds Permanent Building Society (1985–94).

22. A further irony in this debate, and a trend that acknowledges the popular appeal of car-boot sales, is that some metropolitan authorities now run their own boot sales on existing market sites (see Gregson et al. 1997).

23. For contrasting readings of gentrification see: Bondi, 1991, 1998; Hamnett, 1991, 2000; Lees, 1994; Ley, 1996.

24. Fuelled by Julia Roberts's dress at the 2001 Oscars Ceremony, this is now the subject of considerable coverage in the fashion press (Alexander, 2000; Armstrong, 2000a, 2000b; 2001; McDowell, 2000; Picardie, 2001).

25. It is worth noting here Top Shop's recent move to retail second hand clothing in its flagship Oxford Circus store in London, a manoeuvre that copies retro retailers' retro-repro juxtaposition, but that simultaneously problematizes any attempt to identify this tactic with 'the alternative'.

26. The exceptions to this tendency are hospice shops and locally based, usually one-shop charities (see Parsons, 2001), both of which are usually located in neighbourhood-oriented shopping parades.

27. See DoE/URBED 1994; Guy, 1998a, 1988b; Hall and Breheny, 1987; Howard, 1989; Lowe, 1998, 2001; Taylor et al. 1996.

28. The rise of the discounters and their importance in the clothing market is well documented in the trade press (see, for example Key Note 1997 Clothing and Footwear Report (London: Keynote) and Key Note 1999 Clothing and Footwear Report (London: Keynote)). Verdict's (2000) Clothing and Retailing Market Report argues that discounters such as Matalan, New Look and Mark One have redefined the lower end of the UK clothing market, by offering both fashionability and value. In 1999 the discount sector's sales grew by 17 per cent, whereas the clothing market as a whole grew by only 0.8 per cent. Verdict estimates that the discount sector will increase their share of the UK market to 13.9 per cent by 2004 (1999: 8.4 per cent), and that this will continue to threaten the trading position of middle-market retailers. Furthermore, growth will have significant implications for buyer-supplier relations, with price becoming an increasingly important element for supply–chain management strategies.

29. As we write, this is further confirmed by speculations over joint 'out-of-town' ventures by some of the large charity retailers (Charity Finance Report, 2001, p 47). Indicative of the effects of a 33 per cent rent increase across the sector over the past three years, during which time average profits have fallen by 25 per cent, this is – as yet – just talk.

30. Oxfam is the market leader in these tendencies (see Revell, 1997), and at the same time has recently diversified into further niche markets opening specialist book shops and craft-only shops in key university towns and cities such as York, Durham and Canterbury (Benady, 1997).

31. By comparison, amateur or occasional sellers are marked out by their lack of knowledge about value regimes, which means that they often attempt to sell inappropriate goods in inappropriate locations, or that they try to sell 'over the odds'. More 'commercial' traders would include those like Mal and Fran who utilize geographical variations in value-regimes to buy in bulk from car-boot sales in certain locations to sell on in others, market

traders and those like refuse collectors and household-waste site workers, whose access to household 'rubbish' allows them to deal – illegally – in the second-hand market.

32. More recent examples of Daphne and Phil's 'lead' items include a 'gold pheasant' and a 'horn of plenty', both part of an Avon perfume promotion, and both of which were 'snapped up' by a woman who was collecting them. The current 'lead' item is a condiment set in the style of a hard-boiled egg.

33. The use of language more commonly associated with the racecourse is a feature of car-boot sales and another means through which differences from other sites of exchange are signalled.

34. Dress is an important facet of car-boot-sale participation, with dressing down being critical to enabling the capture of value. Scruffy trainers, old track-bottoms and T shirts, then, are very much part of the serious buyer's performance and are seen as key props to getting the bargain.

35. Even allowing for the small amounts of money usually involved in each transaction (typically < £5), being able to constitute exchange as a game and to take risks is clearly dependent on having sufficient income for 'mistakes' not to matter. Furthermore, not reading the codes of boot sales accurately can have significant implications for purchasing, increasing the chances of buying 'the dud', the fake or indeed the counterfeit. In the course of our research, however, we encountered few transparent instances of the latter while those on limited incomes consistently showed that they were as well versed in the skills of 'the game' as those with more to play with.

36. Hiring is a strategy that an increasing number of retro retailers are turning to. Although some stock, inevitably, is lost in this way, hire costs are priced commercially, at at least 50 per cent of the full sale price.

37. Although this is an important group of shoppers, to research why they do not engage in second-hand shopping is a difficult exercise. At the outset of this research, then, we experimented with talking with a few individuals about why they didn't go to car-boot sales and charity shops, but like many other researchers before us found that getting people to articulate why they didn't do what we were researching problematic in the extreme (Barker and Brooks, 1998). Not only were we, by our very positioning as researchers – and in two occasions through styles of dress – identified positively with these practices, but individuals proved either unable or unwilling to articulate their reasons for shopping exclusively first hand. Likewise, many of our respondents revealed that this was something that did not get readily talked about within wider friendship networks. Left to the assumed and imagined, a lot of this speculation reiterated notions of stigma, bodily dirt and consumerism.

38. It is important to emphasize too that these three instances involve all three researchers. They therefore suggest that elision and slippage is a consistent pattern of talk among our respondents.

39. It is important to emphasize that practices are not associated exclusively with particular individuals, and that while individuals' talk and practice might be predominantly located within one practice, it can extend to include others. This becomes apparent in the sections that follow, where certain individuals crop up on more than one occasion.

40. This is to do with the way in which young children are allowed to play in these spaces – with toys that are 'for sale' for example (Chapter 4), and the ways in which volunteers frequently talk and/or occupy them while adults 'shop'. At the same time, there is none of the stress of potential breakages – a major worry for those on limited incomes when shopping in first-cycle spaces with young children.

41. Intriguingly, Christina talking about the same problem – for her potential rather than actual – is intent on resisting these tendencies. Whether this talk translates into practice, however, is in our minds open to question.

42. This is further confirmed by numerous instances observed during our participant observation work in charity shops, where women in this age group, accompanied by their male partners, engaged in practices of looking (and buying) while the men hovered outside or on plastic chairs at the front of the shop. Judy describes her husband doing exactly this, and cites this as one of the reasons why she prefers to shop alone. Similarly Val modifies her charity-shopping visits when away on holiday with her husband by looking only at bric-a-brac or for her mother and not for herself – 'because I wouldn't dream of wasting his time'.

43. It is worth noting that both Kate and Nicky – both regular wearers of second hand clothing – routinely engage in this practice too.

44. It is fair to say that this relative absence may be indicative of our research design, in that we did not deliberately set out to talk to individuals known for their activism around consumer politics – by snowballing from local wholefood co-ops for example. Rather, we wanted to see how widespread such articulations were within groups that were not defined already by such practices. That we encountered only five such individuals in more than 80 depth interviews is to our minds salutary.

45. It is important to note that within this household, while some agree totally with Chris's practices, others resist them. Chris's daughter for example is labeled by her mother as 'a bit of a snob really' because of her preference for new and 'designer' clothes for herself and her baby son. By comparison, her younger son – then at university – was lauded for his accord with his mother's views. Intriguingly, the elder son's preference for 'the new' was

explained by Chris as the result of his girlfriend's clothing practices, and by the fact that she worked for Next.

46. Although Thompson's *Rubbish Theory* is a noticeable exception here. See too Chase, 1999; Strasser, 2000; Rathje and Murphy, 2001.

47. Thompson draws on the work of two physicists here to explain how we are predisposed (by our theories, or world-view) to notice some things and ignore others. As one's subject position changes, so the things that we notice or ignore change. He uses the term 'relevate' to describe the way in which a theory makes things noticeable, and 'irrelevate' to describe how things are obscured from view.

48. Of course in practice sourcing and disposal strategies don't follow one another in a neat and linear sequence but are commonly run together, as individuals and traders both acquire desired commodities and dispose of unwanted things at one and the same time. It is, however, difficult to convey such continuity and multiplicity through the written word, whose order and structure is, of necessity, linear.

49. Although less common, there are two other disposal dispositions which we encountered in our research. The first we term indiscriminate jettisoning. Exemplified by Louise, this strategy involves periodic chucking-out of anything and everything in sight, including books, men's, women's and children's clothes (much of it bearing designer labels), toys, electrical items and so on. In one particular week, for example, she cleared out a cupboard and threw away a bin-liner full of almost-new childrenswear (including hardly-worn Marese, Miniman and Gap items as well as more mass-market M&S, Adams and Debenhams labels), two cassette players, a record player, about 50 white cot and cot-bed sheets, pillow-cases and blankets, and a computer box full of sun cream, mosquito repellant and other holiday-sundries. While it is interesting to speculate where Louise's junk may end up (in a landfill site to be raked over by refuse collectors perhaps), there is little more to say about this strategy in conceptual terms, save that it is indicative of overconsumption and the result of limited interest in, commitment to and time available for sorting and sifting through a range of commodities in order to evaluate their potential value to others. It is good housekeeping at its most radical and unreflexive, possession-purging on a grand scale. The final disposal disposition that we identify is the hoarder who has a reluctance to dispose of anything. This of course is not in itself a disposal strategy but it does nonetheless provide the opportunity for potential future rediscovery and revalorization. And given our comments about the central presence of women in space-making good housekeeping practices, we suggest here that a number of men may fall into the hoarder category, using sheds and garages as repositories for 'you never know when you might need it' commodities.

50. The case of retirees is interesting here, in that we see how both men and women feel able to discard smart 'work' clothes. In part this seems connected to a more relaxed approach to body dressing and management practices; dress codes become less of a regulated work-related performance.

51. We encountered several instances of women who have two 'wardrobes', for 'fat' and thin' phases and/or days respectively. And while some hold onto 'thin' clothes as a positive reminder of what once was, and what might be again, others (such as those who have been dieting and/or exercising and have lost weight) hold on to 'fat' clothes as a negative reminder of what must never be again (and see too Guy et al. 2001).

52. It needs to be noted here that the philanthropic disposition connects to particular disposal sites – charity shops, charity car-boot sales and jumble sales.

53. It is important to acknowledge here that this argument may say rather more about the specificities of the second-hand sites we investigated, and their limitations/possibilities for money-making. Clearly, disposal through charity shops is the counter case to this disposition. But there are other second-hand sites – such as dress agencies – that are spaces where disposal is governed by money-making. And our – admittedly limited – knowledge of these sites would suggest that they are for the most part frequented by women. Moreover, it needs to be recognized that, of the sites we investigated, it was primarily car-boot sales (and market stalls) that were associated with disposal as money-making. In the case of the former, it is entirely possible that some of the arguments we make in this section say rather more about the interweavings of masculinities with class at certain car-boot sales than about the gendering of this disposal disposition.

54. See Perry (1998) on the working lives of San Francisco's refuse collectors 'The Scavengers' and Tooke (2000) for a participant observational study of refuse collectors in the UK context.

55. The case of Elton John, for example, whose sale of his entire wardrobe of designer clothes raised $0.5m in 1996 reveals multiple motivations for disposal: in part to do with good housekeeping, in part to do with anxieties over body size and fit and in part to do with philanthropic, cause-related motivations (all proceeds from the auctioning of his clothes went to AIDS charities), Elton's indiscriminate jettisoning of late can be traced back to earlier phases of excessive consumption and to former hoarding tendencies, which includes clothes, record and car collections, all of which he has now sold off. When Christie's auctioned 20 of his cars in 2001 they fetched £1.8 million in what was described as an 'absolutely electric auction . . . we had to use two sale rooms there were so many bidders' (CNN, 2001: 2 – http://www.CNN.com). And see too Branigan (2001) who

discusses Vivienne Westwood's recent wardrobe clear-out and Brampton (1999), Christie's (1998), Garber (1992), The Hayward Gallery (1998), Showalter (2001), The Tyne and Wear Museum (1993), Vogue Daily (1998) and Windsor (1988) for retrospective celebrity fashion exhibitions and auctions.

56. McCracken talks, for example, about how infant's clothing may have to undergo a 'cooling off' period during which it is stored away for a while so that it will be cool, distant enough in meaning to allow disposal (1986). For others, such as Helen and Ian, their infants' clothes are so sacred, so impregnated with meaning and memory that they are priceless, cherished, singular, never to be disposed of.

57. There are, of course, others who venerate other historical eras – most notably the 1940s and 1950s (see Beardsall (1999) and McDowell (2000)), but more recently too the 1970s and 1980s (Alexander (1999, 2000), Edelstein and McDonagh (1990), Frankel (1997), Gerard (1996), Kennedy (1994), McDermott (1987), Rettenmund (1996)).

58. It is important to note that these modes are analytical categories. So, while individuals can, and do, demonstrate forms of object attachment that correspond exclusively with one mode of meaning creation, others reveal practices that run the two together. Examples of both singularity and blurring occur in what follows.

59. Here we draw on Kopytoff's discussion of the cultural biography of things.

60. This echoes the ways in which certain of the retro traders we interviewed are having to look further and further afield for affordable quality items.

61. While women did talk about their second-hand consumption in terms of imagined histories, this was almost exclusively confined to musings about familial histories. Rachel, for example, talks about 'This bag my gran gave me . . . I do have clothes from my gran. I just go up and raid her wardrobe; she gave me this lovely black top with silver sparkly stripes on . . . my mum thinks I'm a reject from the 60s, like hippy things . . . my gran says "I've been here before"'. Far less evident were the kind of romantic imaginings about unknown others which typify men's discussions about the meaning of their second-hand clothes.

62. Just a few of our respondents – interestingly, all men – admitted to occasionally not bothering about washing purchases. However, all acknowledged washing to be what ought to occur; they saw washing then as the normative practice. Rather than see their actions, then, as openly transgressive, we would interpret such lapses as 'permissable slips' (for men) to make, and 'permissable slips' to admit to us as women.

63. A number of our interviewees did, however, make the point about not buying outerwear which would require dry-cleaning, except in exceptional

circumstances. Much of this is to do with the way in which paying for dry-cleaning is seen to add to the cost of the garment and therefore negates any sense of capturing the saving through the bargain.

64. These practices clearly resonate with those of other subcultures – see for example the discussion of punk in Chapter 4 – and indicate how various second-hand sites, but particularly charity shops, have comprised key resources for a number of generations.

65. It is important to note that trading standards legislation makes it unlikely that many of these types of commodity would be offered 'for sale' in charity shops.

66. Two exceptions to this practice are where women purchase clothing for babies and children, and good housekeeping practices – where they may dispose of others' clothes.

67. In fact we only encountered one individual who bought second-hand gifts for Christmas. This was Tom, the fine art student from Nottingham who now doesn't shop at all in first-cycle retail stores. He argues that 'At Christmas now for my girlfriend I'd buy her loads of stuff – a record player, 20 records, a jumper. D'you know what I mean?' Here we see that Tom isn't necessarily rejecting the concept of the Christmas gift economy but is altering the way in which he seeks out such gifts.

68. As we have alluded to in Chapter 5, the two key exceptions to this pattern are children's clothes and maternity wear, which are typically 'loaned' (rather than gifted) among friendship and kin groups. It is the second-hand clothes of unknown adult others that are rarely gifted.

69. As we write this has just received a make-over and been converted into a dedicated Oxfam bookshop (see too Chapter 2).

70. 'Interpretive repertoires' is a term used by Hermes (1995) with respect to how women readers make sense of women's magazines. This has been developed further by Jackson (2001), Jackson et al. (2001), and Stevenson et al. (2000) to include how people both make sense of and also talk about, in their case, men's magazines.

Bibliography

Abelson, E. (1989) *When Ladies Go A-Thieving: Middle Class Shoplifters in the Victorian Department Store*, Oxford: Oxford University Press

ACC (1994) 'Time to put the lid on the boot? The implications of car boot sales'. Conference Proceedings, Association of County Councils

ADC (1993) 'Review of street trading legislation', Association of District Councils

ADC (1994) 'Response to the Department of the Environment's Consultation on Market Franchise Rights', Association of District Councils

Alexander, H. (1999) 'Eighties power', *The Telegraph*, 22 December

Alexander, H. (2000) 'The past masters: in Milan fashion has turned its back on the future and revisited the forties, the sixties, the seventies and even the eighties', *The Telegraph* 1 March

Allen, P. (1994) 'I bought it at a car boot sale officer', *The Times*, 3 February

Appadurai, A. (ed.)(1986) *The Social Life of Things: Commodities in Cultural Perspective*, Cambridge: Cambridge University Press

Armstrong, L. (2000a) 'One step forwards, four decades back', *The Times*, 30 March

Armstrong, L. (2000b) 'Psychedelic returns', *The Times*, 27 March

Armstrong, L. (2001) 'Something old, something new', *The Times*, 4 June

Baker, A. (ed.)(2000) *Serious Shopping: Essays in Psychotherapy and Consumerism*, London: Free Association Books

Barker, M. and Brooks, K. (1998) *Knowing Audiences: Judge Dredd, its Friends, Fans and Foes*, Luton: Luton University Press

Barkham, P. (1999) 'Second to none', *The Guardian*, 6 August

Barrientos, S. (2000) 'Globalisation and ethical trade', *Journal of International Development* 12: 559–70

Baudrillard, J. (1988) 'Consumer society', in M. Poster (ed.) *Jean Baudrillard. Selected Writings*, Cambridge: Polity, pp 26–43

Bauman, Z. (1993) *Postmodern Ethics*, Oxford: Blackwell

Bauman, Z. (1998) *Work, Consumption and the New Poor*, Buckingham: Open University Press

Bauman, Z. (2000) *Globalization: The Human Consequences*, Columbia: Columbia University Press

Beardsall, J. (1999) 'Tea in a time warp: the couple who shut the door on the late C20[th]'*Telegraph Magazine*, 5 June

Becker, H. (1963) *Outsiders*, Chicago: The Free Press

Bedford, T. (2002) 'Ethical consumerism: information, commodity fetishism and connections across the commodity chain', in A. Hughes and S. Reimer (eds.) *Geographies of Commodity Chains*, Harlow: Addison Wesley Longman (forthcoming)

Bedford, T. and Burgess, J. (2001) 'The focus group experience', in M. Limb and C. Dwyer (eds.) *Qualitative Methodologies for Geographers*, London: Arnold, pp 121–35

Belk, R. (1987) 'A child's Christmas in America: Santa Claus as Deity, consumption as religion', *Journal of American Culture* 10: 87–100

Belk, R. (1992) 'Attachment to possessions', in I. Altman and S. Low (eds.) *Place Attachment*, New York: Plenum, pp 114–30

Belk, R. (1995a) 'Studies in the new consumer behaviour', in D. Miller (ed.) *Acknowledging Consumption*, London: Routledge, pp 58–95

Belk, R. (1995b) *Collecting in a Consumer Society*, London: Routledge

Belk, R. and Coon, G. (1993) 'Gift-giving as agapic love: an alternative to the exchange paradigm based on dating experiences' *Journal of Consumer Research* 20: 393–417

Belk, R., Sherry, J. and Wallendorf, M. (1988) 'A naturalistic enquiry into buyer and seller behaviour at a swap meet', *Journal of Consumer Research* 14: 449–70

Belshaw, C. (1965) *Traditional Exchange and Modern Markets*, New Jersey: Prentice Hall

Benady, D. (1997) 'Charity shops adapt to survive', *Marketing Week*, 19 June

Benton, T. (1989) 'Marxism and natural limits: an ecological critique and reconstruction', *New Left Review* 178: 51–86

Bingham, N. (1996) 'Object-ions: from technological determinism towards geographies of relations', *Environment and Planning D: Society and Space* 14: 633–57

Bjerkan Weller, K. (1998) 'You think it's all over – but retro style is back in a big way', *Ideal Home and Lifestyle* (September) pp 24–31

Blomley, N. (1996) "I'd like to dress her down all over': masculinity, power and retail space', in N. Wrigley and M. Lowe (eds.) *Retail Capital and Consumption*, Harlow: Longman, pp 238–56

Blowfield, M. (1999) 'Ethical trade: a review of developments and issues', *Third World Quarterly* 20: 753–70

Blowfield, M., Mahlins, A., Nelson, V., Maynard, W. B., Gallat, S. and Robinson, D. (1999) *Ethical Trade and Sustainable Rural Livelihoods*, Chatham: Natural Resource Institute

Boggan, S. (1994) 'Punters make light of black market', *The Independent* 10 January

Bondi, L. (1991) 'Gender divisions and gentrification: a critique', *Transactions Institute of British Geographers* 16: 190–8

Bookchin, M. (1990) *Remaking Society: Pathways to a Green Future*, London: Black Rose Books

Bourdieu, P. (1977) *Outline of a Theory of Practice*, Cambridge: Cambridge University Press

Bourdieu, P. (1984) *Distinction: A Social Critique of the Judgement of Taste*, Cambridge MA: Harvard University Press

Bowlby, R. (1985) *Just Looking: Consumer Culture in Dreiser, Gissing and Zola*, New York: Methuen

Bowlby, R. (1987) 'Modes of modern shopping: Mallarmé at the Bon Marché', in N. Armstrong and L. Tennenhouse (eds.) *The Ideology of Conduct. Essays in Literature and the History of Sexuality*, London: Methuen, pp 185–205

Bowring, F. (1998) 'LETS: an eco–socialist initiative?', *New Left Review* 232: 91–111

Brampton, S. (1999) 'Biba girl puts a glittery era up for sale', *The Times*, 25 September, 3

Branigan, T. (2001) 'Old style success: Vivienne Westwood clears out her wardrobe' *The Guardian*, 5 September

Bret, D. (2001) 'Lipstick and lace: forget designer labels, go for romantic vintage clothes', *The Times*, 4 June

Breward, C. (2001) 'Manliness, modernity and the shaping of male clothing', in J. Entwistle and E. Wilson (eds.). *Body Dressing* Oxford: Berg, pp 165–82

Brewer, J. and Porter, R. (1993 eds.) *Consumption and the World of Goods*, New York: Routledge

British Broadcasting Corporation (1981–94) *Only Fools and Horses*, London: British Broadcasting Corporation

Brooke, S. (2000) 'Wayne's world of sixties kitsch', *The Times*, 19 February

Brown, I., O'Connor, J. and Cohen, S. (2000) 'Local music policies within a global music industry: cultural quarters in Manchester and Sheffield' *Geoforum* 31: 437–51

Burns Howell, T. (1993) 'In the country: are boot sales become loot sales?', *Daily Telegraph* 10 July

Bussmann, J. (1998) 'In praise of bad taste', *Sunday Times Style Magazine*, 11 October

Callon, J. (ed.)(1998) *The Laws of the Market*, Oxford: Blackwell

Campbell, C. (1987) *The Romantic Ethic and the Spirit of Modern Consumerism*, Oxford: Blackwell

Campbell, C. (1992) 'The desire for the new: its nature and social location as presented in theories of fashion and modern consumerism', in R. Silverstone and E. Hirsch (eds.) *Consuming Technologies: Media and Information in Domestic Spaces* London: Routledge, pp 48–63

Carrier, J. (1995) *Gifts and Commodities: Exchange and Western Capitalism since 1700*, London: Routledge

Carrier, J. (ed.)(1997) *Meanings of the Market*, Oxford: Berg

Carter, A. (1982) 'Notes for a theory of 1960s style', in A. Carter *Nothing Sacred* London: Virago

Champion, S. (1991) *And God Created Manchester*, Manchester: Wordsmith

Chaney, D. (1983) 'The department store as a cultural form', *Theory Culture and Society* 1: 22–31

Chaney, D. (1990) 'Subtopia in Gateshead: The MetroCentre as a cultural form', *Theory Culture and Society* 7: 49–68

Chapman, D, and Larkham, P. (1995) 'The use of Article 4 Directions in planning control', Research Paper, Faculty of the Built Environment, University of Central England, Birmingham

Chase, R. (1999) *Rubbish*, London: Simon and Schuster

Cheal, D. (1988) *The Gift Economy*, London: Routledge

Cheary, N. (1997) 'Oxfam forced to import goods as donations slide' *Marketing Week*, 19 June

Christie's (1998) *Street Fashion Exhibition Catalogue*, London: Christie's

Clarke, A. (1998) 'Window shopping at home: classified, catalogues and new consumer skills', in D. Miller (ed.) *Material Cultures*, London: UCL Press, pp 73–99

Clarke, A. (2000) '"Mother swapping": the trafficking of nearly new children's wear', in P Jackson et al. (eds.) *Commercial Cultures: Economies, Practices, Spaces*, Oxford: Berg, pp 85–100

Cockle, J. (2001) 'Obsessions: when one woman's trash is another woman's treasure', *M* August pp 8–12

Commoner, B. (1990) *Making Peace with the Planet*, London: New Press

Constant, J. (1993) 'Pirates ahoy at the boot sale', *The Times*, 13 May

Cooper, T. (2000) 'Hoxton, the new Hollywood' *This Is London*, 3 August

Corbett, G. (2000) 'Women, body image and shopping for clothes', in A. Baker (ed.) *Serious Shopping*, London: Free Association Books, pp 114–32

Crang, P. (1996) 'Displacement, consumption and identity' *Environment and Planning A* 28: 47–67

Crang, P. and Malbon, B. (1996) 'Consuming geographies: a review essay', *Transactions Institute of British Geographers* 21: 704–11

Crewe, L. (1996) 'Material culture: embedded firms, organizational networks and the local economic development of a fashion quarter', *Regional Studies* 30: 257–72

Crewe, L. (2001) The besieged body, *Progress in Human Geography* 24: 629–40

Crewe, L. (2002) 'A thread lost in an endless labyrinth: unravelling fashion's commodity chains' in A. Hughes and S. Reimer (eds.) *Geographies of Commodity Chains,* Harlow: Addison Wesley Longman (forthcoming)

Crewe, L. and Beaverstock, J. (1998) 'Fashioning the city: cultures of consumption in contemporary urban spaces', *Geoforum* 29: 287–308

Crewe, L. and Davenport, E. (1992) 'The puppet show: buyer supplier relations in clothing retailing', *Transactions Institute of British Geographers* 17: 183–97

Crewe, L. and Forster, Z. (1993) 'Markets, design and local agglomeration: the role of the small independent retailer and the workings of the fashion system', *Environment and Planning D: Society and Space* 11: 213–29

Crewe, L. and Gregson, N. (1998) 'Tales of the unexpected: exploring car boot slaes as marginal spaces of contemporary consumption', *Transactions of the Institute of British Geographers* 23: 39–53

Crewe, L. and Lowe, M. (1996) 'Gap on the map: Towards a geography of consumption and identity', *Environment and Planning A* 29: 1877–98

Crewe, L. Gregson, N. and Brooks, K. (2002) 'The spaces of creative work: retro retailers and the production of consumption', in R. Lee, A. Leyshon and C. Williams (eds.) *Alternative Economic Spaces,* Sage, London (forthcoming)

Crewe, L., Gregson, N. and Brooks, K (2002) 'The discursivities of difference: retro retailers and the ambiguities of the alternative', *Journal of Consumer Culture* (forthcoming)

Crossik, G. and Gaumain, S. (eds.)(1998) *Cathedrals of Consumption,* London: Ashgate

Csikszentmihalyi, M. and Rochberg-Halton, E. (1981) *The Meaning of Things: Domestic Symbols and the Self,* Cambridge: Cambridge University Press

DoE (1988) 'General Development Order Consolidation', Circular 1988/22, Department of the Environment, London: HMSO

DoE (1993) *Consultation Paper on Market Franchise Rights*, Department of the Environment

DoE/URBED (1994) *Vital and Viable Town Centres: Meeting the Challenge*, London: HMSO

De Shalit, A. (1995) *Why Posterity Matters: Environmental Policies of Future Generations*

Davis, F. (1992) *Fashion, Culture and Identity*, Chicago: University of Chicago Press

Davis, J. (1992) *Exchange*, Buckingham: Open University Press

Dewar, D. and Watson, V. (1990) *Urban Markets: Developing Informal Retailing*, London: Routledge

Dilley, R. (ed.)(1992) *Contesting Markets: Analyses of Ideology, Discourse and Practice*, Edinburgh: Edinburgh University Press

Dittmar, H. (1992) *The Social Psychology of Material Possessions: To Have is To Be*, Hemel Hempstead: Harvester Wheatsheaf

Dobson, A. (ed.)(1991) *The Green Reader*, London: André Deutsch

Dobson, A. (1995) *Green Political Thought* (2nd Edition), London: Routledge

Domosh, M. (1996) 'The feminised retail landscape: gender, ideology and consumer culture in nineteenth century New York City', in N. Wrigley and M. Lowe (eds.) *Retailing, Consumption and Capital* Harlow: Longman, pp 257–71

Dorfles, G. (1979) *Kitsch: The World of Bad Taste*, New York: Universe Books

Douglas, M. and Isherwood, B. (1979) *The World of Goods: Towards an Anthropology of Consumption*, Harmondsworth: Penguin

Dowling, R. (1993) 'Femininity, place and commodities: a retail case study' *Antipode* 25: 295–319

du Gay, P. (1996) *Consumption and Identity at Work*, London: Sage

Dyson, J. (1998) 'Why Bath is the new Notting Hill', *Daily Express*, 30 July, pp 48–9

Edelstein, A. and McDonagh, M. (1990) *The Seventies: From Hot-pants to Hot-tubs*, New York: Penguin

EFTA (1998) *From Fair Trade to Responsible Consumption: the Power of the Citizens of Europe to Change the Conditions of North/South Relations*, Maastricht: European Fair Trade Association

Elkington, J. and Hailes, J. (1988) *The Green Consumer Guide*, London: Gollancz

Ewen, E. and Ewen, S. (1982) *Channels of Desire: Mass Images and the Shaping of American Consciousness*, New York: McGraw-Hill

Ewen, S. (1976) *Captains of Consciousness: Advertising and the Social Roots of Consumer Culture*, New York: McGraw Hill

Featherstone, M. (1991) *Consumer Culture and Postmodernism*, London: Sage

Fletcher, S. (2000) 'Forget Soho, go Sosho', *This Is London*, 14 July

Forty, A. (1986) *Objects of Desire*, London: Thames & Hudson

Frankel, S. (1997) 'Remembrance of padded shoulders past', *The Guardian*, 12 March

Freedman, A. (1976) 'Garage sale folklore', *New York Folklore* 2: 167–76

Frith, S. (1997) 'Formalism, Realism and Leisure: The case of punk', *The Subcultures Reader*, London: Routledge: 163–74

Fuentes, A. and Ehrenrich, B. (1983) *Women in the Global Factory*, Boston: South End Press

Gamman, L. (2000) 'Visual seduction and perverse compliance: reviewing food fantasies, large appetites and grotesque bodies', in S. Bruzzi and P. Church-Gibson (eds.) *Fashion Cultures*, London: Routledge, pp 61–78

Garber, M. (1992) 'Overcoming auction block: stories masquerading as objects', *Critical Quarterly* 34(4):74–96

Gelber, S. (1992) 'Free market metaphor: the historical dynamics of stamp collecting', *Comparative Studies in Society and History* 34: 42–69

Gelder, K. and Thornton, S. (eds.)(1997.) *The Subcultures Reader*, London: Routledge

Gerard, J. (1996) 'From naff to classic in two decades', *The Telegraph*, 14 September

Gereffi, G. (1994) 'The organisation of buyer-driven global commodity chains: how US retailers shape overseas production networks', in G. Gereffi and M. Korzeniewicz (eds.) *Commodity Chains and Global Capitalism*, Connecticut: Greenwood, pp 93–122

Gereffi, G., Korzeniewicz, M. and Korzeniewicz, R. (eds.)(1994) *Commodity Chains and Global Capitalism*, Connecticut: Greenwood

Giddens, A. (1991) *Modernity and Self-Identity: Self and Society in the Late Modern Age*, Cambridge: Polity

Glennie, P. and Thrift, N. (1992) 'Modernity, urbanism and modern consumption', *Environment and Planning D: Society and Space* 10: 423–43

Glennie, P. and Thrift, N. (1993) 'Modern consumption: theorizing commodities and consumers' *Environment and Planning D: Society and Space* 11: 603–6

Gold, M. (2001) 'Only one careful wearer' *The Times*, 1 September

Goodall, R (2001) 'Charity shops back on target', *Charity Finance* (July), pp 42–57

Gordon, G. (1985) 'The trouble with garage sales', *Journal of Consumer Research* 14: 449–70

Goss, J. (1993) 'The magic of the mall: an analysis of form, function and meaning in the contemporary retail built environment', *Annals of the Association of American Geographers* 83: 18–47

Goss, J. (1999) 'Once-upon-a-Time in the commodity world: an unofficial guide to Mall of America', *Annals of the Association of American Geographers* 89: 45–75

Gottdiener, M. (1986) 'Recapturing the centre: a semiotic analysis of shopping malls', in M. Gottdiener and A. Lagoupolos A (eds.) *The City and the Sign: an Introduction to Urban Semiotics*, New York: Columbia University Press, pp 288–302

Gregory, C. (1982) *Gifts and Commodities*, London: Academic Press

Gregson, N. and Crewe, L. (1994) 'Beyond the high street and the mall: car boot fairs and the new geographies of consumption in the 1990s', *Area* 26: 261–67

Gregson, N. and Crewe, L. (1997a) 'The bargain, the knowledge and the spectacle: making sense of consumption in the space of the car boot sale' *Environment and Planning D: Society and Space* 15: 87–112

Gregson, N. and Crewe, L. (1997b) 'Performance and possession: rethinking the act of purchase in the light of the car boot sale' *Journal of Material Culture* 2: 241–63

Gregson, N., Crewe, L. and Longstaff, B. (1997) 'Excluded spaces of regulation: car boot sales as an enterprise culture out of control?', *Environment and Planning A* 29: 1717–37

Gregson, N. and Crewe, L. (1998) 'Dusting down *Second-hand Rose*: gendered identities and the world of second-hand goods in the space of the car boot sale', *Gender Place and Culture* 5: 77–100

Gregson, N., Brooks, K. and Crewe, L. (2000) 'Narratives of consumption and the body in the space of the charity shop', in P. Jackson, M. Lowe, D. Miller and F. Mort (eds.) *Commercial Cultures: Economies, Practices, Spaces*, Oxford: Berg, pp 101–22

Gregson, N., Brooks, K. and Crewe, L. (2001) 'Bjorn Again? Rethinking 70s revivalism through the reappropriation of 70s clothing' *Fashion Theory* 5: 3–28

Gregson N, Brooks K and Crewe L (2002a) 'Discourse, displacement and retail practice: some pointers from the charity retail project', *Environment and Planning A* (forthcoming)

Gregson, N., Crewe, L. and Brooks, K. (2002b) 'Shopping, space and practice', *Environment and Planning D: Society and Space* (forthcoming)

Grogan, S. (1999) *Body Image* London: Routledge

Guy, A., Green, E. and Banim, M. (eds.)(2001) *Through the Wardrobe: Women's Relationship with their Clothes*, Oxford: Berg

Guy, C. (1998) 'Off centre retailing in the UK: prospects for the future and the implications for town centres', *Built Environment* 24: 16–30

Hale, A. (2000) 'What hope for ethical trade in the globalised garment industry?', *Antipode* 32: 349–56

Hall, P. and Breheny, M. (1987) 'Urban decentralization and retail development: Anglo American comparison', *Built Environment* 13: 244–61

Hamnett, C. (1991) 'The blind men and the elephant: the explanation of gentrification' *Transactions Institute of British Geographers* 16: 259–79

Hamnett, C. (2000) 'Gentrification, post industrialization and restructuring', in G Bridge and S Watson (eds.) *A Companion to the City*, Oxford: Blackwell

Hansard (1994) House of Commons Standing Committee F, Deregulation and Contracting Out Bill, Clause 21, columns 513–99, London: HMSO

Harris, D. (1994) 'Federation targets the high street charity shop; your own business', *The Times*, 17 May

Hartwick, E. (1998) 'Geographies of consumption: a commodity chain approach', *Environment and Planning D: Society and Space* 16 423–437

Hartwick, E. (2000) 'Towards a geographical politics of consumption', *Environment and Planning A* 32: 1177–92

Harvey, D. (1996) *Justice, Nature and the Geography of Difference*, Oxford: Blackwell

Hayward Gallery (1998) *Addressing the Century: 100 Years of Art & Fashion*, London: Hayward Gallery

Hebdige, D. (1979) *Subculture: the Meaning of Style*, London: Methuen

Hermes, J. (1995) *Reading Women's Magazines*, Cambridge: Polity

Herrmann, G. and Soiffer, S. (1984) 'For fun and profit: an analysis of the American garage sale', *Urban Life* 12: 397–421

Hirst, J. (1993) 'Boots are made for hawking' *The Guardian*, 15 September

Hoff, A. (1997) *Thrift Score*, London: Harper Collins

Homer, K. (2001) 'Second-hand bargains', *The Times* 8 August

Hopkins, J. (1990) 'West Edmonton Mall: landscapes of myth and elsewhereness', *Canadian Geographer* 34: 2–17

Horne, S. (2000) 'Charity shops in the UK', *International Journal of Retail Distribution and Management* 26: 155–61

Howard, E. (1989) *Prospects for Out-of-Town Retailing: the Metro Experience*, Harlow: Longman

Hughes, A. and Reimer, S. (2002 eds.) *Geographies of Commodity Chains*, Harlow: Addison Wesley Longman (forthcoming)

Hulanicki, B. (1983) *From A to Biba*, London: Hutchinson

Hutcheon, L. (1994) *Irony's Edge: the Theory and Politics of Irony*, London: Routledge

Hyman, R. (1999a) 'Doom and gloom engulfs the high street', *The Independent*, 28 September

Hyman, R. (1999b) 'M&S cranks up the retail war', *The Guardian*, 8 March

Imrie, S. (1989) *Beyond Green Consumerism*, London: Friends of the Earth

Jackson, J. (1993) 'Sweet charity', *Drapers Record*, 21 August

Jackson, L. (1998) *The Sixties*, London: Phaidon

Jackson, P. (1993) 'Towards a cultural politics of consumption', in J. Bird *Mapping the Futures: Local Cultures, Global Change*, London: Routledge, pp 207–228

Jackson, P. (1999) 'Commodity Cultures: The traffic in things', *Transactions Institute British Geographers* 24: 95–108

Jackson, P. (2000) 'Rematerialising social and cultural geography', *Social and Cultural Geography* 1: 9–14

Jackson, P. (2001) 'Making sense of qualitative data', in M. Limb and C. Dwyer (eds.) *Qualitative Methodologies for Geographers*, London: Arnold, pp 199–214

Jackson, P. and Holbrook, B. (1995) 'Multiple meanings: shopping and the cultural politics of identity' *Environment and Planning A* 27: 1913–30

Jackson, P., Stevenson, N. and Brooks, K. (2001) *Reading Men's Magazines*, Cambridge: Polity

Johns, R. and Vural, L. (2000) 'Class, geography and the consumerist turn: UNITE and the sweatshops campaign', *Environment and Planning A* 23: 1193–1213

Johnson, P. (1996) *Straight Outa Bristol*, London: Sceptre

Keating, M. (1998) 'Charity shops: faith, hope and tax relief', *The Guardian*, 15 December

Kennedy, P. (1994) *Platforms: A Microwaved Cultural Chronicle of the 1970s*, New York: St. Martin's Press

Key Note (1997) *Clothing and Footwear Report*, London: Key Note

Key Note (1999) *Clothing and Footwear Report*, London: Key Note

Kingsley, M. (1998) 'Charity shop chic', *Home and Life* 9 (February): 35–8

Klein, N. (2000) *No Logo*, London: Flamingo

Kopytoff, I. (1986) 'The cultural biography of things: commodification as a process', in A. Appadurai (ed.) *The Social Life of Things*, Cambridge: Cambridge University Press, pp 64–94

LACOTS (1993) 'Car boot sales: a discussion paper designed to stimulate debate on the implications of the success of car boot sales', Local Authorities Coordinating Body on Food and Trading Standards

Laermans, R. (1993) 'Learning to consume: early department stores and the shaping of modern consumer culture, 1860–1914', *Theory Culture and Society* 10: 79–102

Lancaster, W. (1995) *The Department Store: A Social History*, London: Pinter

Landry, C. (2000) *The Creative City*, London: Earthscan

Larkham, P. (1995) 'Controlling the car boot sale', *Area* 27: 74–6

Lash, S. and Friedman, F. (1992 eds.) *Modernity and Identity*, Oxford: Blackwell

Latour, B. (1993) *We Have Never Been Modern*, Cambridge, MA: Harvard University Press

Laurence, C. (1997) 'When men were men and knew it', *Daily Telegraph*, 4 October

Laurier, E. (1998) 'Geographies of talk: "Max left a message for you"', *Area* 30: 36–45

Lavelle. P. (1995) 'Dodgy dealings with the real life Del Boys', *Northern Echo*, 19 April

Leach, W. (1984) 'Transformations in a culture of consumption: Woman and department stores, 1890 – 1925', *Journal of American History* 71: 319–42

Leadbeater, C. (1999) *Living on Thin Air*, Harmondsworth: Penguin

Leadbeater, C. and Oakley, K. (1999) *The Independents* London: Demos

Lee, R. (1996) 'Moral money? LETS and the social construction of local economic geographies in SE England', *Environment and Planning A* 28: 1377–94

Lees, L. (1994) 'Rethinking gentrification: beyond the positions of economics or culture' *Progress in Human Geography* 18: 137–50

Lehtonen, T. and Mäenpää, P. (1997) 'Shopping in the East Centre Mall', in P. Falk and C. Campbell (eds.) *The Shopping Experience*, London: Sage, pp 136–65

Lemire, B. (1991) 'Peddling fashion: salesmen, pawnbrokers, tailors, thieves and the second-hand clothes trade in England c. 1700–1800', *Textile History* 22: 67–82

Leslie, D. and Reimer, S. (1999) 'Spatialising Commodity Chains' *Progress in Human Geography* 23: 401–20

Ley, D. (1996) *The New Middle Classes and the Remaking of the Central City*, Oxford: Oxford University Press

Lobental, J. (1990) *Radical Rags: Fashions of the 1960s*, New York: Abbeville Press

Lowe, M. (1998) 'The Merry Hill regional shopping centre controversy: PPG6 and new urban geographies', *Built Environment* 24: 57–69

Lowe, M. (2001) 'From Victor Gruen to Merry Hill: reflections on regional shopping centres and urban development in the US and UK', in P. Jackson, M. Lowe, D. Miller and F. Mort (eds.) *Commercial Cultures: Economies, Practices, Spaces*, Oxford: Berg, pp 245–59

Lunt, P. and Livingstone, S. (1992) *Mass Consumption and Personal Identity*, Buckingham: Open University Press

Lury, C. (1996) *Consumer Culture*, Cambridge: Polity

McCann, P. (1997) 'Charity doesn't begin at home any more', *The Independent*, 19 June

McConnell, S. (1999) 'EC1 is the place for fringe benefits', *The Guardian*. 28 September

McCracken, G. (1988) *Culture and Consumption*, Bloomington IN: Indiana University Press

McCree, C. (1984) 'Flea market', *Psychology Today* 18: 46–53

McDermott, C. (1987) *Street Style: British Design in the 1980s*, London: The Design Council

McDowell, C. (2000) 'Vintage rock'n'roll memorabilia', *Sunday Times Style*, 14 May

McKendrick, N., Brewer, J. and Plumb, J. H. (1982) *The Birth of a Consumer Society: the Commercialization of Eighteenth Century England*, London: Hutchinson

McRobbie, A. (1989) *Zoot Suits and Second-hand Dresses: an Anthology of Fashion and Music*, Basingstoke: Macmillan

McRobbie, A. (1998) *British Fashion Design: Rag Trade or Image Industry*, London: Routledge

McRobbie, A. (1999) *In the Culture Society: Art, Fashion and Popular Music*, London: Routledge

Maddrell, A. (2000) '"You just can't get the staff these days"': the challenges and opportunities of working with volunteers in the charity shop – an Oxford case study', *International Journal of Nonprofit and Voluntary Sector Marketing* 5: 125–39

Maffesoli, M. (1991) *The Times of the Tribes*, London: Sage

Maisel, R. (1976) 'The flea market as action scene', *Urban Life* 24: 488–505

Malinowski, B. (1922) *Argonauts of the Western Pacific*, London: E. P. Dutton

Malson, H. and Swann, C. (1999) 'Prepared for consumption: (dis)orders of eating and embodiment', *Journal of Community and Applied Social Psychology* 9: 369–406

Mauss, M. (1954) *The Gift: the Form and Reason for Exchange in Archaic Societies*, New York: W W Norton

Miles, S. (1998) *Consumerism – as a Way of Life*, London: Sage

Miller, D. (1987) *Material Culture and Mass Consumption*, Oxford: Blackwell

Miller, D. (ed.)(1993) *Unwrapping Christmas*, Oxford: Oxford University Press

Miller, D. (ed.)(1995) *Acknowledging Consumption: A Review of New Studies*, London: Routledge

Miller, D. (1998) *A Theory of Shopping*, Cambridge: Polity

Miller, D. (2000) 'The birth of value', in P. Jackson, M. Lowe, D. Miller and F. Mort (eds) *Commercial Cultures: Economies, Practices, Spaces*, Oxford: Berg, pp 77–84

Miller, D., Jackson, P., Thrift, N., Holbrook, B. and Rowlands, M. (1998) *Shopping Place and Identity*, London: Routledge

Miller, M. (1988) *The Bon Marché: Bourgeois Culture and the Department Store*, London: Allen & Unwin

Miller, M. (1981) 'Patterns of exchange in the rural sector: flea markets along the highway', *Journal of American Culture* 11: 55–9

Mintel (Marketing Intelligence) (1997) *Charity Shop Retailing*, London: Mintel

Moorehouse, H. (1991) *Driving Ambitions: an Analysis of the American Hot-Rod Enthusiasm*, Manchester: Manchester University Press

Morris, M. (1988) 'Things to do with shopping centres', in S. Sheridan (ed.) *Grafts: Feminist Cultural Criticism*, London: Verso, pp 193–225

Mort, F. (1996) *Cultures of Consumption*, London: Routledge

Muggleton, D. (2000) *Inside Subculture*, Oxford: Berg

Murphy, A. (1997) 'Seconds to go', *The Observer*, 19 January

NABMA (1991) *Annual Report: Proceedings of the 43rd Annual Conference*, National Association of British Market Authorities

NABMA (1994) 'Response to the Department of Environment's consultation paper on market franchise rights: the case for the retention of market franchise rights, National Association of British Market Authorities

Nava, M. (1996) 'Modernity's disavowal: women, the city and the department store', in M. Nava and P. O'Shea *Modern Times: Reflections on a Century of English Modernity*, London: Routledge, pp 38–76

NGO Finance (1996) *NGO Finance Charity Shops Survey* High Street Wars Hot Up: Charity Shops Face Rates Offensive, London: Plaza

NGO Finance (1997) *NGO Charity Shops Survey* Coming of Age in the High Street – A Brighter Future for Charity Shops, London: Plaza

NGO Finance (1998) *NGO Charity Shops Survey* Charity Shops Sailing Fair – But Storm Cloud Blots Retail Horizon, London: Plaza

NGO Finance (1999) *NGO Charity Shops Survey* Working on the Chain Gang: Hard Labour for Charity Shops, London: Plaza

Nixon, S. (1996) *Hard Looks: Masculinities, Spectatorship and Contemporary Consumption*, London: UCL Press

North, P. (1999) 'Explorations in heterotopia: local exchange trading systems (LETS) and the micropolitics of money and livelihood', *Environment and Planning D: Society and Space* 17: 69–86

North, R. (1995) *Life on a Modern Planet: a Manifesto for Progress*, Manchester: Manchester University Press

North, R. (1997) 'Turning back the tables on all that's new', *Electronic Telegraph* 16th September

O'Connor, J. (1998) 'Popular culture, cultural intermediaries and urban regeneration', in T. Hall and P. Hubbard (eds.) *The Entrepreneurial City*, Chichester: Wiley, pp 225–40

O'Connor J, Lovatt A and Milestone K (1993) *Culture and the Northern Quarter* MIPC: Manchester

O'Neill, P. and Gibson-Graham, J. K. (1999) 'Enterprise discourse and executive talk: stories that destabilize the company', *Transactions Institute of British Geographers* 24: 11–22

Ong, A. (1987) *Spirits of Resistance and Capitalist Development: Factory Women in Malaysia*, Albany: State University of New York Press

Pacione, M. (1997) 'Local exchange trading systems as a response to the globalisation of capitalism', *Urban Studies* 34: 1179–99

Palmer, I. (1999) 'Supermodel Thrift', *Elle* (November)

Parrish, R. (1986) 'A garage sale is never as simple as you think: there's always something that stays to haunt you', *Smithsonian* 17: 133

Parsons, E. (2001) Participating in charity retailing: shopping, volunteering and managing in charity shops. Unpublished PhD thesis, University of Bristol

Pavia, T. (1993) 'Dispossession and perceptions of self in late stage HIV infections', *Advances in Consumer Research* 17: 425–8

Pearce, D., Markandya, A. and Barbier, E. (1989) *Blueprint for a Green Economy*, London: Earthscan

Pearce, S. (1995) *On Collecting*, London: Routledge

Pease, J. and Chitty, J. (1990) *Law of Markets and Fairs*, Croydon: Charles Knight

Pepper, D. (1993) *Eco Socialism: From Deep Ecology to Social Justice*, London: Green Print

Perry, S. (1998) *Collecting Garbage*, London: Transaction

Picardie, J. (2001) 'Is vintage old hat?', *Vogue* (October) pp 127–30

Polan, B. (1999) 'Boho a go go', *Daily Mail*, 30 August

Polhemus, T. (1994) *Streetstyle*, London: Thames & Hudson

Polhemus, T. and Proctor, L. (1978) *Fashion and Anti Fashion*, London: Thames & Hudson

Polhemus, T. and Proctor, L. (1984) *Pop Styles: Where Fashion Meets Rock n Roll*, London: Vermilion

Porter Benson, S. (1986) *Counter Culture: Saleswomen, Managers and Customers in American Department Stores, 1890–1940*, Urbana: University of Illinois Press

Powell, P. and Peel, L. (1988) *'50s and '60s Style*, Secaucus, NJ: Chartwell

Quant, M. (1967) *Quant on Quant*, London: Pan Books

Radner, H . (2001) 'Embodying the single girl in the 1960s', in J. Entwistle and E. Wilson (eds) *Body Dressing*, Oxford: Berg, pp 183–200

Raikes, P,. Jensen, M. and Ponte, S. (2000) 'Global commodity chain analysis and the French filière approach: comparison and critique', *Economy and Society* 29: 390–417

Rathje, W. and Murphy, C. (2001) *Rubbish: the Archaeology of Garbage*, Tucson: University of Arizona Press

Rawlinson, R. (1992) 'Charity retail success sparks high street row', *Drapers Record* 1 August

Razzouk, N. and Gourley, D. (1982) 'Swap meets: profile of shoppers', *Arizona Business* 29: 8–12

Reardon, L. (1994) 'The legal aspects of car boot sales and markets', *Journal of Planning and Environmental Law* 94: 13–19

Redclift, M. (1996) *Wasted: Counting the Costs of Global Consumption*, London: Earthscan

Redhead, S. (1993) *Rave Off: Politics and Deviance in Contemporary Youth Culture*, Aldershot: Ashgate

Reekie, G. (1993) *Temptations: Sex, Selling and the Department Store*, Sydney: Allen & Unwin

Renard, M. (1999) 'The interstices of fair trade', *Sociologia Ruralis* 39: 484–500

Rettenmund, M. (1996) *Totally Awesome '80s*, New York: St Martin's Griffon Press

Revell, P. (1998) 'Famine to feast', *The Guardian*, 25 February

Richards, X (1996) 'Ladies of fashion: pleasure, perversion or paraphilia' *International Journal of Psychoanalysis* 77: 337 – 51

Rickey, M. (1999) 'All the trends are born on these stalls', *Daily Telegraph*, 26 May

Rickey, M. (2000) 'Tat is where it's at', *Daily Telegraph*, 26 April

Rickey, M. (2001) 'Get the hippy hippy chic and prepare for a Summer of Love Revival', *The Times*, 16 July

Roddick, A. (2000) *Business as Unusual*, London: HarperCollins

Ross, A. (1997) *No Sweat: Fashion, Free Trade and the Rights of Garment Workers*, London: Verso

Rudmin, F. (1991) *To Have Possessions: a Handbook of Ownership and Property*, Corte Madera, CA: California Select Press

Rudmin, F. and Richens, M. (eds)(1992) *Meaning, Measure and Morality of Materialism*, Utah: Association for Consumer Research

Samuel, R. (1994) *Theatres of Memory*, London: Verso

Sanders, C. (2001) 'Dirty tricks', *Vogue* (August) pp 219–220

Saunders, G. (2001) 'It's Vintage', *Elle* (August)

Sayer, A. (1997) 'The dialectic of culture and economy', in R. Lee and J. Wills (eds.) *Geographies of Economies*, London: Edward Arnold, pp 16–26

Schouten, J. (1991) 'Selves in transition: symbolic consumption in personal rites of passage and identity construction', *Journal of Consumer Research* 17: 412–25

Schrift, A. (1997) *The Logic of the Gift*, London: Routledge

Sconce, J. (1995) '"Trashing" the academy: taste, excess and an emerging politics of cinematic style', *Screen* 36: 371–93

Scott, A. (1999) 'The US recorded music industry: on the relations between organisation, location and creativity in the cultural economy', *Environment and Planning A* 31: 1965–84

Sherry, J. (1990) 'A sociocultural analysis of a Midwestern American flea market', *Advances in Consumer Research* 17: 13–30

Sherry, J. and McGrath, M. (1989) 'Unpacking the holiday presence: a comparative ethnography of two gift stores', in C. Hirschman (ed.) *Interpretive Consumer Research*, Provo, UT: Association for Consumer Research, pp 148–67

Sherry, J., McGrath, M. and Levy, S. (1992) 'The disposition of the gift and many unhappy returns', *Journal of Retailing* 68: 40–65

Sherry, J., McGrath, M. and Levy, S. (1993) 'The dark side of the gift', *Journal of Business Research* 28: 225–44

Shields, R. (1989) 'Social spatialisation and the built environment: West Edmonton Mall', *Environment and Planning D: Society and Space* 7: 147–64

Shields, R. (ed.)(1992) *Lifestyle Shopping: the Subject of Consumption*, London: Routledge

Showalter, E. (2001) 'Fade to greige', *London Review of Books* 23 (14 January), 1–9

Sibley, D. (1995) *Geographies of Exclusion*, London: Routledge

Skeggs, B. (1997) *Formations of Class and Gender: Becoming Respectable*, London: Sage

Slater, D. (1993) 'Going shopping: markets, crowds and consumption', in C. Jenks (ed.) *Cultural Reproduction*, London: Routledge, pp 188–209

Slater, D. (1997) *Consumer Culture and Modernity*, Cambridge: Polity

Slater, D. (2000) 'Consumption without scarcity: exchange and normativity in an internet setting', in P. Jackson, M. Lowe, D. Miller and F. Mort (eds) *Commercial Cultures: Economies, Practices, Spaces*, Oxford: Berg, pp 123–142

Slater, D. and Tonkiss, F. (2000) *Market Society: Markets and Modern Social Thought*, Cambridge: Polity

Smith, C. (1989) *Auctions: the Social Construction of Value*, Hemel Hempstead: Harvester Wheatsheaf

Smith, N. (1979) 'Toward a theory of gentrification: a back to the city movement by capital not people', *Journal American Planners Association* 45: 538–48

Smith, N. (1996) *The New Urban Frontier: Gentrification and the Revanchist City*, London: Routledge

Smith, N. and Williams, P. (eds)(1986) *Gentrification of the City*, London: Unwin Hyman

Smith, S. (2001) 'Doing qualitative research: from interpretation to action', in M. Limb and C. Dwyer (eds.) *Qualitative Methodologies for Geographers*, London: Arnold, pp 23–40

Soiffer, S. and Herrmann, G. (1987) 'Visions of power: ideology and practice in the American garage sale', *Sociological Review* 35: 48–83

Spencer, E. (1997) *The London Fashion Guide: Shopping for Style in the Capital*, London: Evening Standard Books

Spindler, A. (1994) 'Looking back: all the bustle over retro', *New York Times*, 15 November

Stallybrass, P. and White, A. (1986) *The Politics and Poetics of Transgression*, London: Methuen

Stevenson, N., Jackson, P. and Brooks, K. (2000) 'Ambivalence in men's lifestyle magazines', in P. Jackson, M. Lowe, D. Miller and F. Mort (eds.) *Commercial Cultures: Economies, Practices, Spaces*, Oxford: Berg, pp 189–212

St Leger, M. (1993) 'Shops operated by the top 400 charities', in S. K. E. Saxon-Harrold and J. Kendall (eds.) *Researching the Voluntary Sector*, London: Charities Aid Foundation

Strasser, S. (1998) 'The convenience is out of this world: The garbage disposer and American Consumer Culture', in S. Strasser, C. McGovern and M. Judt (eds) *Getting and Spending: European and American Consumer Societies in the Twentieth Century*, Cambridge: Cambridge University Press

Strasser, S. (2000) *Waste and Want: a Social History of Trash*, New York: Owl Books

Strathern, M. (1988) *The Gender of the Gift*, Berkeley: University of California Press

Tannock, S. (1995) 'Nostalgia critique', *Cultural Studies* 9: 453–64

Taylor, I., Evans, K. and Fraser, P. (1996) *A Tale of Two Cities: Global Change, Local Feeling and Everyday Life in the North of England: A Study in Manchester and Sheffield*, London: Routledge

Thames Television (1979–94) *Minder*, London: Thames Television

Thompson, M. (1979) *Rubbish Theory: the Creation and Destruction of Value*, Oxford: Oxford University Press

Thorne, L. (1996) 'Local exchange trading systems in the UK – a case of re-embedding' *Environment and Planning A* 28: 1361–76

Thornton, P. (1990) 'Flared to Death', *The Face* 2(19) pp. 56–7

Thornton, S. (1995) *Club Cultures: Music, Media and Subcultural Capital*, Cambridge: Polity

Thrift, N. and Olds, K. (1996) 'Refiguring the economic in economic geography', *Progress in Human Geography* 20: 311–37

Time (1966) *London: The Swinging City* 87(15):30–4

Trainer, T. (1985) *Abandon Affluence!* London: Zed Books

Tranberg Hanson, K. (2000a) 'Other people's clothes? The international second-hand clothing trade and dress practices in Zambia', *Fashion Theory* 4: 245–74

Tranberg Hanson, K. (2000b) *Salaula: The World of Second-hand Clothing and Zambia*, Chicago: University of Chicago Press

Tyler, S. (1997) 'Postmodern ethnography', in K. Gelder and S. Thornton (eds) *The Subcultures Reader*, London: Routledge, pp 254–61

Tyne and Wear Museum (1993) 'Biba: the label, the lifestyle, the look', *Exhibition Catalogue* Tyne and Wear

Verdict (2000) *UK Retailing Report*, London: Verdict

Vogue Daily (1998) 'The high price of fashion: Sotheby's Passion for Fashion Auction', *Vogue Daily* 26 November

Watson, L. (2001) 'Why old is the new new', *Sunday Times Style*, 8 April

Waundby, C. (1995) 'Have crooks hijacked car boot sales?', *Sheffield Star*, 7 July

Webb, I. (1998) 'First look – history class: designers plunder the past for today's retro chic', *Elle* (August)

Whatmore, S. (1997) 'Dissecting the autonomous self: hybrid cartographies for a relational ethics', *Environment and Planning D: Society and Space* 15: 37–53

Whatmore, S. (1999) 'Hybrid geographies: rethinking the 'human' in human geography', in D. Massey, J. Allen and P. Sarre (eds.) *Human Geography Today*, Cambridge: Polity, pp 24–39

Which? (1994) 'Car boot bargains?', (May) pp 30–3

Whitear, R. (1999) 'Charity shop volunteers: a case of tender loving care', *International Journal of Nonprofit and Voluntary Sector Marketing* 4: 107–20

Williams, C. (1997) 'Local exchange and trading systems: a new source of work and credit for the poor and unemployed?', *Environment and Planning A* 28: 1395–1415

Williamson, J. (1992) 'I-less and gaga in West Edmonton Mall: towards a pedestrian feminist reading', in D. Currie and V. Raol (eds.) *The Anatomy of Gender: Women's Struggle for the Body*, Ottawa: Carlton University Press, pp 97–115

Willis, P. (1990) *Common Culture*, Milton Keynes: Open University Press

Willis, P. (1997) 'Theoretical confessions and reflexive method', in K. Gelder and S. Thornton (eds.) *The Subcultures Reader*, London: Routledge, pp 246–53

Wilson, E. (1991) *The Sphinx in the City: Urban Life, the Control of Women and Disorder*, Berkeley: University of California Press

Wilson, E. (1992) 'The invisible flâneur', *New Left Review* 191: 90–110

Windsor, J. (1988) 'Bid for a Biba', *The Independent*, 2 September

Wolff, J. (1985) 'The invisible *flâneuse*: women and the literature of modernity', *Theory Culture and Society* 2: 37–47

Woodall, V. (1999) 'The genius of the lamp', *Hotline Business Magazine* London: Virgin

Woods, J. (1998) 'Nicole Farhi's flea market finds', *Electronic Telegraph*, 4 November

Young, J. (1971) *The Drugtakers: The Social Meaning of Drugs*, London: Paladin

Young, R. (1993) 'Car boot sales out of control' *The Times*, 12 August

Index

aesthetics, 62–7, 73, 138, 147–8, 190
aesthetic obsolescence, 116
aesthetic principles, 119
agency, 12, 107, 145, 171–2, 182, 192, 194, 200
alternative economies, 106–7, 197–200
altruism, 175–7
anti-consumerism, 86, 93, 106
art, 146
aura, 175, 183–4, 189, 192–3
authenticity, 52, 77, 146–55 passim, 171

bargain, 3–4, 11, 58, 76, 81, 94, 102–4, 198
   examples of, 138–9
Bauman, Z., 12
biographies, 2–12 passim, 84, 111–13, 115, 154, 169–72, 200–1
boast value, 100
body, 7, 134, 155–63, 171
   boundaries, 157–162
   presence, 122, 155–7, 180, 229n62
   see also cleansing rituals
Bourdieu, P., 4, 149
brand dilution, 116
branding, 5, 11, 49, 86, 106, 198
browsing, 68, 74

car-boot sales, 13–14, 25–33, 54–62, 207
   differentiation, 56, 60, 138
   proliferation, 21–2
   regulation and exclusion, 27–33, 214, 221n15–16
      criminalizing, 28–9
      escalation, 31
      unfair competition, 30–1
      see marginality
   research methods, 206–9, 214
   sites, 26–8
   transience, 21
career biographies, 136
carnival, 4, 61
casting out, 2, 6–7, 15, 111–29 passim, 201
   deserving others, 6, 112, 123
      see also philanthropy
   self-surveillance, 7, 112
      see also housekeeping strategies
cathedrals of consumption, 13
charity 53, 78–9, 107
charity finance report, 47, 221n12–13
charity retail, 14, 40–7, 75–82, 221n11
   class and, 80
   gender and, 155
   limits to, 195–6, 221n12

professionalization, 20, 41–4, 75
    critique of, 44–7, 79–83, 107
proliferation, 21–2, 40
regulation, 76–8
research methods, 209–14
research sites, 45, 209–11
specialization, 45–6
the body and, 156–63, 171
Christmas, 181–2
circuits of meaning, 142
class, 8, 11–12, 86, 91–4, 104,
    159–60, 179–80, 182, 190, 214
see also masculinity
cleansing rituals, 7, 162–3
clever consumption, 11–12, 179
clothing, 7, 14–15, 80, 170–1
    as gifts, 180–1
    children's, 91–3, 125, 198,
      229n56
    death and, 160–2
    disposal, 129
    first-cycle infusion, 167–8
    gender and, 121–3
    history and, 148, 152–5
    transformation, 163–6, 198
    underwear, 93, 158–60
    see also discount stores
    see also rituals of possession
collecting, 8–9, 113, 173–5, 183–94
    cycle of, 187
    insecurity and, 190–2
    literature, 183, 187, 202
    the 'hunt', 9, 185–7
    see also aura
    see also display
commercial-merchanting model,
    133–7
commodity chains, 4–5, 11, 141–2,
    154, 199, 219n3
    see biographies
commodity circulation, 131, 138

commodity journeys, 111, 142, 146,
    154, 182
commodity production, 198
communities of practice, 36
constitutive consumption, 190
consumer culture, 9–13
consumerism, 21
consumption
    counter readings of, 3–4, 72–4,
      78–81, 111–12
    definition, 9–10
    literature, 1–9, 144–5, 155, 175–6,
      183
    social regulation and, 175
    see also second-hand consumption
consumption cycles, 2, 144, 172, 193
consumption work, 7, 12, 68, 86,
    91–4, 112, 118, 175–9
corporeality, 171
creative restoration, 77
critical consumption, 11, 86–7,
    103–7, 198–9
    see also ethical consumption
    see also green consumption
cultural capital, 74, 100–3, 147, 149,
    165, 192, 200
cultural distance, 48
cultural economy, 140
cultural intermediary, 134
cycle of de/recommodification, 133,
    144, 172
cycle of de/revalorisation, 15, 111,
    143, 200–2
cycles of re-enchantment, 112
cycles of use, 154

devalorization, 191, 193
devaluation, 117
discount stores, 44–5, 224n28
discovery, 68, 74, 81–3, 185–6
discursive communities, 86, 98–103

discursive markers, 216
display, 150–1, 168, 187–9, 192
disposal dispositions, 118–29
disposal strategies, 113, 118–29, 144
    car-boot sales and, 122–3
    motives, 123–9
distinction, 4, 8, 11, 21, 35, 46,
        71–3, 86, 102–3, 141, 149, 172,
        181, 193, 198
    see cultural capital
    see also subcultural consumption
divestment rituals, 7, 15, 77, 144–5,
        155–63
    charity shops and, 53, 156–62
    see body
    see cleansing rituals
division of labour, 134
dual-pricing, 73

economic regeneration, 36
elite, 8, 39, 71, 149–50, 175
ethical consumption, 10–11, 105,
        124–5
ethnography, 207, 210, 217
exchange, 2–3, 14, 17–18, 35, 61,
        115
exchange imperative, 48
exchange relations, 82
exchange values, 126, 128

familialism, 121
familial history, 152–3
fashion, 24, 36, 62, 151, 168
fetishism, 172
first-cycle
    as accessory, 167–8
    as release, 93
    sites, 48
    see second-hand / first-cycle
        relationship
food, 8, 219n5

fun, 3, 61, 69–72, 90, 99, 177–9
functional commodities, 118–19

gift economy, 9, 174, 181
gifting, 8–9, 113, 173–83, 194
    limits to, 180–2
    literature, 175–6
gender, 96–7, 102–3, 108, 112–13,
        120–7 passim, 141–2, 146–7,
        155, 163–6, 176
    see housekeeping strategies
    see also masculinity
generation, 147
gentrification, 33, 36–7
geographies of exchange, 32
geographies of exclusion, 26
green consumption, 10, 86, 93, 104,
        124, 197–8
Goffman, E., 187

home, 150, 168, 187
hospice shops, 47
house clearances
housekeeping strategies, 6, 112–13,
        118, 120–3, 142

identity, 103, 108, 122, 145, 181, 202
    formation, 87, 99–100, 143, 149
    literature, 6, 145
    see also distinction
imaginative potential, 112, 145–6,
        153–5
imagined histories, 8, 15
imagined others, 147, 154, 160
interpretive repertoires, 230n70
investment, 215–6
investment rituals, 146
irony, 52, 69, 99, 102, 115

jumble sales, 82, 90–1, 135, 220n9
junk, 115, 118

kitsch, 52, 69, 115
knowledges, 4–11 passim, 61, 67–8,
    86, 117, 128, 133, 147–51, 163,
    183, 188, 193
  commodity, 139
  geographical, 56, 137–9
  situated, 36, 86, 140–1
  see also sourcing
knowledge exchange, 61

landscapes of power, 48–9
leisure, 95
local authority, 25–31 passim, 206–7
locality, 6, 47, 86–7, 137–8, 196–7,
    224n26
location geographies, 19–20, 47–9, 56
  alternative-mainstream, 20, 33–40,
    45–8
  centre-margin, 13–14, 17–18, 32–3
  first-cycle, 41–4
  see locality
  see marginality

marginality
  regulatory power and, 20, 25–6,
    32–3
Marks and Spencer, 5, 42, 97
masculinity, 126–7, 141
  class and, 147, 152–5
material culture, 7–8, 14, 145
material practices, 12–13
material realities, 111
meaning creation, 146–7
  historical reconstruction and,
    147–51
  imagined history making and,
    151–5
media, 21, 44, 125, 139, 206, 209
memorabilia, 144, 148
merchanting intermediaries, 133
methodology, 15, 205–14

analysis, 12–13, 214–18
  issues, 21–2, 208, 210, 213–14
money-making, 126–7
moral economy, 4, 86, 106, 108,
    113, 124–5, 142, 196, 199
mothering strategies, 92
multiple identities, 108
music, 147–9

nostalgia, 8, 147, 153, 188, 190

objectification, 10
originality, 147–51

personalization, 111–12, 146
philanthropy, 123–4
political economy, 103, 124–6
politics of consumption, 16
  see critical consumption
post-purchase rituals, 143, 162
post-sourcing rituals, 133
post-transformation practices, 167
premises of exchange, 3, 46, 51,
    62–82, 200, 219n2
  counter-readings of, 72–3, 78–84
principles of exchange, 3, 13, 51–62,
    200
production of space, 3

quality, 149, 154

race, 213
rationalization, 195–7
recovery, 144, 146
redistribution, 4, 86–7, 90
regimes of commodity production,
    111
regimes of representation, 3, 17,
    51–4, 68, 75–84 passim, 98
  see premises of exchange
  see principles of exchange

regimes of value, 115
regulatory framework, 33, 48
regulatory power, 20, 33
    see car-boot sales
regulatory practice, 189–92
relational slippage, 90
relations of looking, 51–2, 68, 72,
    82–3
repro-retro, 38, 45, 191
    see also retro retail
retail capital, 48–9, 104–5, 111,
    172
retailer-shopper
    discordance, 72–3
    performance, 57–8
retro retail, 14, 33–40, 62–74
    agglomeration, 24, 35–6
    alternative-mainstream, 33–9
    closure, 195–7
    commercialization, 36–8, 69–74,
        197
    historical retreat, 38–9
    proliferation, 22–4
    research methods, 209–14
    research sites, 23–4, 35–6, 62–7,
        120, 136, 211
    'staples', 53, 62, 71
    transience, 23, 37–8, 211
reuse, 10, 138, 198–9, 202
revalorization, 33, 111, 116–18,
    142–3, 155, 167, 184
ritual of consumption, 175–7, 181
ritual of participation, 184–5
rituals of possession, 143–5, 170
    see divestment rituals
    see meaning creation
    see transformation
romantic imaginings, 151–2
rubbish, 115, 118, 127, 132, 183,
    192, 201–3
rummaging, 68, 74, 95

sacralization, 187–9
second-hand consumption
    as community, 99–100
    as enjoyment, 94–7
    as necessity, 90–4
    as resistance, 96, 108
second-hand exchange
    diversity, 19, 21, 196
    internal divisions/linkage, 6, 15,
        49, 85, 87–90, 100, 109, 130–1,
        205–6
    limits to, 92, 167–8
        see also charity shops
        see also rationalization
    proliferation and growth, 19,
        21–5, 200
    the 1960s and, 7, 147–51
second-hand / first-cycle relationship,
    3–14 passim, 17–18
    consumers and, 85–6, 90, 101–9
        passim, 115–19, 167–8, 177,
        198, 200
    producers and, 20, 40–9 passim,
        53, 77–8, 82–4
sense of place, 87, 108
single parents, 80, 91–2, 99
sites of exchange, 1–2, 13–15,
    see car-boot sales
    see charity shops
    see retro shops
social exclusion, 12, 87, 91–4, 108
sourcing, 117–8
    commercial, 133–7
    limits to, 134–5, 196
    individual, 130–3
    overseas, 148, 196–7
space-making, 120
spatial fix, 142, 196–7, 201
spatialities of exchange, 17
    see location geographies
    see regimes of representation

subculture, 86, 99–101, 108, 149
supply chains, 5, 71, 77
survival strategy, 91
symbolic commodity value, 8, 100,
    177–9
  see collecting
  see gifting
symbolic positioning, 47–9, 100
  charity shops, 41, 44
  retro retailing 20, 33–6, 39

talk, 1, 87–90, 215–18
taste aesthetics, 8
taste communities, 100, 108, 175,
    180–2, 188
taste cycle, 129, 143
thrift, 11, 103, 113
transformation, 7, 131–2, 144,
    163–7

alteration, 164–55
decline of, 166
repair, 163
trash, 52, 69, 73, 115
treat, 94–8
triangulation, 217

value, 4, 14, 46, 76, 83–4, 86, 106,
    111–13, 142, 145–7, 170–2
value regimes, 57, 115, 138, 184,
    190, 192–3, 198, 201, 224n31
value systems, 146
value transformations, 115–17
volunteer labour poaching, 196
volunteers, 133–4

worth, 111–12

youth culture, 147